China's Integration with the Global Economy

ADVANCES IN CHINESE ECONOMIC STUDIES

Series Editor: Yanrui Wu, *Professor in Economics, University of Western Australia, Australia*

The Chinese economy has been transformed dramatically in recent years. With its rapid economic growth and accession to the World Trade Organization, China is emerging as an economic superpower. China's development experience provides valuable lessons to many countries in transition.

Advances in Chinese Economic Studies aims, as a series, to publish the best work on the Chinese economy by economists and other researchers throughout the world. It is intended to serve a wide readership including academics, students, business economists and other practitioners.

Titles in the series include:

China's Integration with the Global Economy

WTO Accession, Foreign Direct Investment and International Trade

Edited by

Chunlai Chen

The Australian National University, Australia

ADVANCES IN CHINESE ECONOMIC STUDIES

Edward Elgar

Cheltenham, UK • Northampton, MA, USA

Published by
Edward Elgar Publishing Limited
The Lypiatts
15 Lansdown Road
Cheltenham
Glos GL50 2JA
UK

Edward Elgar Publishing, Inc.
William Pratt House
9 Dewey Court
Northampton
Massachusetts 01060
USA

A catalogue record for this book is available from the British Library

Library of Congress Control Number: 2009925925

Mixed Sources
Product group from well-managed
forests and other controlled sources
www.fsc.org Cert no. SA-COC-1565
© 1996 Forest Stewardship Council
FSC

ISBN 978 1 84844 214 6

Printed and bound by MPG Books Group, UK

Contents

PART III AGRICULTURAL TRADE AND ENERGY DEMAND

Contributors

Vivienne Bath, Senior Lecturer, Faculty of Law, and Director of the Centre for Asian and Pacific Law, University of Sydney, Australia.

Chunlai Chen, Senior Lecturer, Crawford School of Economics and Government, the Australian National University, Australia.

Tingsong Jiang, Senior Economist, Centre for International Economics, Canberra, Australia.

Xia Kang, Research Fellow, Academy of State Administration of Grain, China.

Kunwang Li, Professor, Deputy Director, School of Economics, Nankai University, China.

Warwick McKibbin, Executive Director of Centre for Applied Macroeconomic Analysis, Professor of College of Business and Economics of the Australia National University, Professorial Fellow of Lowy Institute for International Policy, Australia, and Non-Resident Senior Fellow of the Brookings Institution, the United States.

Huanguang Qiu, Associate Professor, Center for Chinese Agricultural Policy, Chinese Academy of Sciences, China.

Yu Sheng, Research Economist, Australian Bureau of Agriculture and Resource Economics, Australia.

Ligang Song, Associate Professor, Crawford School of Economics and Government, the Australian National University, Australia.

Xiaosong Wang, PhD candidate, School of Economics, Nankai University, China.

Yanrui Wu, Professor, School of Economics and Commerce, University of Western Australia, Australia.

Lilai Xu, Senior Research Fellow/Senior Lecturer, School of Economics, Finance and Marketing, RMIT University, Australia.

Jun Yang, Associate Professor, Center for Chinese Agricultural Policy, Chinese Academy of Sciences, China.

James Xiaohe Zhang, Senior Lecturer, School of Economics, Politics and Tourism, Faculty of Business and Law, University of Newcastle, Australia.

Zhangyue Zhou, Professor, Director, Centre for AusAsia Business Studies, School of Business, James Cook University, Australia.

Preface

This edited volume contains selected papers presented at the International Conference on 'China's Conformity to the WTO: Progress and Challenges' held at the Australian National University in Canberra, Australia on 13–14 July 2007. This focused conference brought together scholars, government officials and representatives from international organizations and discussed the key issues and challenges surrounding China's conformity to the WTO five years after China became a formal member of the organization. All the selected papers were reviewed anonymously by scholars in the field. The authors then revised their papers following the comments made by the reviewers. The conference was organized jointly by the Association for Chinese Economic Studies (Australia) (ACESA) and the China Economy and Business Program, Crawford School of Economics and Government at the Australian National University (ANU).

I thank all contributors for their participation in this project and for their cooperation in finalizing the chapters in time. I thank all the anonymous reviewers for their valuable comments on the selected papers. I also thank Professor Ron Duncan from the Australian National University and Professor Christopher Findlay from the University of Adelaide for their help in reading through some of the chapters. I would also like to thank Professor Yanrui Wu from the University of Western Australia (UWA) for his valuable advice in drafting the book proposal. And I also thank Edward Elgar Publishing for publishing the book.

I am indebted to my colleagues in the Crawford School of Economics and Government of the Australian National University and the Association for Chinese Economic Studies (Australia) for their support in organizing the conference. Many of them kindly acted as either a chairperson or a discussant at the conference. In particular, I would like to thank Professor Ross Garnaut (Chairperson, China Economy and Business Program), Professor Andrew MacIntyre (Director, Crawford School of Economics and Government), Associate Professor Ligang Song (Director, China Economy and Business Program) and Dr Sizhong Sun (James Cook University) for their major role in organizing the conference.

Finally, I would like to thank the Ford Foundation Beijing Office for providing financial support to enable two Chinese scholars to participate in the conference, and the Education Department of the Chinese Embassy in Australia for its support to the conference.

Chunlai Chen
The Australian National University
Canberra

1. China's economy after WTO accession: an overview

Chunlai Chen

China's accession to the World Trade Organization (WTO) in December 2001 is widely regarded as a major milestone in the development of the Chinese economy as well as the multilateral trading system. There is no doubt that the accession has led to deepened integration of the Chinese economy into the global economy and moved China towards a more rules-based economic system. However, at the same time, meeting China's commitments to the WTO under the protocol of its accession raises enormous problems and challenges to China, its trading partners and the WTO itself.

China's full conformity to the WTO is strategically important for China, its trading relations with others and the multilateral trading system. This book provides a remarkable background of information about China's economy after WTO accession and analyses many important issues concerning China's economic growth, international trade, transparency of trade policy, regional trade arrangements, foreign direct investment, banking sector liberalization, exchange rate reform, agricultural trade and energy demand. The book is an indispensable source for scholars and students interested in Chinese economic studies and many chapters should also be of interest to a wide range of readers.

This introductory chapter will first present a brief review of China's fast economic growth after WTO accession and discuss the sources contributing to China's economic growth. Then it will discuss the increasing integration of China's economy with the global economy and analyse the issues associated with the rapid expansion of China's international trade. Subsequently, it will discuss a number of problems in China's economy and the challenges that China faces in future economic and social development. Finally, it will present the outline of the chapters in this book.

SURGING ECONOMIC GROWTH

Since China's entry into the WTO in 2001, China's economy has experienced a new period of high and stable growth, with real GDP growth rate on average in excess of 10 per cent for the period 2002–07. China's fast economic growth has had a significant impact on the world economy. In 2007, China's total GDP reached US$3.43 trillion and it became the world's fourth largest economy[1] after the United States, Japan and Germany, although it is still a lower-middle-income economy based on per capital GDP – China's per capita GDP reached US$2500 in 2007.

The fast economic growth has led to significant structural changes in China's economy. The share of the secondary industry and services sectors as a proportion of China's total GDP has increased from 85.6 per cent in 2001 to 88.3 per cent in 2006, while the share of agriculture has declined from 14.4 per cent to 11.7 per cent in the same period.[2] Undoubtedly, such dynamic expansion in economic growth and structural change reflect the positive effect of WTO entry on China's economy.

The high growth of China's economy after WTO accession is contributed to by a number of factors. On the supply side, for a large and populous country like China with abundant labour supply, one of the main sources of economic growth is the transfer of its surplus labour from the low-productivity agricultural sector to the high-productivity industrial and services sectors. The share of urban population increased from 37.7 per cent in 2001 to 43.9 per cent in 2006.[3] Therefore, rapid development of industrialization and urbanization is one of the major driving forces of China's recent strong economic growth.

Apart from the growth of factor inputs, China's high economic growth is also linked with rapid growth in total factor productivity (TFP). Though economists are still debating the role of TFP in economic growth, most empirical studies show that TFP growth has played an important role in China's recent economic growth (Wu, 2006).

On the demand side, domestic investment is the most important factor in driving the growth of China's economy, followed by domestic final consumption and net exports of goods and services (external demand). During 2002–07, the average annual contribution of domestic capital formation to GDP growth was 48.9 per cent, while the average annual contributions of domestic final consumption and net exports to GDP growth were 38.7 per cent and 12.4 per cent respectively in the same period (Table 1.1).

In most economies, final consumption takes up more than 70 per cent of their GDP. However, China has an unusually high rate of capital formation. As Figure 1.1 shows, the share of final consumption in total GDP has been declining, from 59.6 per cent in 2002 to 36.7 per cent in 2007, while

Table 1.1 GDP growth rate and contributions to GDP growth by the three-expenditure approach in China (%)

	2002	2003	2004	2005	2006	2007	Average 2002–07
GDP growth rate	9.1	10.0	10.1	10.4	11.1	11.4	10.4
Contribution by:							
Domestic investment	48.8	63.7	55.3	37.7	41.3	46.8	48.9
Domestic final consumption	43.6	35.3	38.7	38.2	39.2	37.2	38.7
Net exports	7.6	1.0	6.0	24.1	19.5	16.0	12.4

Sources: Calculated from various issues of the National Bureau of Statistics of China (NBS), *China Statistical Yearbook*, Beijing: China Statistics Press.

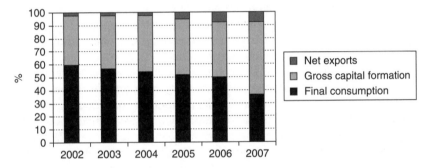

Sources: Calculated from various issues of the National Bureau of Statistics of China (NBS), *China Statistical Yearbook*, Beijing: China Statistics Press.

Figure 1.1 Composition of GDP by expenditure approach in China

the share of capital formation in total GDP has been increasing, from 41.0 per cent to 55.6 per cent in the same period.

With regard to investment financing, China's total investment in fixed assets is predominantly financed by domestic sources. As Figure 1.2 shows, over 95 per cent of total investment in fixed assets were financed by domestic sources. Among the domestic sources of financing, privately self-raised funds and others have taken the dominant position and their share in total investment financing has been increasing in recent years. In 2006, privately self-raised funds and others accounted for 74.2 per cent of the total sources of investment in fixed assets, while government budget

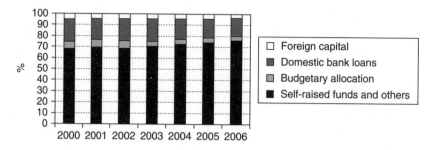

Sources: Calculated from various issues of the National Bureau of Statistics of China
(NBS), *China Statistical Yearbook*, Beijing: China Statistics Press.

*Figure 1.2   Composition of sources of financing in total investment in
           China*

allocation and bank loans accounted for only 21.6 per cent of the total.
Although China attracted large amounts of FDI inflows, the contribution
of FDI to China's total investment in fixed assets has been low. During the
period 2000–06, foreign investment as a percentage of China's total investment in fixed assets was around 4–5 per cent.

It is clear that China's high economic growth, especially after WTO
accession, has been predominantly driven by high levels of investment,
especially by domestic financing. This has raised the question of whether
China's high levels of domestic investment are sustainable enough to
support the high level of economic growth in the long run. Therefore,
the Chinese government needs to take measures to expand domestic consumption to provide a more balanced source of economic growth for the
future.

Another source of economic growth is external demand. China's fast-
growing exports have been its major external demand and have contributed to its economic growth. After the entry into the WTO, net exports
as a share of GDP have increased rapidly, increasing from 2.6 per cent in
2002 to 7.7 per cent in 2007. Consequently, the contribution of net exports
to China's GDP growth has also increased significantly. As Table 1.1
shows, the contribution of net exports to China's GDP growth on average
was around 5 per cent during 2002–04. However, it increased to around
20 per cent during 2005–07 as exports have been growing much faster
than imports. Apart from the direct contribution of exports to China's
economic growth, there are also a lot of indirect economic activities generated by the export sector. For example, large portions of local services and
local investment are connected with the export industries whose employees
also generate multiplier effects on the economy.

INCREASING INTEGRATION WITH GLOBAL ECONOMY

China's economy after WTO accession has become much more closely integrated with the global economy, leading to a large inflow of foreign direct investment (FDI) and the rapid expansion of the export-oriented manufacturing activities. FDI inflows into China reached US$74.8 billion in 2007, an increase of 60 per cent on those in 2001. The manufacturing sector has been the most attractive sector to FDI. After WTO accession, average annual FDI inflows into the manufacturing sector surged to US$36.44 billion during 2002–06, an increase of 34.86 per cent on those during 1997–2001, and accounting for 68.74 per cent of the total FDI inflows into China. Furthermore, the WTO accession has led to the opening up of many domestic sectors, especially the services sectors, to greater foreign competition. This in turn has led to a sharp rise in domestic investment for economic expansion.

Since the entry into the WTO in 2001, China's international trade has been increasing rapidly. Total international trade (export plus import) reached US$2.18 trillion in 2007, 3.27 times that of 2001 (Figure 1.3). China has now become the world's third largest trading country only after the United States and Germany. In particular, export growth has been much faster than import growth. In 2007, China's exports reached US$1.22 trillion, contributing to a record high level trade surplus of US$262.2 billion.

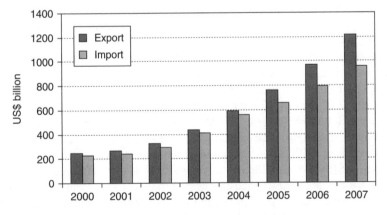

Sources: Calculated from various issues of the National Bureau of Statistics of China (NBS), *China Statistical Yearbook*, Beijing: China Statistics Press.

Figure 1.3   China's international trade (at current prices)

China's integration with the global economy

Table 1.2   *Shares of China's exports by destination and imports by source*
             in 2007

Region/Country	Export Destination (%)	Import Source (%)
Japan	8.38	14.01
Asian NIEs	24.11	24.59
ASEAN-4	4.09	9.09
The United States	19.14	7.27
The European Union	18.19	11.09
Rest of the world	26.10	33.94

Source: Calculated from the United Nations Statistics Division, Commodity Trade
Statistics Database, COMTRADE.

Because of fast economic growth, large amounts of FDI inflows and rapid
expansion in international trade after WTO accession, China has become
not just a leading engine of economic growth for Asian economies, but
also one of the major drivers of world economic growth. Because of its
size and scale, China's levels of production, consumption, imports and
exports carry significant global implications. Apart from being an important source of global economic growth, China has also operated as one of
the world's most significant integrating forces, as it is a crucial link in the
world's many production networks.

Table 1.2 shows the pattern of China's direction of trade in 2007. For
exports, the Asian newly industrializing economies (NIEs)[4] were China's
top market, accounting for 24.11 per cent, followed by the United States
(19.14 per cent), the EU (18.19 per cent) and Japan (8.38 per cent).
ASEAN-4[5] took up 4.09 per cent of China's exports.

On the import side, Asian NIEs again captured the largest share of the
Chinese markets (24.59 per cent), followed by Japan (14.01 per cent), the
EU (11.09 per cent) and ASEAN-4 (9.09 per cent). The United States
captured 7.27 per cent of the Chinese market.

Figure 1.4 shows the pattern of China's trade balance with its major
trading partners. In 2006 and 2007 China continued to run substantial
trade deficits with its neighbouring economies, from Taiwan, South
Korea, ASEAN-4 and Japan to Australia. However, China had a large
trade surplus with the United States and the EU.[6] As a result, China still
had an overall trade surplus. China's trade deficits with its neighbours
means that China has opened up its vast domestic market for their exports
(both manufactured products and primary commodities),[7] thereby, oper-
ating as an engine for their economic growth. This will further add to
China's rising geo-political and geo-economic influence in the region.

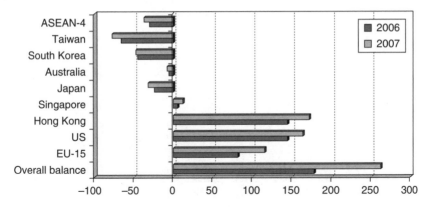

Source: Calculated from the United Nations Statistics Division, Commodity Trade Statistics Database, COMTRADE.

Figure 1.4   China's trade balance with selected economies (US\$ billions)

China's trade pattern and trade balance with its trading partners have important economic implications in China's integration with the global economy, particularly with East and Southeast Asian economies. Since most of China's exports are processing trade (53 per cent of total exports in 2006)[8] or final products (57 per cent of total exports in 2005)[9] generally with low domestic value-added and low domestic content, China must import raw materials, semi-finished products, parts and components in order to export. Also, since over half of China's foreign trade is handled by foreign-invested enterprises (59 per cent in 2006),[10] particularly those from Japan, South Korea, Taiwan, Hong Kong and the ASEAN economies, China's foreign trade has become a critical link in the East and Southeast Asian supply chains. It can further be argued that China is becoming an important 'integrator' of global production networks. China's exports embody raw materials, semi-finished products, parts and components, technology and financial services from different Asian economies to serve the world markets.

However, China's huge trade surplus has led to increasing pressures from its major trading partners to revaluate its currency. As a result, China revaluated the RMB (renminbi) by 2.1 per cent in July 2005. Since then the RMB has appreciated, with an accumulated rate of 12.1 per cent by 2007, even though the Chinese government has announced that the RMB exchange rate adjustment would follow a slow and gradual process.

Apart from the political pressures from the United States and the EU, China's monetary authorities have been confronted with not only an

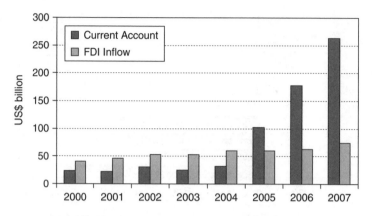

Sources: Calculated from various issues of the National Bureau of Statistics of China (NBS), *China Statistical Yearbook*, Beijing: China Statistics Press.

Figure 1.5 China's current account and FDI inflow (at current prices)

enormous problem of how to sterilize the large increase in foreign reserve to prevent the higher growth of money supply in the domestic economy, but also a big problem of recycling profitably its huge foreign reserves back to the international monetary system. The problem has been worsening since 2005, because of China's huge 'twin surpluses' on both capital and current accounts (Figure 1.5).

The structural factor for the accumulation of the twin surpluses include China's underdeveloped financial market, which cannot smoothly channel China's huge domestic saving into the needed areas of investment (Riedel, Jin and Gao, 2007). But the main causes of China's 'twin surpluses' come from policy biases such as preferential policies towards FDI, and excessive export promotion such as export tax rebates and an undervalued exchange rate.

The persistence of such twin surpluses is not desirable. On the financial side, apart from being a clear case of misallocation of valuable financial resources, the existence of large twin surpluses hampers China's effective participation in the global economy. As has already happened, China's persistent twin surpluses have resulted in the rapid growth of China's foreign exchange reserves, which now stand as the world's largest, reaching US$1.7 trillion by April 2008. This in turn adds pressure on the RMB to appreciate further. On the trade side, the twin surpluses have led to rising protectionism in the developed countries against China's exports, and have given rise to numerous trade frictions for China with the United States and the EU.

However, China has recently taken concrete measures to slow down the growth and even to reduce the twin surpluses. China started to cut or eliminate export tax rebates for 2831 commodities representing 37 per cent of the total number of items listed on customs tax regulations on 1 July 2007 (*People's Daily* Online, 2007). China has taken measures to encourage outward FDI. China's overseas investment increased rapidly, with an annual average growth rate of 60 per cent during 2002–06 (*China Daily*, 2007). In the first half of 2008, China's non-financial outward FDI reached US$25.7 billion, 2.3 times the level recorded in the same period in 2007 (AFP, 2008). Therefore, China has increased efforts to channel its huge financial surpluses into the international financial system.

PROBLEMS AND CHALLENGES

After accession to the WTO, despite China's rapid economic growth and increasing importance in the global economy, it still faces a number of important social and economic challenges.

First, the high economic growth has sparked fears of overheating, which materialized in 2007. The inflation rate, the consumer price index (CPI), increased from 1.5 per cent in 2006 to 4.8 per cent in 2007, exceeding the government's target of 3 per cent. Food prices, which accounted for a third of the index, were up 12.3 per cent during 2007. As a result, the predominant task for the Chinese government in 2008 was to take measures to fight against inflation and to start rebalancing and reorienting development policies.

The IMF cut China's economic growth forecasts to about 9 per cent in 2008 (*China Daily*, 2008) owing to decelerating exports and a weakening global outlook. The slowdown in economic growth could reduce inflationary pressure and contribute to China's rebalancing. However, there remains the immediate issue concerning the ability of monetary policy to combat rising inflation. In this regard, a more flexible exchange rate regime could enable China to operate a more independent monetary policy, which would be better suited to ensuring a low and stable rate of inflation, and therefore contribute to a macroeconomic environment more conducive to sustained strong economic growth.

Second, China's economy is characterized by a number of imbalances. In particular, there is the imbalance in sources of growth in the economy, which has been driven much more by investment and exports than by consumption, as reflected in China's growing current account surplus. Moreover, the efficient allocation of the vast amount of investment within the economy has been hampered by an underdeveloped capital market.

China needs to increase government spending on social services, such as health and education, and thus human capital, as well as basic pensions, thereby possibly reducing the need for precautionary saving and thus raising consumption. These and other measures to increase consumption would not only reduce China's reliance on exports for growth, and hence its vulnerability to economic slowdowns abroad, but would also narrow the gap between national saving and gross domestic investment and therefore help to reduce China's large current account surplus. Another way of reducing China's high propensity to save would be by channelling savings into the most profitable investments, thus improving the productivity of capital in the economy as a whole. Therefore, China needs to accelerate ongoing reform of the banking system and the capital market.

Third, income inequality has widened among regions and between urban and rural residents. One of the primary causes of widening income inequality is wage differentials reflecting differences in labour productivity. Therefore, the challenge is to accelerate the movement of surplus labour from relatively low-productivity agriculture into other activities, especially services. Moreover, as growth in the labour force slows, technological progress will assume much greater importance as a source of economic growth and productivity improvement, so that China needs to continue to pursue its goal of substantially raising expenditure on R&D.

Fourth, the pace of China's growth and industrialization has exacerbated environmental problems. That more and more environmental accidents have happened recently should be a signal that the time has come for China to act urgently on its environmental problems. Impediments to the efficient allocation of land, energy, water and other natural resources, such as price controls, need to be gradually dismantled; this would help protect the environment, especially if supplemented by market-based tax and non-tax instruments, for example based on the 'polluter pays' principle, to correct market failure.

Overall, China's economy after WTO accession has achieved remarkable progress; however, it also faces many problems and challenges for future economic development. Fortunately, the Chinese government has realized the urgent need to rebalance and reorient economic and social development policies, which is reflected in the Eleventh Five-year Plan 2006–10. It has broadly embraced the need to change and launched some new development policies, like green GDP, balanced development and harmonized society. However, it still has a long way to go to implement these policies and to achieve desired results.

OUTLINE OF THE CHAPTERS

The ten core chapters of the book are grouped into three parts, with each focusing on a specific topic, namely, economic growth and globalization (Part I), foreign direct investment and exchange rate (Part II), and agricultural trade and energy demand (Part III).

In Part I, Chapter 2 examines the trend of China's international trade growth, the changes in trade pattern and the implication of trade expansion for the world economy after China's WTO accession. Kunwang Li and Xiaosong Wang show that the rapid growth of China's international trade since 2001 has relied mainly on the exports of labour-intensive products based on its underlying comparative advantages. They argue that the continued and large amount of FDI inflows have helped China upgrade its trade structure rapidly. Their analysis also shows that China has taken advantage of globalization and played a very important role in the international segmentation of production. However, they point out that China still deeply depends on developed economies' markets for its final products. The increasing trade imbalance between China and developed economies raises the question of the sustainability of China's export growth strategy.

Yanrui Wu in Chapter 3 conducts valuable research on measuring China's capital stock. The lack of capital stock statistics for empirical research on the Chinese economy has for a long time been one of the major impediments. Though many authors have attempted to derive their own data series, most authors have focused on investigations at the national level and their findings are not without controversies. Few studies have provided estimates of capital stock for China's regional economies. This chapter adds to the literature in several ways. First, it presents a critical review of the methods and findings in the existing literature. Second, it proposes an alternative approach to estimate China's regional capital stock values. And most importantly, the author applies the derived capital stock series to examine growth, disparity and convergence in China's regional economies.

Vivienne Bath in Chapter 4 examines the WTO and China's transparency requirements. The aim of this chapter is to look at the way in which the Chinese government has dealt with the obligation of transparency in terms of its approach to regulation and the law, to assess the degree of compliance and to consider to what extent the changes have made or could make a substantial difference to the experience of businesses (both local and foreign) in trading in and with China. An important obligation of signatories to the WTO is the requirement to engage in transparency in decision-making and in regulation. For China, what this has meant is a commitment to publish laws and regulations, administer them in a uniform, impartial and reasonable way and to provide impartial and independent tribunals to review administrative decisions on WTO-related legislation. The author argues that since accession, the Chinese government has made major changes in reforming its regulatory and legislative system to comply with these requirements. The period since 2001 has seen improved publication and availability of legislative and regulatory information, the initiation of public discussion on important legal issues, and major changes in the administrative approval and licensing system, which plays such a major role in business in China. In particular, the Administrative Licensing Law, which came into effect in 2004, represents an ambitious effort to reform the way in which members of the public and organizations deal with government. Although international satisfaction with the result is not universal, China has undoubtedly made considerable progress in relation to its commitments on transparency.

The final chapter in Part I (Chapter 5) examines the impact of the proposed Free Trade Area of the Asia-Pacific (FTAAP) on China and its regional economies. The authors, Tingsong Jiang and Warwick McKibbin, applied a suite of general equilibrium models: APG-Cubed, a dynamic global model; GTAP, a static global model; and CERD, a static China model with regional dimension. The impact on the Chinese economy of the FTAAP is also compared with those of other forms of FTAs such as the ASEAN+1 and ASEAN+3. The authors find that China benefits from all three FTAs, and the Eastern region gains the most. They also find that China's benefit increases along with the increase in coverage of the FTAs, that is, the FTAAP has the biggest positive impact on the Chinese economy among the three FTAs considered in the study. In terms of sectors, the textile, clothing and footwear sector gains the most from the FTAAP, while the motor vehicle and parts sector loses the most.

Part II has three chapters, addressing foreign direct investment (FDI), foreign banks in China and the impact of RMB revaluation. Chunlai Chen in Chapter 6 examines the characteristics and changes of FDI in China since WTO accession. The author shows that FDI inflows into China have increased rapidly after China's WTO accession. Over 70 per cent of FDI inflows were in the manufacturing sector and FDI firms have become a major part of China's manufacturing sector. The author reveals that after China's accession to the WTO, FDI firms in the manufacturing sector have undergone both rapid expansion and structural changes. FDI inflows into the manufacturing sector have shifted from concentrating in labour-intensive industries toward increasing investment in technology-intensive and capital-intensive industries. FDI firms on average are more advanced and superior than domestic firms in terms of firm size, physical capital intensity and labour productivity. However, the relative superiority of FDI firms over domestic firms in physical capital intensity and labour productivity has been lessening. In labour-intensive industries, both physical capital intensity and labour productivity of FDI firms have fallen below those of domestic firms, though FDI firms still have relatively higher physical capital intensity and labour productivity in capital-intensive and technology-intensive industries than do domestic firms. The author argues that these changes indicate that through enterprise reform and competition, China's domestic firms have been catching up with FDI firms, especially in labour-intensive industries.

Lilai Xu in Chapter 7, using Shanghai as a case study, explores the implications on, and opportunities in, China's banking sector from greater foreign competition. China's financial services industry is experiencing profound changes and continues to undergo a steady transformation to a more open and competitive environment as a result of its membership of the WTO. It is evidenced that foreign banks in China initially try to exploit market niches where they have competitive success in other countries; eventually they may attempt to compete more broadly as they gain experience in the domestic market. In assessing the ensuing regulatory and structural changes, the author strives to characterize and extrapolate the impact of such foreign participation on competition and performance in the sector. It is suggested that as long as an adequate supervisory and regulatory system is in place, there is a need to speed up the reform in the area of foreign exchange control and further facilitate financial innovations if China wants to benefit more from the presence of foreign banks in its domestic market.

James Xiaohe Zhang in Chapter 8 applied a multicountry computable general equilibrium model (the GTAP model) to analyse the impact of the RMB revaluation on China and the world economy. The author found that the revaluation of the RMB would not be appealing to the Chinese. To some extent it would further reduce the competitiveness of China's exports and the growth of GDP. Furthermore, the impact of RMB revaluation will be different for different industries and for different regions. While the capital-intensive industries in China and labour-intensive industries in the rest of the world benefit, labour-intensive industries in China and the rural sector in particular are more likely to suffer. As a result, some additional policies may need to be implemented to remove the adverse impact.

Part III of the book presents three topics, covering China's agricultural trade, the impact of regional trade arrangement on China's agricultural development and the relationship between economic development and energy demand. Zhangyue Zhou and Xia Kang in Chapter 9 examine China's implementation and management of grain TRQs (tariff-rate quotas) since its accession to the WTO in late 2001. The authors show that since 2001 China's total grain trade volume has increased significantly and net grain imports have also increased. They argue that while China has done well to fulfil its WTO entry commitments, its trade policies have been generally in favour of encouraging domestic grain production. Mainly influenced by domestic supply–demand situations coupled with policies promoting domestic supply, China's grain imports and exports in the past five years fluctuated and the utilization of the grain TRQs has been low. Whether China's grain TRQ usage will increase and how its grain trade policy will evolve will continue to be affected by domestic grain supply and demand, and also by the outcomes of bilateral and multilateral free trade negotiations.

Jun Yang, Huanguang Qiu and Chunlai Chen in Chapter 10 examine the impact of ASEAN-China Free Trade Area (ACFTA) on China's economy and its regional agricultural development by using the Global Trade Analysis Project model (GTAP) and the China Agricultural Decision Support System (CHINAGRO). Their analysis shows that, first, ACFTA will improve resource allocation efficiencies for both China and ASEAN and will promote bilateral agricultural trade, hence having positive effects on economic development of both sides. Second, ACFTA will accelerate China's export of agricultural commodities in which it has comparative advantages, such as vegetables, wheat and horticultural products, but at the same time bring about a large increase in imports of commodities such as vegetable oil and sugar. Third, ACFTA will have different impacts on China's regional agricultural development due to the large disparity in agricultural production structure in each region. Their results indicate that agriculture in the North, Northeast and East regions of China will benefit from ACFTA, whereas agriculture in South China will suffer. The regional specific impacts caused by ACFTA are quite different from the effects brought by multilateral trade liberalization such as the WTO, which have positive effects on the Southern region of China but negative impacts on the Northern and Western regions of China.

Finally, Chapter 11 by Ligang Song and Yu Sheng examines the linkage between economic development and energy demand in the world and China. The authors use the difference and system general method of moment (GMM) to estimate an energy demand function with a dataset covering a 65-country and over 40-year period of 1965–2005. Their estimated results for the cross-country income and price elasticities of energy usage show that countries in different stages of economic development would demonstrate different levels of demand for energy consumption. The authors argue that, combined with the long-term pattern of energy supply, this finding can be used to explain how the wave-by-wave economic development across countries may lead to a cyclical fluctuation of energy price, to predict the changing trade pattern of energy products in the world market, and also can be used to explain the recent booms in energy products demand in India and China.

NOTES

1. According to the WTO (2008), China was the world's third largest economy only after the United States and Japan in 2007.
2. Calculated from *China Statistical Yearbook* (2007).
3. Calculated from *China Statistical Yearbook* (2007).
4. Asian NIEs include Hong Kong, Taiwan, South Korea and Singapore.
5. ASEAN-4 include Malaysia, Indonesia, the Philippines and Thailand.
6. China also ran a substantial trade surplus with Hong Kong. But most of China's exports to Hong Kong are re-exported to the United States and the EU.
7. China and ASEAN signed the Framework Agreement on Comprehensive Economic Cooperation in November 2002 to establish the ASEAN-China Free Trade Area (ACFTA) for goods trade by 2010 for China and the older ASEAN members, including Brunei, Indonesia, Malaysia, the Philippines, Singapore and Thailand, and by 2015 for China and the newer ASEAN member states, Vietnam, Laos, Cambodia and Myanmar. The Early Harvest Program (EHP), implemented on 1 January 2004, specifies that China and all older member countries of ASEAN should phase out mutual import tariffs on almost all agricultural goods; newer ASEAN members have until 2015 to eliminate tariffs on these commodities. The enforcement of the Agreement on Trade in Goods of July 2005 signals the operational phase of the ACFTA.
8. Calculated from *China Statistical Yearbook* (2007).
9. See Table 2.6 in Chapter 2 of this book.
10. Calculated from *China Statistical Yearbook* (2007).

REFERENCES

AFP (2008), 'China's overseas investments more than double in first half: govt', 23 July 2008, http://afp.google.com/article/ALeqM5gv8GifdvuO9Q7RITM4jUiS WpJkQA, accessed 21 August 2008.

China Daily (2007), 'China's overseas investment rises 60% annually', 2 October 2007, http://www.chinadaily.com.cn/bizchina/2007-10/02/content_6150523.htm, accessed 21 August 2008.

China Daily (2008), 'IMF cuts Chinese economic growth forecasts to about 9%', 9 May 2008, http://www.chinadaily.com.cn/bizchina/2008-05/09/content_6672331. htm, accessed 21 August 2008.

National Bureau of Statistics of China (NBS) (various issues), *China Statistical Yearbook*, Beijing: China Statistics Press.

People's Daily Online (2007), 'China to adjust export rebate policy on 2,831 commodities', 20 June 2007, http://english.people.com.cn/200706/20/ eng20070620_385830.html, accessed 21 August 2008.

Riedel, J., J. Jin and J. Gao (2007), *How China Grows: Investment, Finance, and Reform*, Princeton and Oxford: Princeton University Press.

United Nations Statistics Division, Commodity Trade Statistics Database, COMTRADE. http://unstats.un.org/unsd/comtrade/default.aspx.

World Trade Organization (WTO) (2008), 'Trade Policy Review – China 2008', Secretariat report, WT/TPR/S/199, 16 April 2008, http://www.wto.org/english/tratop_e/tpr_e/tp299_e.htm, accessed 21 August 2008.

Wu, Y. (2006), 'Introduction', in Y. Wu (ed.), *Economic Growth, Transition and Globalization in China*, Cheltenham, UK and Northampton, MA, USA: Edward Elgar, pp. 1–10.

PART I

Economic Growth and Globalization

2. China's foreign trade: trends and issues after WTO accession

Kunwang Li and Xiaosong Wang

INTRODUCTION

China's rising role in world trade has been much more outstanding since its accession into the World Trade Organization (WTO) in 2001. The rapid expansion of foreign trade has contributed to China's economic growth. Such outstanding trade performance can be attributed to many factors, especially its abundant labour endowment, huge inflows of foreign direct investment (FDI), extensive and deep involvement in international division of production and trade liberalization particularly after WTO accession.

China reduced its average most favoured nation (MFN) tariffs for agricultural and non-agricultural products to 15.3 per cent and 8.8 per cent respectively by 2007. Non-tariff measures have also been reduced significantly. Import quotas and trading rights were eliminated at the end of 2004. Import licensing has been reduced progressively and the administration of the import licensing regime has been simplified. China has liberalized its services in line with its schedule in the General Agreement on Trade in Services (GATS), and its specific commitments to the GATS are very extensive by developing country standards, covering nine out of the 12 large sectors in the GATS list.

This chapter first examines the growth trends, changing patterns and the driving forces of China's foreign trade after its WTO accession. Then, we will analyse the impact of China's growing foreign trade on the United States, the EU, Japan and other Asian economies. Finally, we will discuss some issues in China's foreign trade, including China's exports growth strategy, the sustainability of China's exports, upgrading the structure of China's export products and new trade protectionism from developed countries.

TRENDS AND CHANGING PATTERNS OF CHINA'S FOREIGN TRADE AFTER WTO ACCESSION

China's foreign trade has increased rapidly since its accession to the WTO in December 2001. During the period 2002–07, the total value of China's foreign trade increased from US$620.7 billion to US$2173.8 billion, with its exports increasing from US$325.6 billion to US$1218.0 billion and imports increasing from US$295.1 billion to US$955.8 billion (see Table 2.1). The annual growth rates of total trade, exports and imports were 27.5 per cent, 28.9 per cent and 25.9 per cent respectively, which are almost twice those (14.8 per cent, 14.6 per cent and 15.3 per cent) during the period 1991–2001.[1] China has become the third largest trading nation in the world after the United States and Germany.

Because of the faster growth in exports than in imports, China's trade surplus has risen sharply, from US$22.5 billion in 2001 to US$262.2 billion in 2007. The trade surplus has been contributed to by a sharp rise in the trade surplus in the manufacturing sector. In particular, machinery, electronic appliances and transportation equipment account for more than half of the trade surplus. The rapid increase in trade surplus has contributed to the accumulation of foreign reserve. China's foreign reserve has amounted to US$1.6 trillion in 2007.

China's trade is more concentrated in the Asia-Pacific region, especially in East Asia. Comparing pre- and post-WTO accession, there have been some changes in the relative importance of China's major trading partners (see Tables 2.2 and 2.3). Although the United States and Japan continue to be China's major export markets, their relative importance has been diminished by the EU, especially after China's accession to the WTO. The proportions of China's export to Japan and the United States in China's total export have declined from 16.9 per cent and 20.4 per cent respectively

Table 2.1   China's foreign trade 2001–07 (US$ billion)

Year	Total	Exports	Imports	Trade balance
2001	509.7	266.1	243.6	22.5
2002	620.7	325.6	295.1	30.5
2003	851.0	438.2	412.8	25.4
2004	1154.5	593.3	561.2	32.1
2005	1428.0	762.0	666.0	96.0
2006	1760.7	969.1	791.6	177.5
2007	2173.8	1218.0	955.8	262.2

Source: China Customs Statistics.

Table 2.2   Shares of China's merchandise exports by destination (%)

Region/Country	1995	2000	2001	2002	2003	2004	2005	2006	2007
Japan	19.2	16.7	16.9	14.9	13.6	12.4	11.0	9.5	8.4
Asian NIEs	23.2	27.6	26.2	26.9	26.1	26.1	25.3	25.2	24.1
ASEAN-4	1.4	3.6	3.8	4.1	4.0	4.1	4.1	4.0	4.1
US	16.6	20.9	20.4	21.5	21.1	21.1	21.4	21.0	19.1
European Union	13.6	16.4	15.4	14.8	16.4	16.8	17.7	17.4	18.2

Source: Calculated from the United Nations Statistics Division, Commodity Trade Statistics Database, COMTRADE.

Table 2.3   Shares of China's merchandise imports by source (%)

Region/Country	1995	2000	2001	2002	2003	2004	2005	2006	2007
Japan	22.0	18.4	17.6	18.1	18.0	16.8	15.2	14.6	14.0
Asian NIEs	24.2	25.1	26.8	28.6	27.6	27.2	27.3	25.9	24.6
ASEAN-4	3.4	5.8	6.8	7.7	8.4	8.2	8.4	8.6	9.1
US	12.2	10.0	10.8	9.2	8.2	8.0	7.4	7.5	7.3
European Union	13.9	13.9	14.6	13.1	12.9	12.1	10.9	11.0	11.1

Source: Calculated from the United Nations Statistics Division, Commodity Trade Statistics Database, COMTRADE.

in 2001 to 8.4 per cent and 19.1 per cent in 2007, though the absolute value of China's export to these two major trading partners has increased. In contrast, the share of China's export to the EU increased from 15.4 per cent in 2001 to 18.2 per cent in 2007. A possible explanation of this phenomenon is that China's accession to the WTO helps to decrease trade barriers in the EU more than those in the United States and Japan, thus facilitating China's export to the EU.

As for the Asian newly industrializing economies (NIEs)[2] and the ASEAN-4,[3] the shares of China's export to these economies have not changed much during the post-WTO period (25 per cent for the Asian NIEs and 4 per cent for the ASEAN-4). This is partly due to the comparative advantages shared by China and these economies – abundance of labour, which makes the production structure of these economies similar to that of China.

In terms of China's import, a similar trend can be observed for the changes in the relative importance of the United States, Japan and the EU. In addition, an interesting phenomenon is that the proportion of China's import from the ASEAN-4 has been increasing, which reflects the effect of international reorganization of production.

Table 2.4   Structure of China's exports (%)

Year	Primary Goods	Manufactured Goods	Manufactured goods	
			Electrical goods (appliances and machinery)	High-tech products
1995	14.4	85.6	29.5	6.8
2000	10.2	89.8	42.3	14.9
2001	9.9	90.1	44.6	17.5
2002	8.7	91.3	48.2	20.8
2003	7.9	92.1	51.9	25.2
2004	6.8	93.2	54.5	27.9
2005	6.4	93.6	56.0	28.6
2006	5.5	94.5	56.7	29.0
2007	5.1	94.9	57.6	28.6

Source: Calculated from China Customs Statistics.

Table 2.5   Structure of China's imports (%)

Year	Primary Goods	Manufactured Goods	Manufactured goods	
			Electrical goods (appliances and machinery)	High-tech products
1995	18.5	81.5	44.8	16.5
2000	20.8	79.2	45.7	23.3
2001	18.8	81.2	49.5	26.3
2002	16.7	83.3	52.7	28.1
2003	17.6	82.4	54.5	28.1
2004	20.9	79.1	53.8	28.8
2005	27.4	77.6	53.1	30.0
2006	23.6	76.4	54.0	31.2
2007	25.4	74.6	52.2	30.0

Source: Calculated from China Customs Statistics.

The commodity structure of China's foreign trade has also changed (see Tables 2.4 and 2.5). Following the trend throughout the whole 1990s, the proportion of primary goods export in China's total export continued to fall after China's accession to the WTO. From 2001 to 2007, the share of primary goods export in China's total export declined from 9.9 per cent to 5.1 per cent, while the proportion of manufactured goods export increased from 90.1 per cent to 94.9 per cent. Moreover, a decomposition of the manufactured goods exports shows that the export shares of electrical goods (appliances and machinery) and high-tech goods have presented an increasing trend in China's export. In 2007, electrical goods accounted for 57.6 per cent of China's total export, and the share of high-tech export reached 28.6 per cent of China's total export. This implies that China's overall export structure has become more sophisticated. This feature is largely attributed to the processing trade – the assembly of duty-free intermediate inputs.

Manufactured goods are also the largest component of China's import, with its share maintaining above 70 per cent. But the changes in commodity structure of China's import seem to favour primary goods after China's accession to the WTO. Since 2002 the share of primary goods in China's import has increased significantly. The most important factor driving such large increase is the increased demand from China for energy and raw materials from the rest of the world. Similar to export, China has increased the import of electrical and high-tech goods after WTO accession. Though the growth rate was not very high and there were fluctuations, the trend was evidently upward.

SOURCES OF CHINA'S TRADE BOOM

The remarkable performance of China's foreign trade in recent years is attributed to many factors. Among them the following factors are the most important.

First, China has the most abundant labour supply in the world. According to neoclassic theory of international trade, China will specialize in labour-intensive activities and export labour-intensive products. Although there has been increasing competition from some Asian developing economies in recent years, China still has strong comparative advantage in labour-intensive activities due to its abundant and cheap labour supply, and dominates the export of many labour-intensive products in the world market.

Along with its strong comparative advantage in labour-intensive activities, China has also increased its comparative advantages in capital-intensive and technology-intensive activities due to accelerated physical capital and human capital accumulation, which have benefited from fast economic growth and large amount of FDI inflows in the past three decades. As a result, the structure of China's international trade has changed gradually. Following the trend in the late 1990s, China's export after accession to the WTO has been increasingly shifting towards capital-intensive and technology-intensive products. As Figure 2.1 shows, during

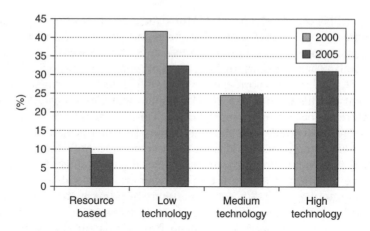

Source: Calculated from China Customs Statistics.

Figure 2.1   Structural change of China's manufactured exports

the period 2000–05, China's export structure shifted significantly towards high-technology products. Although unskilled labour-intensive products (low-technology products) still dominated China's manufactured exports, its share has declined sharply while the share of high-technology-intensive products has increased significantly.[4]

Second, the rapid growth of China's foreign trade is highly associated with the growing FDI inflows into China. FDI has contributed more and more to China's export growth, particularly after China's accession to the WTO. During the period 1996–2001, foreign-invested firms (FIFs) contributed 64.3 per cent of China's export growth, and it increased to 78.5 per cent during the period 2002–07.[5]

FIFs account for more than half of China's total trade and carry out the overwhelming share of processing trade. In 2007, the processed export made up over 50 per cent of China's total export, and the import for processing accounted for 38.5 per cent of China's total import.[6] During 2002–07, FIFs' processed export has accounted for around 45 per cent of China's total export, and FIFs' import for processing accounted for around 35 per cent of China's total import.[7] In general, the rapid growth of China's foreign trade is mainly based on the expansion of assembly activities, and the lion's share of assembly operation is taken by FIFs.

The inflows of FDI have also improved the technological upgrading of China's trade. As mentioned above, the share of high-technology products in China's manufactured exports has increased rapidly. This is mainly attributed to FIFs. FIFs' exports and imports both rapidly shifted towards high-technology products. In 2004, the shares of high-technology products in FIFs' exports and imports reached 80 per cent and 71 per cent respectively.[8] This indicates that FIFs have played an increasingly important role in upgrading China's trade structure.

Finally, globalization has provided new opportunities for China to enter international trade through vertical specialization. International production sharing or international production fragmentation is a widespread phenomenon in the global economy, especially in East Asia. China has taken advantage of this vertical specialization within the production process and it has become an assembly centre for firms located in East Asia. In other words, firms in East Asia have moved production facilities to China, which reorganized their industrial capacities and extended their production and trade networks (Gaulier, Lemoine and Ünal-Kesenci, 2005).

Cross-border production and trade networks explain the rapid growth of China's trade in intermediate goods. The pattern of China's trade by stage of production reveals China's position in the international segmentation of production processes. As shown in Table 2.6, after China's WTO accession, although the share of import declined marginally, it was still more than 60 per cent in 2005. For intermediate goods, the import of parts and components increased from 18.9 per cent in 1997 to 30.5 per cent in 2005. On the export side, final goods are the most important category, within which consumer goods take the overwhelming share. In 2005, the share of final goods export in total export was 57.1 per cent and consumer goods accounted for 36.4 per cent of the total export. The rapid increase in trade of parts and components indicates the deepening of China's engagement in international division of production and it is the core of China's rapid trade expansion.

Table 2.6   China's trade pattern by stage of production (%)

	Import		Export	
	1997	2005	1997	2005
Primary goods	10.6	11.2	5.1	2.6
Intermediate goods	65.9	61.2	33.4	40.3
Semi-finished goods	47.0	30.7	25.2	21.9
Parts and components	18.9	30.5	8.2	18.4
Final goods	23.5	27.6	61.5	57.1
Consumer goods	4.4	6.0	48.9	36.4
Capital goods	19.1	21.6	12.6	20.7
Total	100.0	100.0	100.0	100.0

Sources: Gaulier et al. (2005) and authors' calculations from China Customs Statistics.

THE IMPACT OF CHINA'S TRADE EXPANSION ON THE WORLD ECONOMY

The impact of China's rise on the world economy can be seen in various areas, but the most direct impact will be on trade. China's rapid trade growth and its increasing participation in international specialization have introduced competition as well as opportunities to the world economy.

Undoubtedly, China's rising position in the international market after its WTO accession has intensified the competitive pressure on both developed and developing countries. From the developed countries' point of view, the expansion of China's export, especially the expansion of export of labour-intensive products to their markets, will adversely affect employment, especially of unskilled labour, and consequently their income. As a result, there are surges in trade protectionism in developed countries against Chinese exports.

There are also anxieties among developing countries over the rising trade from China. In particular, some developing countries with similar exports to China have felt the pressure of intensified competition resulting from the rise of Chinese exports to the world market. They are concerned that Chinese exports will replace their exports in the third market.

It is difficult to quantify the various effects of China's trade expansion on the world economy. However, our discussion is only focused on two questions: has China become an engine of intra-regional trade in Asia? And what is the implication of China's increasing trade imbalance with the United States?

The Impact on Asian Neighbours

China's trade expansion has been mainly due to international production sharing between China and its neighbours in Asia, which has led to a reorganization of industrial production in the region (Gaulier, Jean and Ünal-Kesenci, 2004). Since WTO accession, 60 per cent of China's imports from Asian NIEs and 40 per cent of China's imports from Japan have been related to supplying inputs, intermediate goods and machinery for the processing industries (Gaulier, Lemoine and Ünal-Kesenci, 2006). This strong intensity of Asian export to China can be explained by international splitting up of the value-added chain within the region. Therefore, the Asian NIEs and Japan are the major sources of inputs for China's processing activities (Ng and Yeats, 2003).

Based on the above background, China's rapid increase in foreign trade could have the following impact on Japan. The supply of Japanese parts and components to China are mainly directed to foreign export platforms set up in the Chinese mainland. Processing activities played a dominant role in the bilateral trade, and the move of the final stage of production to China meant Japan's import of final goods shifted from advanced economies to China. Also, China has become a major exporter of final goods to the United States, having overtaken Japan as its major supplier of capital goods and consumer goods. In 2003 China became the largest supplier to the United States of capital goods (Gaulier et al., 2006). So Japan's export of capital goods and consumer goods slowed down after China's WTO accession.

The major impact of China's trade expansion on the Asian NIEs is that their trade has been shifting from Japan to China. The share of the Asian NIEs' imports of capital goods from China increased from 6 per cent in 1995 to 23.1 per cent in 2005.[9] Also, the Asian NIEs have gradually taken Japan's position as a major supplier of capital goods to China. In terms of consumer goods, China has already become the dominant supplier to the Asian NIEs, while Japan has been losing its position (Lee and Kim, 2004; Masuyama, 2004).

China has become an important player in the international production chain through its increasing share of trade in parts and components with its main trading partners. China has now been incorporated into the regional production network consisting of Korea, Japan, Hong Kong, Taiwan and the six ASEAN countries and is engaged in trading relationships with North American and European economies. The accession of China into such a regional production network provided an enlarged market for all the regional economies. As a result, all parties involved will gain from participating in this dynamic process (Li, Song and Zhao, 2007).

To assess the impact of China on its trading partners in the region, we estimated the contribution of China to its Asian trading partners' export expansion on the demand side during the period 1990–2005 by employing the approach of Li and Song (2005). We estimated the contribution of three large economies – the United States, China and Japan – to the region, respectively. The results show that the proportion of the United States' contribution to the regional demand effect is 19.1 per cent, the largest contributor among the three, closely followed by China (16.2 per cent). Japan's proportion of contribution is comparatively low, 4.6 per cent during the period. By looking at the results over different periods, it can be seen that China's contribution to the demand effect in this region's export growth is continuously on the rise. Before 2000, the United States' contribution was always in the leading position. However, China's role increased rapidly, rising to 27.9 per cent during 2000–05. The United States' role declined drastically, falling from 33.2 per cent during 1995–2000 to 13.6 per cent during 2000–05. Japan's role increased slightly from 4.2 per cent during 1995–2000 to 6.3 per cent during 2000–05. Our finding indicates that China

Table 2.7   The US trade deficit, 2001–06

Year	GDP (US$ billion)	Current Account Deficit (US$ million)	Current Account Deficit / GDP (%)	Goods Trade Deficit (US$ million)	Goods Trade Deficit to China (US$ million)	Goods Trade Deficit to China/Total Goods Trade Deficit (%)
2001	10 128.0	389 456	3.85	410 933	83 171	20.24
2002	10 469.6	475 211	4.54	470 291	103 149	21.93
2003	10 971.2	519 679	4.74	535 652	124 139	23.18
2004	11 734.3	668 074	5.69	651 735	162 035	24.86
2005	12 479.4	788 492	6.32	766 561	197 265	25.73
2006	13 176.1	874 500	6.64	849 572	223 616	26.32

Source: United States Government Printing Office (2008), *2008 US Economic Report of the President*.

has surpassed the United States and has become the most powerful engine in bringing about the region's trade expansion. China's role has become more important to ASEAN's trade expansion due to the implementation of the ASEAN-China Free Trade Area agreement in recent years.

China's Trade Imbalance with the United States

When the trade relationship between China and the United States is ana-lysed, it is inevitable that the huge current account deficit of the United States should be addressed first. As shown in Table 2.7, from 2001 to 2006, the value of current account deficit has enlarged by 1.25 times, and the ratio of current account deficit to GDP increased rapidly from 3.85 per cent to 6.64 per cent. In 2001, the US goods trade deficit with China was US$83.1 billion, but it surged to US$223.6 billion in 2006. The share of the US goods trade deficit with China in the total goods trade deficit increased from 20.24 per cent in 2001 to 26.32 per cent in 2006.

There are many factors contributing to China's rising trade surplus, but one of the main reasons is related to China's increasing involvement in international production sharing. As a result, a triangular trade pattern has emerged. That is, China is used as an export base for the advanced Asian economies, which instead of exporting finished goods to the US and European markets, now export intermediate goods to China. In this triangular trade pattern, the United States and the EU have increased their trade deficits with China, while their trade deficits with Japan and the Asian NIEs have declined.

In the financial arena, China has made an important impact on the United States. The global saving surplus has made it easier for the United States to finance its current account deficit. China, by buying the US financial assets, has helped keep the US bond yields lower than they would otherwise be. The huge amount of China's foreign exchange reserve is rooted in its savings from trade surplus. That is to say, China's trade surplus guarantees low US bond yields. If fast-growing China generates more saving than it is willing to invest, then the United States could continue financing its large current account deficit for some time. However, China's buying the US financial assets may have also sent misleading price signals to the private and government sectors in the United States, contributing to excessive borrowing, a house price bubble and a large fiscal deficit.

In the meantime, the United States must confront the situation that lower-skilled jobs have been lost, either indirectly from competition, or directly as multinational corporations shift production to low-cost China. Moreover, nor are the job losses limited to low-tech industries. The information technology revolution has made it possible to offshore low value-added stages of production of high-tech industries. The challenge of the United States is to find ways to assist the losers in Sino-US trade and help them find their new positions.

SUSTAINABILITY, UPGRADING AND OTHER CHALLENGES OF CHINA'S FOREIGN TRADE

Sustainability of China's Export Expansion

China's trade expansion has been propelling its economic growth. However, whether such a trend would be sustainable is in question. China's trade dependency already climbed to 67 per cent in 2006. More generally China's economic growth has been mainly driven by investment and export. According to the Asian Development Bank (2007), the contribution of China's household consumption to economic growth has been falling, while investment and export has become more and more important instead. This evolution has been even more exacerbated during the recent surge in economic growth since 2003.

A high trade dependency may incur a series of problems for China. First, other economies, especially advanced countries such as the United States, have a large trade deficit with China. As a result, protectionists in these economies may be active in hindering trade with China; they will have an excuse to oppose free trade. Then China may face more and more disputes with other countries in the trade area, and the development of trade may be blocked. Second, when the global economy fluctuates, China's export may decline dramatically. Goods previously sold abroad may surge towards the domestic market, but China's residents' consumption demand is very limited, and its economy may suddenly shrink. Last, while the segmentation of the production process has boosted intra-Asia trade in intermediate goods, China mainly depends on the developed economies outside Asia for its export of final goods. Because the final demand, which eventually drives the international segmentation of the production process, is still located in the United States and European countries, and China's imports are mainly from Asian countries, so China's performance of export strongly depends on the Western countries' markets. Therefore, China's export growth strategy cannot be sustained in the long run. According to the OECD report (2005), China's growth and industrial profits both rose during the first three years after its WTO accession. But this trend slowed remarkably in 2005 and this is especially the case in downstream sectors, where firms face fierce competition in the world market. The firms in downstream sectors have been forced to lower their selling prices, while the recent price rise of energy and raw materials has increased their production costs. Despite the productivity gains and the flexibility of wages, there are indications that the diverging trends in the costs of inputs and the prices are squeezing profit margins of manufacturing firms in individual sectors in which the high level of investment has led to a situation of over-capacity.

In 2007, the Chinese government implemented a series of policies to decrease the country's trade surplus. The government listed many categories of goods, the exporters of which had feasted on tax-reimbursement policy previously. And the Chinese Ministry of Commerce modified the regulations of processing trade, which will restrain its billowing development. The new Law of Labour Contract has a series of regulations on employment, wages and contract, which will evidently increase cost of labour. Along with the appreciation of the RMB, these measures will alter the situation of China's imbalanced trade. The Chinese government has realized that to ensure a sustainable and high growth, China has little choice but to return to a more balanced growth in favour of domestic consumption. Enhancing the social security system should support household consumption.

Development of High-tech Industries

As shown in Table 2.4 and Table 2.5, in 2007, high-tech trade accounted for 28.6 per cent and 30 per cent in China's total export and import, respectively. As analysed above, the rapid technological upgrading of China's trade has been associated with an increased dependence on foreign capital. Thus, an interesting issue is whether this dependence is due to an everlasting tendency or whether China will develop its own technological capacity in the future (Blanchard and Giavazzi, 2005).

Since the economic reform, China has heavily relied on FIFs for technological upgrading and this trend has been sustained up to now. However, there is evidence that FIFs have not had all the positive effects that were expected by the Chinese government. The acquisition of technology through imports incorporating high technology is usually less favourable to its dissemination than other channels such as patents or licences. But the bulk of China's high-tech imports is handled by FIFs, which is likely to have increased the obstacles to the dissemination of high technology. On the other hand, there is evidence that high-tech imports have been used as a substitute for local expenditures in R&D in China.

According to the OECD (2005) report, China's high-tech imports have had a rather limited effect on the domestic innovative capacity. FIFs remained relatively isolated from the local technology market. The performance of the Chinese firms in terms of productivity and innovation has been determined by their own efforts and the acquisition of foreign technology has had a positive effect only when associated with in-house R&D expenses. The shortcomings of this reliance on imported technology have thus become evident and at the end of the 1990s the authorities began to implement a new policy that put emphasis on the development of domestic innovative capacities.

As a result, China's R&D expenditures have increased. In 2006, China's R&D expenditure reached US$136 billion and China became the second largest R&D expending country in the world. Also, China's R&D expenditure share in GDP rose from 0.7 per cent in 1997 to 1.2 per cent in 2004 and reached 1.4 per cent in 2006 (UNCTAD, 2007). A key element of this new policy is the effort made by the authorities to define new Chinese standards, and to impose them instead of the existing technical standards to companies (multinational or local firms) operating in China. This strategy also aims at promoting national industries in the new context created by Chinese entry into the WTO, which limits the instruments available to protect domestic producers.

On the other hand, expansion of FDI may also help China to catch up. FIFs investing in China tend to increase their involvement in R&D activities. This is not only the result of political pressure from the Chinese government to intensify technology transfer but is also part of multinational firms' strategy in order to consolidate their presence in the Chinese market and strengthen their position in inter-firm rivalry. All multinational companies in China have built one or several R&D centres in China. Although their programmes may include mainly expenses for the development of products and their adaptation to the domestic market, they indicate a clear change in the strategy of foreign firms investing in China (Subbaraman and Sun, 2007).

Fortunately, there have been a small number of domestic firms that have emerged as important actors in the sectors of new technology. Their partnerships with multinational firms have helped them to build up their capacity to develop new technical standards. They are now both partners and competitors of world giants in strategic alliances. Although these firms are still more the exception than the rule, they raise the question of whether China can shift from its present position of rapid follower to a position of leader.

The gap between China and industrialized countries remains huge but China has made impressive progress in the field of scientific and technical innovation. The share of R&D expenditures in GDP is still low compared with that in advanced East Asian economies, but China's performance has improved significantly in the area of patent applications and grants, especially for innovation patents. However, in the number of patents applications at world level, China still plays a very marginal part, accounting for 0.2–0.3 per cent of the total, and stands well behind the Asian NIEs.

Facing New Trade Protection from Developed Countries

Until June 2008, the China–US trade surplus and the China–EU trade surplus continued to increase, causing a significant escalation in concern about China's unfair trading practices and the gross undervaluation of the RMB.

As the traditional measures of protection such as quantitative restriction have been prohibited by the WTO's rules, developed countries have employed more and more new types of trade protection on China's export. These new measures include antidumping duty (AD), countervailing duty (CVD), safeguards, technical barriers to trade (TBT), and so on.

After China's WTO accession, more and more AD cases filed have been toward Chinese goods. As shown in Table 2.8, the frequency and intention of US antidumping cases toward China have heightened since 2001. The number of investigations related to China was 37, which was 2.8 times more than the second largest target, India. The share of cases ruled as injury by the US International Trade Commission (ITC) was extraordinarily high, more than two-thirds. At the same time, the mean duty of cases related to Chinese goods was 150.3 per cent, much higher than the level of cases related to other trading partners.

The second largest target of US AD measures was India, another large developing country, but both the number of investigations and the share of injury cases were much lower than their Chinese counterparts. Japan, which was the most important object of US AD measures in the 1980s, was the third largest target after China's WTO accession. Although the mean duty related to Japanese goods was fairly high, the share of injury

Table 2.8 *US antidumping measures against its most frequently investigated trading partners, 2001–05*

Rank	Partner	Investigations	Injury (share %)	Only Country in Investigation	Mean Duty
1	China	37	25 (67.6%)	17 (45.9%)	150.3%
2	India	13	6 (46.2%)	3 (23.1%)	32.6%
3	Japan	10	3 (30.0%)	2 (20.0%)	71.1%
4	South Africa	10	1 (10.0%)	3 (30.0%)	116.0%
5	Canada	8	2 (25.0%)	7 (87.5%)	8.5%
6	Germany	8	1 (12.5%)	0	17.0%
7	Mexico	7	3 (42.9%)	0	44.3%
8	South Korea	7	3 (42.9%)	0	26.3%
9	Brazil	6	2 (33.3%)	1 (16.7%)	66.7%
10	Taiwan	6	1 (16.7%)	1 (16.7%)	2.4%
	Total	112	47 (42.0%)	34 (30.4%)	53.5%

Source: Office of Investigations, the United States International Trade Commission (ITC) (2008), Import Injury Investigation Case Statistics (FY 1980–2006).

cases and the share of cases only targeted to Japan were both very low, so, it is evident that in this period, there was great discrimination in US antidumping measures toward China.

Another area of trade policy where China has faced discriminatory treatment has arisen since its WTO accession. The terms of the accession agreement give WTO members the authority to enact 'China safeguards' in the case of surges of imports of products from China. In the GATT/WTO system, safeguards have traditionally been distinct from the 'unfair trade' laws such as antidumping in that users of safeguards do not need to establish that the foreign country or exporting firms have done anything unfair. All that is necessary is for the domestic industry to show that it has been injured or that there is a reasonable threat of injury, and that this injury is associated with an increase in imports (Bown and McCulloch, 2005).

At least, in principle, safeguard protection is applied to all sources of imports, in keeping with its use when injury to the domestic industry is not due to any unfair act of specific foreign suppliers. However, there are at least two new safeguards facing China alone. The first, authorized by Section 421 of the US trade law, is applicable to all products imported from China. It is administered in much the same way as the standard, WTO-authorized safeguard law of Section 201. Under both laws, the US ITC is charged with investigating injury, and in the case of an affirmative finding, making a remedy recommendation, which the US president then has the discretion to modify, accept or reject. The second new safeguard facing imports from China, which is administered by the Office of Textiles and Apparel in the US Department of Commerce, is applicable to all US imports of textile and apparel products from China.

To the end of 2007, six ITC investigations of Chinese exporters have been conducted under the China safeguard law. In three of the six cases, the ITC voted that the petitioning US industry was either injured or threatened with injury by Chinese exports and recommended that the US president use a trade remedy such as a tariff or quota to protect the domestic industry. However, in each case, the president exercised discretion and declined to implement the ITC's trade remedy recommendations. But in the future, as the use of AD and CVD measures will be restricted under WTO's rules, China safeguard law will be used more frequently and more severely.

After China's WTO accession, all circles in the United States have blamed the fact that the RMB exchange rate system leads to imbalance in Sino-US bilateral trade and they considered that the Chinese government manipulates China's currency. So they asked the US government to urge China to take action to rectify the RMB exchange rate system, the core of which is to achieve a large yuan appreciation immediately.

In September 2003, the US Treasury Secretary, John Snow, pointed out that the Chinese government should fulfil its international obligations to eliminate the imbalance of global payment. And RMB appreciation is the key approach. In the meantime, two famous economists at the Institute for International Economics in Washington, Goldstein and Lardy (see Goldstein, 2004 and Goldstein and Lardy, 2006), argued that a 15 to 25 per cent appreciation of the RMB is in China's favour so that China's foreign reserve can be controlled.

In 2004, the notorious Schumer–Graham bill asked the United States government to press China to reform the exchange rate regime, otherwise the United States would impose a 27.5 per cent additional import tariff on all Chinese goods. However, it is evident that the various myths mentioned above about RMB exchange rate and imbalance in Sino-US trade are absurd.

CONCLUSION

Since China's WTO accession, its huge trade expansion and significant shift of trade pattern is nothing short of spectacular. Among various driving factors, we have emphasized the effect of international segmentation of production. The outsourcing strategy of multinational corporations has transferred the labour-intensive stages of production processes to China.

Although high-tech trade has been playing a more important role in China's foreign trade, we cannot believe that China has already upgraded its domestic capabilities in actuality. China's high-tech trade just reflects the country's position in the international segmentation of production process, and there is a long way to go before its own technological upgrading.

China's trade expansion has a series of implications for the world economy. The position of advanced economies in global trade has been weakened. Emerging economies in Asia, however, though confronting competition with China, have not incurred large losses from the competition; instead they have exported more products to China in recent years.

China's trade performance is outstanding, but the country still deeply depends on developed economies' markets for its final products. And the imbalanced trade has raised a series of problems for itself and the rest of the world. The sustainability of China's export growth strategy is the most important and decisive one. China has little choice but to return to a more balanced growth in favour of domestic consumption.

NOTES

1. Calculated from China Customs Statistics.
2. Asian NIEs include Hong Kong, Singapore, South Korea and Taiwan.
3. ASEAN-4 are Malaysia, Philippines, Thailand and Indonesia.
4. The classification is based on Lall and Albaladejo (2004); Lall, Albaladejo and Zhang (2004).
5. Calculated from China Customs Statistics.
6. Calculated from China Customs Statistics.
7. Calculated from China Customs Statistics.
8. Calculated from China Customs Statistics.
9. Calculated from COMTRADE.

REFERENCES

Asian Development Bank (2007), *Asian Development Outlook 2007*, Asian Development Bank.

Blanchard, O. and F. Giavazzi (2005), 'Rebalancing Growth in China: A Three-handed Approach', Massachusetts Institute of Technology, Department of Economics, Working Paper No. 05-32, November.

Bown, C. and R. McCulloch (2005), 'US Trade Policy Toward China: Discrimination and its Implications', Paper presented at the PAFTAD 30th conference, the East-West Center, Honolulu, February 2005.

China Customs, *China Customs Statistics*, http://www1.customs.gov.cn/Default.as px?tabid=2453&moremoduleid=3760&moretabid=4370.

Gaulier, G., S. Jean and D. Ünal-Kesenci (2004), 'Regionalism and the Regionalization of International Trade', CEPII Working Paper No. 2004-16, November.

Gaulier, G., F. Lemoine and D. Ünal-Kesenci (2005), 'China's Integration in East Asia: Production Sharing, FDI and High-tech Trade', CEPII Working Paper No. 2005-09, June.

Gaulier, G., F. Lemoine and D. Ünal-Kesenci (2006), 'China's Emergence and the Reorganization of Trade Flows in Asia', CEPII Working Paper No. 2006-05, March.

Goldstein, M. (2004), 'Adjusting China's Exchange Rate Policies', Institute for International Economics Working Paper No. 04-1, http://www.iie.com/publications/wp/wp04-1.pdf, accessed 28 July 2008.

Goldstein, M. and N. Lardy (2006), 'China's Exchange Rate Policy Dilemma', *American Economic Review*, **96** (2), 422–6.

Lall, S. and M. Albaladejo (2004), 'China's competitive performance: a threat to East Asian manufactured exports?', *World Development*, **32** (9), 1441–66.

Lall, S., M. Albaladejo and J. Zhang (2004), 'Mapping Fragmentation: Electronics and Automobiles in East Asia and Latin America', QEH Working Paper Series No. 115, February.

Lee, K. and M. Kim (2004), 'The Rise of China and the Korean Firms Looking for a New Division of Labour', Proceedings on Rising China and the East Asian Economy, Korean Institute of International Economic Policy, Korea.

Li, K. and L. Song (2005), 'China's Trade Expansion and the Asia Pacific Economies', in Ross Garnaut and Ligang Song (eds), *China Boom and its Discontent*, Australian National University, Canberra: Asia Pacific Press, pp. 240–62.

Li, K., L. Song and X. Zhao (2007), 'Component Trade and China's Global Economic Integration', in Ross Garnaut and Ligang Song (eds), *China Linking Market for Growth*, Australian National University, Canberra: Asia Pacific Press, pp. 71–94.

Masuyama, S. (2004), 'The Asian Strategy of Japanese Multinationals: Focus on China', Tokyo Club Research Meetings, 9 February.

Ng, F. and A. Yeats (2003), 'Major Trade Trends in East Asia: What Are Their Implications for Regional Cooperation and Growth', World Bank Policy Research Paper Working Paper Series No. 3084, June.

OECD (2005), *Economic Surveys, China*, Volume 2005/13, September.

Office of Investigations, the United States International Trade Commission (ITC) (2008), Import Injury Investigation Case Statistics (FY 1980–2006), http://www.usitc.gov/trade_remedy/Report-01-08-PUB.pdf, accessed 28 July 2008.

Subbaraman, R. and M. Sun (2007), 'China's Re-emergence in the World Economy: Assessing the Implications', Lehman Brothers Working Paper, January.

UNCTAD (2007), *Trade and Development Report*, New York and Geneva: United Nations.

United Nations Statistics Division, Commodity Trade Statistics Database, COMTRADE, http://unstats.un.org/unsd/comtrade/default.aspx.

United States Government Printing Office (2008), *2008 US Economic Report of the President*.

3. Capital stock estimates by region and sector

Yanrui Wu

INTRODUCTION

China's economic reforms and, subsequently, rapid growth for three decades (1978–2007) have attracted a lot of attention both inside and outside the country. As a result, a vast literature has emerged.[1] While working on China's economic statistics, researchers have confronted a major problem, that is, no capital stock data are reported in the Chinese statistical system. Subsequently, researchers have attempted to derive China's capital stock data by themselves. Zhang (1991), He (1992) and Chow (1993) are examples of earlier studies on capital stock estimates and economic growth in China. Zhang and He represent two of the pioneering studies conducted by scholars inside China. Their capital stock estimates are based on the statistics of 'accumulation' defined under the traditional material product system (MPS) in China.[2] The latter was replaced by the UN-adopted system of national accounts (SNA) in the earlier 1990s and subsequently reporting of the 'accumulation' information was discontinued in 1993. Chow (1993) is one of the earlier studies published in English. His study covered the period of 1952–85. He derived capital stock series for five economic sectors, that is, agriculture, industry, construction, transportation and commerce. Chow's empirical estimations were based on data of national income, accumulation of fixed assets and circulating funds. He also derived an estimate of capital stock in agriculture by using data of the original value of fixed assets. It is well known that data on 'accumulation or 'original value' of fixed assets suffer from the serious problem of double-accounting (Chen et al., 1988).

Li, Gong and Zheng (1995) derived capital stock series by using the values of fixed and current assets. Their estimates suffer from the same problem as those in Chow (1993). Subsequently, Borensztein and Ostry (1996) and Woo (1998) applied the same database compiled by Li et al. (1995). More recent works include Hu and Khan (1997), World Bank (1997), Maddison (1998), Chow and Li (2002) and Holz (2006). Those studies cited so far mainly focused on capital stock estimates at the national level. There is a lack of investigation at the regional and sector levels.[3] The objective of this study is to review previous methods as well as findings and employs the recently released national accounts figures to derive capital stock series for China's 31 regions and three economic sectors (that is, agriculture, manufacturing and services) within each region. A review of the general methods of capital stock measurement is presented in the next section. This is followed by discussion of the approach employed for the construction of capital stock series for three sectors in China's regional economies. The estimation results and discussion are presented in the next two sections, respectively. Finally, summary remarks are reported in the concluding section.

CAPITAL STOCK MEASUREMENT TECHNIQUES

The approach of estimating capital stock values in this study belongs to the category of the conventional perpetual inventory method. The value of capital stock is estimated using gross investment or capital formation data in each year. Symbolically, the estimation technique can be expressed as

$$K_{ij,t} = (1 - \delta_{ij})K_{ij,t-1} + \Delta K_{ij,t} \qquad (3.1)$$

where $K_{ij,t}$ is the real value of capital stock for the ith sector of the jth region or economy in the tth year, $\Delta K_{ij,t}$ the real value of incremental capital stock or gross capital formation and δ_{ij} the rate of depreciation. Given the initial capital stock, $K_{ij,0}$, for the ith sector of the jth region or economy, equation (3.1) can then be converted into

$$K_{ij,t} = \Sigma_0^t(1 - \delta_{ij})^k \Delta K_{ij,t-k} + K_{ij,0}(1 - \delta_{ij})^t \qquad (3.2)$$

It is clear in equation (3.2) that the value of capital stock can be computed if the initial value of capital stock, $K_{ij,0}$, and the rate of depreciation, δ_{ij}, are known. For the latter, researchers have resorted to various sources such as national accounts, accounting records at the firm level, findings in the existing literature and ad hoc assumptions. As a result, different rates of depreciation have been used, ranging from 3.6 to 17.0 per cent (Table 3.1). Thus, the choice of the rate of depreciation is itself controversial. This study proposes an alternative approach to derive the rates of depreciation for the Chinese regions and economic sectors. In particular, different rates for each sector of China's regional economies are computed. This is the first of its kind in the literature.

As for the derivation of the initial value of capital stock, various

Table 3.1   Selected rates of depreciation and initial values of capital stock

Authors	Depreciation Rates (%)	Initial Value in 1952 (billion yuan in 1952 prices)
Zhang (1991)	n.a.	200.0[b]
He (1992)	n.a.	50.8[b]
Chow (1993)	n.a.	175.0
Hu and Khan (1997)	3.6	175.0
World Bank (1997)	4.0	n.a.
Perkins (1988)	5.0	200.6
Woo (1998)	5.0	n.a.
Meng and Wang (2000)	5.0	180.0[c]
Wang and Yao (2003)	5.0	175.0
Chow and Li (2002)	5.4[a]	221.3
Young (2003)	6.0	n.a.
Maddison (1998)	17.0	n.a.
Wu (2004)[d]	7.0	n.a.
Zhang (2008)[d]	9.6	n.a.

Notes:
a.   This rate was applied for the period of 1978–98 only.
b.   These numbers are cited in Zhang (2008).
c.   This is 1953 value in 1980 prices.
d.   Wu (2004) and Zhang (2008) are regional studies. Wu's approach is similar to this chapter. Thus no initial values of capital stock are needed. Zhang assumes that the initial value of capital stock in 1952 is equal to the value of fixed investment divided by 10%.
n.a. = not available.

approaches have been employed as well. Subsequently, different results have been derived (Table 3.1). While Chow (1993) provided detailed information and conducted sensitivity analysis, Li et al. (1995) and Maddison (1998) did not elaborate how they estimated the initial value, to cite a few. The main approaches employed in the literature are surveyed in the following section.[4] In general, the existing literature has used four categories of techniques in estimating the initial value of capital stock (Wu, 2008). They are here called the backcasting, the integral, the growth rate and other approaches, respectively.

The Backcasting Approach

According to the backcasting method, the data series for $\Delta K_{ij,t}$ in equation (3.2) are backcasted to the year 1900 using data available and thus the time-series sample has more than 100 observations. Accordingly, equation (3.2) is expanded to

$$K_{ij,t} = \Sigma_0^{t-1901}(1 - \delta_{ij})^k \Delta K_{ij,t-k} + (1 - \delta_{ij})^{t-1900} K_{ij,1900} \qquad (3.3)$$

Equation (3.3) implies that, given the value of capital stock in 1900, $K_{ij,1900}$, and an appropriate rate of depreciation, a capital stock series for each sector or region can be derived. Due to capital decay and the long time horizon, $K_{ij,1900}$ can be assumed to be zero. This is reasonable as the life span of capital is far shorter than 100 years and, in particular, as most studies of the Chinese economy only cover the recent decades, that is, the reform period. Thus, extending the data series to the year 1900 avoids the estimation of the initial value of capital stock.

The Integral Approach

The core of this technique is that the value of capital stock in the initial year is assumed to be the sum of all past investments. Symbolically,

$$K_{ij,0} = \int_{-\infty}^{0} \Delta K_{ij,t} dt = \frac{\Delta K_{ij,0} e^{\theta}}{\theta} \qquad (3.4)$$

where $\Delta K_{ij,t} = \Delta K_{ij,0} e^{\theta(t+1)}$, and θ and $\Delta K_{ij,0}$ are estimated by linear regressions using the investment series available. Among the existing studies, Wu (2000) adopted this approach. Obviously, capital decay is not taken into consideration in the integral approach of estimating the initial value of capital stock. In practice, this approach tends to overestimate the growth of capital stock. For example, Wu (2000) derived an average real annual rate of growth of 21.5 per cent for the Chinese economy during the period 1981–95. This figure is twice as big as the estimates derived by other authors. It is 8.86 per cent during 1978–95 according to Maddison (1998) and 7.90 per cent during 1979–95 according to the World Bank (1997), for instance. Furthermore, in order to apply this approach, one must have investment data that are suitable for regression analysis. This could be difficult in some cases.

The Growth Rate Approach

This approach is based on the assumption that the function of investment is to replace depreciation of old capital and create new capital to maintain growth (Harberger, 1978). Thus, the following equations are obtained:

$$\Delta K_{ij,1} = (\delta_{ij} + g_{ij}) K_{ij,0} \qquad (3.5)$$

That is,

$$K_{ij,0} = \frac{\Delta K_{ij,1}}{(\delta_{ij} + g_{ij})} \tag{3.6}$$

Equation (3.5) implies that the incremental capital stock or realized investment in period 1 is the sum of the depreciated capital stock from period 0 and new capital stock created. The latter is assumed to grow at the constant rate of g_{ij}, which is often replaced by the average growth rate of the incremental capital stock in the initial period, say, five years. In practice, authors have also used the rate of growth of investment or GDP when incremental capital stock data are not available. Young (2003) and Islam, Dai and Sakamoto (2006) followed this approach for their work on China.[5] Other applications include Nadiri and Prucha (1996) on the United States and Miyagawa, Ito and Harada (2004) on Japan. The main advantage of this approach is its simplicity and can hence be applied to small samples.

Other Approaches

Apart from the backcasting, integral and growth rate approaches, several other methods have also been proposed in the literature and are broadly called the 'other approaches' here. Examples include Perkins (1988) who assumed that the capital–output ratio was 3 in the year 1953, and Chow (1993) who relied on the statistics of 'accumulation of fixed assets'. He (1992) and Zhang and Zhang (2003) employed similar raw data to Chow (1993).[6] In addition, Holz (2006) applied official depreciation values and rates of depreciation to generate capital stock series for the period of 1978–2003.

As pointed out earlier, there are some capital stock estimates for China at the national and regional level. This study extends the literature and for the first time presents estimates of capital stock series for the sectors within the Chinese regions.

MEASURING REGIONAL AND SECTORAL CAPITAL STOCK

The objective of this section is to estimate capital stock for three sectors within China's regions. The approach employed falls into the category of the conventional perpetual inventory method. Three tasks must be completed first. These include the choice of deflators, estimation of region-and-sector-specific rates of depreciation and determination of the initial value of capital stock.

The first task is to find a time-varying and sector-specific price index for all regions, which is used to convert investment values into real terms. Such an index is not available in the official statistics until recent years.[7] For this purpose, sector-specific price indices for Chinese regions since 1978 are obtained using the following formulae:

$$P_{ijt}^{con} = Y_{ijt}^{cur} / Y_{ijt}^{con} \qquad (3.7)$$

where P_{ijt}^{con}, Y_{ijt}^{cur} and Y_{ijt}^{con} represent price indices in constant prices, income in current prices and income in constant prices for the ith sector of the jth region at period t. Y_{ijt}^{con} is defined as

$$Y_{ijt}^{con} = Y_{ij0}^{cur} \prod_0^t (1 + r_{ijk}) \qquad (3.8)$$

where r_{ijk} is the real rate of growth in income in the ith sector of the jth region in the kth year and Y_{ij0}^{cur} the initial income at current prices. These datasets are available from 1978 onwards for all regions and sectors. The derived region-and-sector-specific price indices are then used for the estimation of capital stock of each sector in every region. As a result, GDP and capital stock data are expressed in 1978 constant prices.[8]

The mean and standard deviation of the derived regional price indices are plotted in Figure 3.1. Several observations are worth noting. First, during 1978–2006, there were two main price hikes in the late 1980s and mid-1990s. Associated with these hikes was considerable regional variation in prices during the same periods. Second, there is some evidence of price convergence in the past decade as shown by the relatively lower values of standard deviation in Figure 3.1. Third, there is variation among the sectors as well. Thus, empirical analyses applying a single deflator for all regions and sectors can be misleading.

The second task is to derive an appropriate rate of depreciation for each sector within the regions. The latter has been assumed to be the same for all regions in the existing literature with the exception of Wu (2008). To remove this assumption, following Wu (2008), a simulation process is adopted to generate different rates of depreciation for the sectors of the regions. This is the first such exercise in the literature. The National Bureau of Statistics (NBS) (various issues) has released the values of depreciation for each sector in the regions since 1978. The simulation process begins by assuming a rate of depreciation for each sector of the regions and then searches for an optimal rate (via repetitive computations) so that the estimated values of depreciation (using the optimal rate) match the actual values of depreciation.[9] The final simulation results are presented in Table 3.2. In general, the rate of depreciation is high in the more developed regions and low in the less developed regions. The three municipal cities (Beijing, Tianjin and

Shanghai) also show relatively low rates of depreciation. This may be due to the fact that these cities have relatively large service sectors in which the rates of depreciation are smaller than those in the manufacturing sectors according to Table 3.2. It is interesting to note that the overall mean of the regional and sectoral rates of depreciation is about 4.2 per cent, which is close to the rates used by Hu and Khan (1997) and the World Bank (1997) and the mean estimated by Wu (2008). Thus, the application of a rate of depreciation of 7 per cent in Wu (2004), 9.6 per cent in Zhang (2008) and 17 per cent in Maddison (1998) would lead to the underestimation of China's capital stock.[10]

The third task deals with the estimation of the initial value of capital stock. For this purpose, the growth rate approach discussed in the preceding section, that is, equation (3.6), is employed here. After the completion of the three tasks, capital stock series for the sectors within the Chinese regions can be estimated using equation (3.2). The estimation results are discussed in the following sections.

ESTIMATION RESULTS

According to the estimates (not shown), China has enjoyed a steady rate of growth (11 per cent per annum) in capital accumulation since the initiative of economic reform in 1978.[11] Among the 31 Chinese regions, in terms of the value of capital stock, Jiangsu, Shandong, Zhejiang and Shanghai were in turn the top four regions in 2006 though Guangdong had the largest share in 1978 and 1990. As expected, the top four regions have achieved above-average growth in capital accumulation during 1978–2006, that is, 13 per cent in Jiangsu, Shandong and Shanghai and 14 per cent in Zhejiang. The western regions have shown a declining trend in capital endowment.[12] The group's share declined from 27.2 per cent in 1978 to 20.9 per cent in 1990 and 17.7 per cent in 2006 even though there has been a substantial increase in investment in the region since 1999.

At the sector level, the general trend is that the service sector is expanding while agriculture shrinks (Figure 3.2). Though declined slightly, the manufacturing sector still dominates the Chinese economy. However, during 1978–2006, the service sector has shown the trend of rapid catch-up.

For a comparison with the estimates by other authors, the growth rates of the derived capital stock in some periods are illustrated in Table 3.3. According to this table, the estimate of capital stock in this study is slightly higher than others cited, with the exception of Zhang (2008). It should be pointed out that the numbers in both Zhang (2008) and this study are

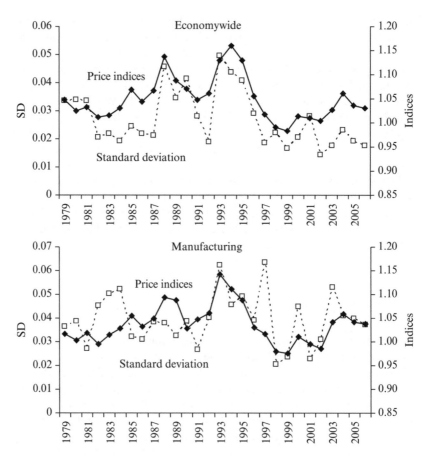

Source: Author's own estimates.

Figure 3.1   Standard deviation (SD) of regional price indices, 1979–2006

based on the arithmetic means of the estimates of regional capital stock data. However, the estimated rate of growth per annum is still below the rate of 11.5 per cent for Singapore, 13.7 per cent for South Korea and 12.3 per cent for Taiwan during the period of 1966–90 (Dougherty and Jorgenson, 1996). The lower estimates derived by other authors are debatable. The explanation may lie in the estimation of the initial capital stock value and the choice of the rate of depreciation. For example, while the World Bank (1997) used a rate of 4 per cent, Maddison (1998) assumed an average asset life of 25 years, equivalent to an annual rate of depreciation of 17 per cent.

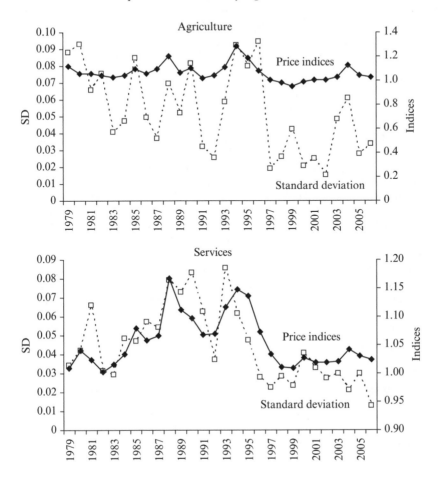

CAPITAL FORMATION AND REGIONAL DISPARITY

Regional disparity and hence convergence have for years been a hotly debated question in China. This question can also be explored in terms of capital stock formation among the regions. Figure 3.3 illustrates the movement of the mean rates of growth in regional capital stock. At the earlier stage of economic reform, capital stock achieved similar growth in agriculture and manufacturing and at the national level. The service sector was an exception. However, during the entire decade of the 1980s, agriculture lagged behind the rest of the economy. The gap has been reduced since the early 1990s.

Table 3.2   Rates of depreciation (%) in the Chinese economy

Regions	Agriculture	Manufacturing	Services	Average	Wu (2008)
Beijing	1.4	5.7	3.2	4.0	3.4
Tianjin	1.0	5.7	3.1	4.3	3.7
Hebei	1.6	6.1	3.5	4.5	4.3
Shanxi	1.2	6.1	3.6	4.7	4.0
Inner Mongolia	1.6	5.0	6.1	4.6	4.3
Liaoning	1.6	7.0	6.3	6.1	5.8
Jilin	1.6	7.0	6.3	5.7	5.1
Heilongjiang	1.6	7.0	6.3	6.2	6.0
Shanghai	0.6	4.8	2.7	3.6	3.4
Jiangsu	2.3	4.2	5.5	4.5	4.2
Zhejiang	2.3	5.3	3.5	4.3	4.0
Anhui	1.6	6.1	3.5	4.2	5.0
Fujian	1.6	6.4	3.5	4.6	4.5
Jiangxi	1.6	6.1	3.5	4.1	3.7
Shandong	2.7	7.0	4.1	5.4	5.0
Henan	1.6	6.1	3.5	4.3	4.1
Hubei	1.6	4.7	5.2	4.5	4.5
Hunan	1.6	5.8	5.2	4.7	4.5
Guangdong	2.3	7.0	5.5	6.0	6.9
Guangxi	2.5	3.7	3.5	3.3	3.3
Hainan	1.6	2.3	3.5	2.5	2.2
Chongqing	1.5	7.0	3.5	4.6	5.0
Sichuan	1.5	7.0	3.5	4.5	4.6
Guizhou	1.3	4.6	3.5	3.4	2.8
Yunnan	0.8	3.5	3.5	2.9	2.7
Tibet	0.6	2.6	3.5	2.6	4.2
Shaanxi	1.8	3.7	3.5	3.4	3.3
Gansu	1.8	3.8	3.2	3.2	2.7
Qinghai	0.6	2.6	3.5	2.7	2.4
Ningxia	1.8	3.2	3.2	3.0	2.8
Xinjiang	1.9	3.0	2.7	2.7	2.6
Mean	1.6	5.2	4.0	4.2	4.0

Source: Author's owner estimates. The 'average' rates are the GDP-weighted means of
regional rates.

Regional disparity and hence convergence can be examined using the
values of standard deviation as shown in Figure 3.4. Several points are
worthy of mention. First, disparity in regional capital formation became
worse immediately after the launch of economic reform in 1978. It peaked
in the mid-1980s and went through a period of improvement for several

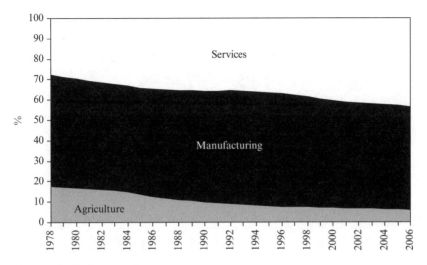

Source: Author's own estimates.

Figure 3.2 Capital stock shares in the sectors

Table 3.3 Growth rates of China's capital stock

Sources	Periods	Growth Rate (%)
Li et al. (1995)	1979–90	9.15
Hu and Khan (1997)	1979–94	7.70
World Bank (1997)	1979–95	7.90
Maddison (1998)	1978–95	8.86*
Zhang (2008)	1979–90	10.27
	1979–95	10.85
	1979–2005	11.79
This study	1979–90	9.71
	1979–95	10.49
	1979–2006	11.09

Note: * Non-residential capital only.

years. Second, regional disparity deteriorated following the economic take-off immediately after the 'southern tour' by Deng Xiaoping in 1992. Third, regional disparity reached the highest level in the mid-1990s. This is followed by a period of convergence. There is, however, more regional difference in terms of regional growth in agricultural capital stock in the last decade.

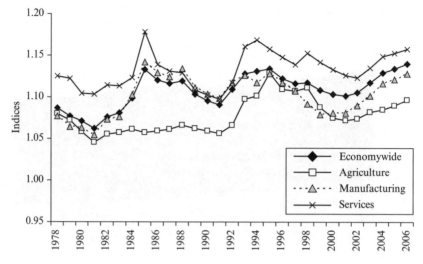

Source: Author's own calculation.

Figure 3.3   Average rates of growth in capital stock, 1978–2006

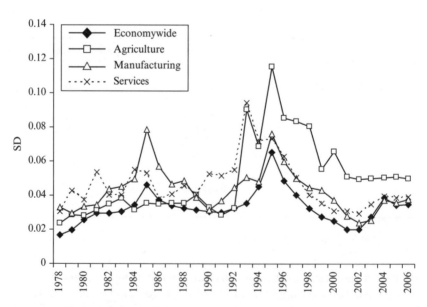

Source: Author's own calculation.

Figure 3.4   Standard deviation of capital stock growth rates, 1978–2006

CONCLUSION

In summary, this study presents a review of the literature and techniques in capital stock measurement and introduces an alternative approach to estimating capital stock series for the three sectors in China's 31 regional economies. This approach overcomes the problem in the existing literature of assuming ad hoc rates of depreciation. In particular, it allows for different depreciation rates for the sectors (agriculture, manufacturing and services) in the regions. The derived capital stock data series are important resources for research on the Chinese economy.

A preliminary examination of the estimated dataset shows that capital stock has expanded substantially among the sectors within China's regional economies. However, in terms of capital endowment, manufacturing still dominates the economy while agriculture is rapidly declining and the service sector is steadily rising. Furthermore, the estimated capital stock series can also shed some light on the debate of regional disparity in China. It is found that regional disparity in terms of capital formation became worse off at the earlier stage of economic reform and in the first half of the 1990s. This may be due to regional variation in responding to reform initiatives at the beginning of economic reform and again after the 'southern tour' by Deng Xiaoping in 1992. There is some evidence of regional convergence, particularly in the past decade. This may be the result of the implementation of the 'go-west' programme since 1999. However, how effective this programme has been needs a more detailed investigation.

Finally, it should be pointed out that empirical application of the estimated capital stock series in this study is subject to several qualifications. First, while the use of sector-and-region-specific rates of depreciation is a major advance in this study, dynamic issues are ignored. That is, the rates could vary over time. Second, due to the non-existence of land markets and hence private land ownership, in particular, rural land market and ownership, land values are not incorporated into the estimates of capital stock. Third, before economic reform began, many Chinese enterprises were located in the interior areas, which are often far away from the border regions for strategic reasons during the Cold War era. Since the beginning of economic reforms in 1978, many of those enterprises have been relocated to the coastal regions or closer to the source of raw materials. These relocation activities may affect regional/sectoral capital stock values and are not reflected in the derived statistics.

NOTES

1. Examples include the World Bank (1997), Maddison (1998), Woo (1998), Bramall (2000), Wang and Fan (2000), Young (2003), Wu (2004, 2008) and Garnaut and Song (2004, 2005).
2. Zhang and Zhang (2003) also used the accumulation data. Wu (1993) presented some discussion comparing MPS with SNA (system of national accounts).
3. Chow (1993) did report estimates for five sectors (agriculture, industry, construction, transportation and commerce) and Wu (1995) considered three sectors (agriculture, urban state and rural industry). More recently, Zhang (2008) and Wu (2008) provided capital stock estimates for China's regional economies.
4. Qian and Smyth (2006) also estimated regional capital stock with 1990 being treated as the initial year. They summed up 'fixed assets accumulation' for all years from 1949 to 1989 as the initial value of capital stock and then assumed a rate of depreciation of 5 per cent to estimate regional capital stock up to the year 2000.
5. Islam et al. (2006) also assumed the rate of depreciation to be 3 per cent during 1952–78, 4 per cent during 1979–92 and 5 per cent during 1993–2002.
6. Detailed descriptions are available in Zhang (2008).
7. Several price indices such as regional CPI are available from 1978 onwards while this study needs sector-specific price information too.
8. It is noted that researchers have attempted to derive their own deflators for samples that are much smaller than the one used in this chapter and that involve either sectoral or nationwide statistics only (for example, Chen et al., 1988 and Woo et al., 1994). Zhang (2008) derived price deflators using implicit deflators of fixed capital formation. The latter has, however, many missing observations that have to be filled by using other price indices.
9. The searching process stops when the two sets of values converge. For example, in this study, the process stops when the difference of two values is less than 0.001 per cent. It should be noted that the simulation process could introduce a time dimension allowing for time-varying rates of depreciation. This is more complicated and beyond the scope of this study.
10. Maddison (1998) assumes that capital has a life span of 25 years, which effectively implies a rate of depreciation as high as 17 per cent and that after 25 years, less than 1 per cent of the original value remains.
11. The estimated dataset is available from the author upon request.
12. The western regions covered under the 'go-west' programme initiated in 1999 include China's 12 administrative areas, that is, five autonomous regions (Guangxi, Inner Mongolia, Ningxia, Tibet and Xinjiang), six provinces (Gansu, Guizhou, Qinghai, Shaanxi, Sichuan and Yunnan) and one municipality (Chongqing).

REFERENCES

Borensztein, E. and J. Ostry (1996), 'Accounting for China's growth performance', *American Economic Review (Papers and Proceedings)*, **86** (2), 225–8.
Bramall, C. (2000), *Sources of Chinese Economic Growth, 1978–1996*, Oxford and New York: Oxford University Press.
Chen, K., H. Wang, Y. Zheng, G. Jefferson and T. Rawski (1988), 'Productivity change in Chinese industry, 1953–85', *Journal of Comparative Economics*, **12** (4), 570–91.
Chow, G. (1993), 'Capital formation and economic growth in China', *Quarterly Journal of Economics*, **108** (3), 809–42.

Chow, G. and K. Li (2002), 'China's economic growth: 1952–2010', *Economic Development and Cultural Change*, **51** (1), 247–56.

Dougherty, C. and D. Jorgenson (1996), 'International comparisons of the sources of economic growth', *American Economic Review (Papers and Proceedings)*, **86** (2), 25–9.

Garnaut, R. and L. Song (eds) (2004), *China: Is Rapid Growth Sustainable?*, Canberra: Asia Pacific Press.

Garnaut, R. and L. Song (eds) (2005), *The China Boom and its Discontents*, Canberra: ANU E Press and Asia Pacific Press.

Harberger, A. (1978), 'Perspectives on Capital and Technology in Less Developed Countries', in M. Artis and A. Nobay (eds), *Contemporary Economic Analysis*, London: Croom Helm, pp. 15–40.

He, J. (1992), 'Estimates of our country's capital' (*Shuliang Jingji yu Jishu Jingji Yanjiu*) *Quantitative and Technical Economics* (8), 24–7.

Holz, C. (2006), 'New capital estimates for China', *China Economic Review*, **17** (2), 142–85.

Hu, Z. and M. Khan (1997), 'Why is China growing so Fast?', *IMF Staff Papers*, **44** (1), 103–31.

Islam, N., E. Dai and H. Sakamoto (2006), 'Sources of Growth', in Y. Wu (ed.), *Economic Growth, Transition and Globalization in China*, Cheltenham, UK and Northampton, MA, USA: Edward Elgar Publishing, pp. 13–60.

Li, J., F. Gong and Y. Zheng (1995), 'Productivity and China's Economic Growth, 1953–1990', in K. Tsui, T. Hsueh and T. Rawski (eds), *Productivity, Efficiency and Reform in China's Economy*, Hong Kong: Chinese University of Hong Kong, pp. 19–54.

Maddison, A. (1998), *Chinese Economic Performance in the Long Run*, Paris: OECD Development Centre.

Meng, L. and X. Wang (2000), 'Assessment of the Reliability of China's Economic Growth Statistics', Monograph, National Economic Research Institute, Beijing.

Miyagawa, T., Y. Ito and N. Harada (2004), 'The IT revolution and productivity growth in Japan', *Journal of the Japanese and International Economies*, **18** (2), 362–89.

Nadiri, M. and I. Prucha (1996), 'Estimation of the depreciation rate of physical and R&D capital in the U.S. total manufacturing sector', *Economic Inquiry*, **34** (1), 43–56.

National Bureau of Statistics (NBS) (various issues), *China Statistical Yearbook*, Beijing: China Statistics Press.

Perkins, D. (1988), 'Reforming China's economic system', *Journal of Economic Literature*, **26** (2), 601–45.

Qian, X. and R. Smyth (2006), 'Growth accounting for the Chinese provinces 1990–2000: incorporating human capital accumulation', *Journal of Chinese Economic and Business Studies*, **4** (1), 21–38.

Wang, X. and G. Fan (eds) (2000), *The Sustainability of China's Economic Growth*, Beijing: Economic Sciences Press.

Wang, Y. and Y. Yao (2003), 'Sources of China's economic growth 1952–1999: incorporating human capital accumulation', *China Economic Review*, **14** (1), 32–52.

Woo, W. (1998), 'Chinese Economic Growth: Sources and Prospects', in M. Fouquin and F. Lemoine (eds), *The Chinese Economy*, Paris: Economica Ltd, pp. 17–48.

Woo, W., W. Hai, Y. Jin and G. Fan (1994), 'How successful has Chinese enterprise reform been? Pitfalls in opposite biases and focus', *Journal of Comparative Economics*, **18** (3), 410–37.

World Bank (1997), *China 2020: Development Challenges in the New Century*, Washington, DC: World Bank.

Wu, H. (1993), 'The "real" Chinese gross domestic product (GDP) for the pre-reform period 1952–77', *Review of Income and Wealth*, **39** (1), 63–86.

Wu, Y. (1995), 'Productivity growth, technological progress and technical efficiency change in China: a three-sector analysis', *Journal of Comparative Economics*, **21** (2), 207–29.

Wu, Y. (2000), 'Is China's economic growth sustainable: a productivity analysis', *China Economic Review*, **11** (3), 278–96.

Wu, Y. (2004), *China's Economic Growth: A Miracle with Chinese Characteristics*, London and New York: RoutledgeCurzon Press Limited.

Wu, Y. (2008), *Productivity, Efficiency and Economic Growth in China*, London and New York: Palgrave Macmillan.

Young, A. (2003), 'Gold into base metals: productivity growth in the People's Republic of China during the reform period', *Journal of Political Economy*, **111** (1), 1220–61.

Zhang, J. (1991), 'Systemic analysis of economic efficiency during the 5th Five Year Plan' (*Jingji Yanjiu*) *Journal of Economic Research* (4), 8–17.

Zhang, J. (2008), 'Estimation of China's provincial capital stock (1952–2004) with applications', *Journal of Chinese Economic and Business Studies*, **6** (2), 177–96.

Zhang, J. and Y. Zhang (2003), 'Re-estimates of China's capital stock' (*Jingji Yanjiu*) *Journal of Economic Research* (7), 35–43.

4. The WTO and China's transparency requirements

Vivienne Bath

INTRODUCTION

When China acceded to the World Trade Organization (WTO) in 2001, it gave a number of specific commitments to improve the 'transparency' of its regulatory regime in relation to trade and trade-related matters. These commitments can be found in Part I, paragraph 2(C) of the Protocol on the Accession of the People's Republic of China (WTO, 2001a). The primary Chinese commitments are mainly based on, and to some extent supplement, the requirements set out in Article X of the General Agreement on Tariffs and Trade (GATT) and Article III of the General Agreement on Trade in Services (GATS). A wider issue that the Chinese government needed to address in order to satisfy these commitments, however, was the overall question of the transparency of the Chinese regulatory regime, in terms of the ready availability of legislation and the ability of the public to have input into legislation and information about (and hence some degree of control over) the exercise of regulatory power by Chinese government and regulatory bodies. In short, the establishment of a more open legislative and regulatory system in China is an integral part of the effective implementation of China's WTO obligations relating to trade.

China has undoubtedly made considerable progress in relation to its commitments on transparency, although international satisfaction with the result is not universal. This chapter addresses a number of issues relating to China's compliance with its requirements and the question of transparency in the Chinese legal and regulatory regime.

WTO REQUIREMENTS

The Protocol sets out three primary commitments under the heading 'Transparency'. China undertook that only published and readily available 'laws, regulations and other measures pertaining to or affecting trade in goods, services, TRIPS or the control of foreign exchange' would be enforced (WTO, 2001a, paragraph (C)(1)). On request, all such laws, regulations or measures would be made available to WTO members before they were implemented or enforced (WTO, 2001a, paragraph 1). Second, China agreed to establish or designate an official journal dedicated to the publication of these laws, regulations and measures and to allow a reasonable period for comment before the implementation of such laws and measures (WTO, 2001a, paragraph 2). Third, China agreed to establish an enquiry point where 'all information relating to the measures required to be published under paragraph 2(C)(1) of this Protocol may be obtained' (WTO, 2001a, paragraph (C)(1)). As noted in the Report of the Working Party on the Accession of China (WTO, 2001b), the representative of China also confirmed that translations into one of the WTO official languages (English, French and Spanish) of 'all laws, regulations and other measures pertaining to or affecting trade in goods, services, TRIPS or the control of foreign exchange' would be made available to WTO members (WTO, 2001b, paragraph 334).

COMPLIANCE

There have been a number of different responses to the question: has China fully satisfied these requirements? The conclusion of the 2006 China's 'Trade Policy Review' reported by the WTO Secretariat is generally positive (WTO, 2006).[1] The report comments favourably on the promulgation of laws and regulations designed to improve transparency and, in particular, on the provisions of the Administrative Licensing Law of the People's Republic of China, which came into effect on 1 July 2004 (NPCC, 2003, Article 83). The requirements of the Law on Legislation relating to soliciting the opinions of the public on proposed legislation are also cited with approval (NPCC, 2000, Articles 35 and 58), as is the promotion of the use of the Internet by government departments to publish legislation and to solicit public input. The report by China for the purposes of the second 'Trade Policy Review' in 2008 (WTO, 2008b, paragraph 83) also cites the promulgation of the Regulations of the People's Republic of China on the Disclosure of Government Information (SCC, 2007a), which came into effect on 1 May 2008, and China's first comprehensive notification of subsidies in 2006 as evidence of its commitment to transparency. The 2008 report by the Secretariat also cites the regulations as an example of China's moves towards increased transparency (WTO, 2008a, pp. 28–9).

In contrast, the report of the United States Trade Representative to Congress at the end of 2006 on China's compliance with its transparency obligations is considerably less favourable. The authors of the 2006 USTR report criticized the Chinese government for its delay in designating a single official journal for the publication of all trade-related measures, and its failure to 'regularize the use of notice-and-comment procedures for new or revised trade-related measures prior to implementation' (USTR, 2006, p. 10). Although China did adopt an official journal in 2007, as discussed below, the United States Trade Representative was still expressing dissatisfaction in relation to transparency in its 2007 report, as follows: 'many of China's regulatory regimes continued to suffer from systemic opacity, frustrating efforts of foreign – and domestic – businesses to achieve the potential benefits of China's WTO accession' (USTR, 2007, p. 11). The 2007 report singles out for criticism China's record on transparency relating to standards, particularly sanitary and phytosanitary standards and the regime relating to agricultural products (ibid., pp. 47–8).

Similarly, the US-China Business Council in 2007 took the view that:

> [t]ransparency is one of the most important problems that companies face in China, both in terms of the ability to do business and China's compliance with a major WTO principle. . .. There can be no question that China's legislative and regulatory processes are far more transparent than ever before . . . Despite the PRC State Council's March 2006 notice requiring all laws and regulations affecting trade in services, intellectual property, or foreign exchange to be published in MOFCOM's *Gazette*, about 60 percent of USBC 2007 survey respondents noted no improvements in transparency in the past year. (US-China Business Council, 2007, pp. 7–8)

There are several questions to be addressed here. First, has China formally complied with its obligations? Second, is this formal compliance reflected in practical improvements in the accessibility of relevant information and materials? Third, to what extent does this demonstrate an overall (and lasting) improvement in the transparency and openness of the regulatory regime?

ENQUIRY POINTS; PUBLICATION AND NOTIFICATION OF LAWS; OFFICIAL GAZETTE

The Chinese government has made significant efforts to meet its obligations in relation to formal compliance with its disclosure obligations. The Ministry of Foreign Trade and Economic Cooperation (MOFTEC) (now the Ministry of Commerce (MOFCOM)) established an enquiry point and method for requests for information to be made in 2002 (MOFTEC, 2002). The official enquiry point for technical barriers to trade (TBT) is now (in English) the WTO/TBT National Notification Authority & Enquiry Point of the PRC, which administers a special website, the WTO/ TBT-SPS Notification and Enquiry of China website, under the General Administration of Quality Supervision, Inspection and Quarantine of the PRC (AQSIQ). The 2007 USTR report (USTR, 2007, p. 107) states that United States companies have generally found the various enquiry points to be 'responsive and helpful'. As noted in the report, various other Chinese ministries and agencies have also set up websites to provide answers and provide information. Although not listed in the 2008 USTR report, these include the Shanghai WTO Affairs Consultation Center, under the Shanghai Municipal Government, and the Guangdong WTO Affairs Consultation Service Center, both of which provide information and services relating to the WTO. The Shanghai WTO Affairs Consultation Center is in fact cited as a successful case study on the WTO website for its success in dealing with WTO inquiries and potential disputes. In fact, the website of the Shanghai WTO Affairs Consultation Center is considerably easier to use as a source of information on China's WTO obligations than the official website of the Ministry of Commerce.

Although less comprehensive than the Chinese version of the website, the English version of the WTO/TBT-SPS Notification and Enquiry of China website provides a lengthy list of notifications and English summaries of standards for TBT (technical barriers to trade) and SPS (sanitary and phytosanitary measures). Full copies of the standards are, however, generally available from the website only in Chinese. The 2007 USTR report complains that the measures notified to the WTO generally do not include measures from such agencies as the Ministry of Health (although there are some notifications from the Ministry of Health on the WTO/ TBT-SPS Notification and Enquiry of China website), the Ministry for Information Industry (now the Ministry for Industry and Information), the State Environmental Protection Administration (now the Ministry of Environmental Protection) and the State Food and Drug Administration (USTR, 2007, p. 48). This suggests that there is an incomplete level of cooperation between the relevant Chinese government agencies in relation to the compilation and systematic notification of information required under the WTO, particularly since the State Food and Drug Administration website does contain information on standards.

An important part of transparency is the easy availability and accessibility of information, particularly where a country uses a language and writing system such as Chinese, which is not easily accessed by non-native speakers. In this regard, although considerable information is available on government-run websites on the Internet, the accessibility to foreigners of English (and Chinese) versions of the relevant websites is an issue.

The links on the Ministry of Commerce website (which is named on the WTO website as China's official WTO website) to the Chinese WTO enquiry points and to other means of providing WTO-related information on laws and regulations are far from complete. Although the WTO/TBT-SPS Notification and Enquiry of China website provides contacts by telephone and e-mail for both TBT and SPS, no information about SPS notifications for China appears on the WTO website. The information about the TBT Enquiry Point on the WTO website for China is under a different name (the Research Center for International Inspection and Quarantine Standards and Technical Regulations) to what now appears to be the official name (the WTO/TBT-SPS Notification and Enquiry of the People's Republic of China) and, although it includes an e-mail contact, does not provide a website reference or link. Similarly, in order to locate a link to the WTO/TBT-SBS Notification and Enquiry of China on the Ministry of Commerce website, it is necessary to go to the sub-heading for the WTO/FTA Consultative Net, which appeared, when checked, to have no functioning English version. There is no similar link on the English language website of the Ministry of Commerce, even through the WTO Affairs Department. There also appears to be no link to the Ministry of Commerce website on the WTO/TBT-SPS Notification and Enquiry of China website. As a result, searching for the relevant information can be time-consuming and difficult. The paucity of website links between the different ministries dealing with notifications and even on the Ministry of Commerce website itself to relevant departments within the Ministry of Commerce suggests a lack of internal coherence in the way in which these important issues are dealt with within the administration.

As a related point, the English version of the website of the Ministry of Commerce is not particularly informative in relation to the WTO activities of the Ministry of Commerce, nor is specific information on WTO and WTO compliance particularly accessible or easy to locate from the English version of this website, although more material is available in Chinese. The website does contain a considerable amount of information that is helpful to foreign businesses and investors, but information specifically related to the WTO is not emphasized in the overall arrangement of the site. Curiously enough, the 'trade in services' group, which has its own sub-heading on the Ministry of Commerce website, has more English language information on the WTO (including WTO documents) than is contained in the WTO Affairs Department's part of the website.

China also made commitments in the Protocol in relation to the publication and notification of laws and regulations. In 2006, in response to pressure particularly from the United States, the State Council issued the State Council Circular on Work Related to Further Fulfilling the

Transparency Provisions in China's Accession Agreement to the World Trade Organization, which designated the *China Foreign Trade and Economic Cooperation Gazette*, a publication issued by the Ministry of Commerce, as the official journal for all laws, regulations and other measures relating to (or affecting) trading in goods, services, intellectual property and exchange control, in accordance with its WTO obligations. The *Gazette* is published by the Ministry of Commerce on its Chinese language website, although an English language table of contents, some English language summaries and some links through to the Chinese versions of the legislation are provided on the English language website.

In practice, at this stage the designation of the *China Foreign Trade and Economic Cooperation Gazette* does not appear to deal with all of the issues relating to the notification of trade-related legislation. First, the location of the English version of the Ministry of Commerce website is problematic as finding it requires going through the sub-heading 'Policy Release'. The *Gazette* sets out a list of laws and regulations in a short version in English and Chinese, but often does not contain links either to a summary or to the full version of the document in either English or Chinese. Links to the full document, when they do occur, are generally to the Chinese version of the legislation. Headings are often unhelpful if no link is provided – for example, 'Announcement No. 13, 2008 of the National Development and Reform Commission of the People's Republic of China' (*China FTEC Gazette*, 2008). Despite the undertaking referred to above in relation to the translation of trade-related legislation into a WTO official language, full translations are not available from this source, although English versions of major pieces of legislation are produced and made available relatively quickly on commercial websites, and on other websites run by various parts of the Chinese government. One example is another website run by the Ministry of Commerce itself, the 'Invest in China' site.

The timing and content of the information in the *Gazette* is also questionable. For example, Decree No. 512 of the State Council, which issued the Regulations for the Implementation of the Law of the People's Republic of China on Enterprise Income Tax, promulgated on 6 December 2007 and effective on 1 January 2008, was not included in the *Gazette* until Issue No. 16, 2008 (posted 5 May 2008). The Law on Mediation and Arbitration of Labour Disputes, which was promulgated on 29 December 2007, had not, at the end of May 2008, been notified in the *Gazette*, despite its potential significance for any company employing labour or dealing with Chinese companies that employ labour in China.

In addition, it is far from clear that the *Gazette* includes all trade-related legislation that is issued by regional governments within China and by ministries other than the Ministry of Commerce. As an example, the first 18 issues of the *Gazette* list 174 laws and regulations, of which only 32 were issued by provincial or regional governments. The Ministry of Commerce itself accounts for by far the largest number of administrative regulations listed in the *Gazette*. It is no wonder, then, that the 2007 USTR report comments that 'adherence to the State Council's notice is far from complete' (USTR, 2007, p. 105).

The Protocol provided that China would only enforce published and readily available laws relating to trade. This has been a long-standing issue for foreigners in China, and, for many years, the standard equity joint venture contract included references to 'published laws' in order to deal with claims by the Chinese party and local government that a transaction is subject to 'internal (*neibu*) requirements which could not be shown to foreigners' (Lubman, 2006). The Law on Legislation now requires that all legislation be published (NPCC, 2000, Articles 52, 62, 70 and 77). In 2003, the Ministry of Commerce attempted to set the standard for government agencies in terms of the publication of information by issuing the Interim Measures of the Ministry of Commerce on Publicizing Government Affairs, which required the publication of legislation in print and on the Ministry of Commerce website and release of rules for a 10-day comment period.

On the positive side, the availability of both Chinese and English versions of recent trade-related legislation on the Internet and elsewhere (not including commercial sites for which a paid subscription is required) has certainly improved over the last 10 years or so. In addition to the links to legislation available through the *Gazette*, another website run by the Ministry of Commerce, 'Invest in China', is an excellent source of central-level legislation, in both English and Chinese, and also includes some summaries of decisions in arbitration and court cases relating to investment and trade disputes. In addition, as the authors of the first 'Trade Policy Review' comment (WTO, 2006), websites run by government departments at the central and local level now include large amounts of information on legislation and government decisions, although the quality of the various sites, particularly in the English version, and the timeliness of the information provided varies considerably. In some cases, for example, local government websites are better sources of information on central government legislation than the central government websites. Again, a significant issue here is that due to the siloed nature of Chinese government (discussed in more detail below), the information included on government websites is focused on materials directly relevant to or issued by that ministry and is rarely linked to websites of other government departments, even when this would be helpful. There is no one government source in China for central or local legislation that would compare with sites such as www.comlaw. gov.au, which makes available all laws and regulations of the Australian federal government, or www.gpoaccess.gov, the United States Printing Office online publishing service. As a result, locating up-to-date Chinese legislation, particularly at a provincial or local level, continues to be a difficult and unreliable process.

ISSUES – STANDARDS

A major issue is the use of standards and non-transparent legal measures in order to impose impediments on trade. This is in many ways a technical issue. However, it should be noted that the United States Trade Representative continues to believe that China uses such methods in relation in particular to agriculture (as noted above) and that in a number of cases its product standard notifications do not comply with its obligations under the Agreement on Technical Barriers to Trade. Issues cited in the 2006 USTR report include the entry into force of technical standards without prior notification to the TBT Committee and without foreign companies having had the opportunity to comment on the standards, and comment periods that importers consider to be unacceptably short (USTR, 2006, pp. 45–6). The 2007 USTR report also includes a number of examples of cases where, it is alleged, legislation on standards that could have a significant effect on importers was brought in without notice (or adequate notice) or consultation (USTR, 2007, p. 48). In its negotiations with the Chinese government in relation to the entry into a free trade agreement (FTA), the Australian government has also raised the issue of transparency in connection with sanitary and phytosanitary assessment for the purpose of imports and in connection with standards generally (DFAT, 2005). We can expect that, in the free trade agreement discussions and elsewhere, the general issue of transparency in relation to the imposition of standards, as well as China's moves towards the creation and imposition of its own distinctive standards, will continue to be raised. However, it should be noted that the provisions on transparency in the recently signed New Zealand-China Free Trade Agreement do not add materially to China's obligations on transparency (MFAT, 2008, Articles 98 and 168). The emphasis in the future is likely to be on enforcement of the existing obligations rather than the introduction of new requirements.

ISSUES – OPENNESS OF THE LEGAL SYSTEM

The second question is the openness of the Chinese system in relation to the publication of laws, regulations and other measures, and solicitation of comments and views from the public and affected parties. Here there are a number of issues that the Chinese government has had to address. The first is the establishment of a coherent legislative system, an issue that arises both from the ad hoc way in which the current Chinese legislative framework of laws, administrative rules and other measures developed historically, and from the 'silo' structure of the Chinese government, which leads to a plethora of possibly inconsistent laws, regulations and other measures and, of course, local protectionism.

The Chinese government system incorporates both horizontal and vertical lines of command. Vertically, the Central Government, and the ministries and agencies under the State Council, is at the top, with the provinces, autonomous regions, municipalities under central control directly under it and municipalities and the various levels of local government (prefectures, cities, countries, towns and townships) below them. Within the various levels of government, there are different ministries and bureaus, each of which has a substantial amount of independence and power and tends to operate autonomously and often without a significant degree of cooperation with ministries and bureaus of the same level. In addition, the ability of the individual ministries to control the offices vertically below them in different levels of government differs. Within a municipal government, therefore, there may be conflicts between the requirements of higher-level government and municipal government policy, and, within a government office, there may be conflicts between the orders of the higher-level ministry and the pressures applied by the local government. The courts are a good example of this structural conflict. Under the Constitution, the Supreme People's Court supervises the administration of justice by the people's courts at all levels (NPCC, 2004, Article 126). Pursuant to Article 128 of the Constitution, however, the local people's courts are responsible to the organs of state power that appointed them.[2] The difficulties posed for judges in attempting to fulfil their responsibilities in this structure (even without taking account of the parallel chain of command created by the Communist Party of China) are self-evident.

The Law on Legislation, based on the legislative structure set out in the Constitution, attempted to resolve some of these problems by defining as clearly as possible which level of government may pass certain types of legislation. Thus, laws (*falu*) may only be passed by the National People's Congress, or the Standing Committee of the National People's Congress (Article 7), while 'administrative regulations' (*xingzheng fagui*) are issued by the State Council (Article 56). Local regulations (*difangxing fagui*) may be issued by the people's congresses and standing committees of provinces, autonomous regions and municipalities directly under the central government (such as Beijing and Shanghai) and, in some circumstances, of larger municipalities (Article 62). Where this system presents particular issues is when a conflict arises between a piece of legislation passed by a local authority and a national law. Pursuant to Article 67(8) of the Constitution, the Standing Committee of the National People's Congress, rather than the courts, has the power to annul any administrative rules or local regulations that contravene the Constitution or any higher-level law or administrative rule or regulation. Articles 86, 87 and 88 of the Legislation Law contain more detail on the way in which inconsistencies between different levels of legislation should be resolved, but, again, these Articles provide for resolution through administrative rather than judicial means. Article 14 of the Administrative Licensing Law, which deals with the establishment and implementation of licensing and approval requirements, attempts to deal with this issue by providing that administrative licensing requirements can be established only by a law or by an administrative regulation, or, in special circumstances, pursuant to a decree of the State Council.

What this means for the discussion on transparency is that although the ability of lower-level entities to pass legislation that directly contradicts higher-level legislation is limited by law, enforcement when this requirement is breached is administrative rather than judicial. The ability of affected individuals and companies to challenge directly local legislation that appears to conflict with the content or intent of higher-level legislation, or with China's international commitments, is restricted. The WTO requirement that all trade-related legislation be notified to the Ministry of Commerce and published in the *Gazette* (as well as the requirement that opportunities for comment should be provided in advance) should in theory mean that legislation is subject to an increased degree of scrutiny at both a government and a public level. This suggests that the Ministry of Commerce should be increasing its efforts to ensure that all local legislation is notified for the purpose of publication in the *Gazette*. It is not clear, however, in view of the earlier discussion about the conflicts within the governmental system, whether the Ministry of Commerce has the practical ability strictly to enforce this requirement. As discussed above, it is doubtful whether all such local government legislation is in fact notified in the *Gazette*.

Another issue that is relevant in terms of the openness of government is the historical reluctance of Chinese government officials to part with information. The disclosure obligations in the Protocol, therefore, required an overall change in the approach of government in China to the question of openness, not merely procedural changes in the way in which legislation is issued and published.

As part of, and side by side with, the changes to the regulatory regime that have resulted from China's WTO accession, the central government has initiated administrative reforms that are designed to streamline and improve the service offered by government officials in China. The implementation of the programme for the promotion of law-based administration in 1999 (Dong, undated) as well as the passage of important pieces of legislation in the administrative law area, including the Administrative Licensing Law, indicates the importance that is attached to administrative reform, at least at the central level of government.

As noted above, China's compliance with provision of a notice and comment period for new legislation has been criticized. There have, however, been a number of well-publicized cases where legislation has been subjected to extensive public commentary before being passed. The recently passed Employment Contract Law, for example, attracted more than 190 000 submissions from the public during the drafting period (*People's Daily* Online, 2007) including submissions from groups representing foreign interests, such as the US-China Business Council. Similarly, in June 2007, the National Development and Reform Commission circulated its Request for Feedback on the Implementing Regulations for the PRC Bidding Law, and included a request for comments on whether the draft regulations dovetailed with the WTO Agreement on Government Procurement. Another example is the solicitation by the State Food and Drug Administration in early 2008 of public comments on its proposed regulations on medical device advertisement examination (SFDA, 2008). A significant issue, however, is that there is no one central point where proposed legislation is published and calls for public comments are publicized.

There is a strong move within the central government for more openness in the administrative and legislative system. As an example, the Communist Party of China, in its 2008 Opinions Concerning Deepening Reform of Administrative Management Mechanisms, called for government administrative modes that reflect 'standardization, orderliness, openness, transparency, convenience for the people and high efficiency' (CPC, 2008).

A potentially highly significant legislative reform came with the passage of the Administrative Licensing Law, which came into effect in mid-2004. The Administrative Licensing Law is not specifically directed at trade or China's WTO obligations. Nevertheless, it applies to many commercial activities conducted in China and has significant potential benefits for foreigners as well as for Chinese corporations and individuals. The law applies to acts whereby administrative organs permit citizens, legal persons or other organizations to engage in special activities. It therefore covers most of the acts for which the permission of a government agency is required. The law strictly restricts the circumstances in which an administrative licensing requirement can be imposed (as noted above) and, as a result of the passage of the law (and of the preceding administrative reforms), a large number of licence requirements have been cancelled (Bath, 2008). The law establishes principles of 'publicity, fairness and impartiality' in relation both to the establishment and the implementation of administrative licences (NPCC, 2003, Article 5). As noted above, it imposes strict limits on the number and type of government organs that may impose licensing requirements. It sets out procedures and criteria, including requirements for public hearings, designed to ensure that the process of applying for and obtaining a licence is fair. It also aims to control and limit the costs that may be imposed in relation to licensing. Article 20 also provides for the periodic evaluation of administrative licences to determine whether a licence is still necessary, and permits citizens and legal persons to put forward their own views about licences. Similarly, under Articles 46, 47 and 48, an open hearing may be required (or may be requested by an affected person) in relation to the implementation of an administrative licence. Article 33 requires the announcement of matters under administrative licence on the Internet and the sharing of information to promote efficiency.

The effect of this new commitment to openness, when combined with China's WTO commitments, can already be seen on the websites of government agencies, which have greatly improved in terms of the information available. An example of this is the website of the State Administration of Foreign Exchange. Although the English language version of the site is considerably less informative than the Chinese version, it includes lists of holders of licences issued by the State Administration of Foreign Exchange (SAFE), such as Qualified Foreign Institutional Investors (QFIIs) with investment quotas granted by SAFE (SAFE, 2006), with the amount of investment quota. The Chinese site contains significantly more information. An examination of local websites for government agencies also shows the impact of the Administrative Licensing Law on the data that is disclosed, although the quality of the websites and the information varies (Bath, 2008).

The most recent foray by the central Chinese government into the area of government transparency is the recently issued Regulations of the People's Republic of China on the Disclosure of Government Information (SCC, 2007a), which came into effect on 1 May 2008. This follows the introduction of open government legislation by a number of major municipalities, including Shanghai, Beijing, Shenzhen and Shantou (freedominfo.org, 2004). Under Article 2 of the regulations, 'government information' refers to 'information made or obtained by government agencies in the course of exercising their responsibilities and recorded and stored in a given form'.

Article 9 requires government agencies to disclose certain information 'on their own initiative'. Article 13 allows citizens, legal persons and other organizations to file requests for information based on special needs such as their livelihood and scientific and technological research. Article 14 provides an exception for state secrets, commercial secrets and confidential information.

Of particular interest in the context of the WTO transparency requirements are the provisions of Articles 10 to 12 of the regulations, which set out the types of information that should be provided. The listed items include administrative rules, regulations and regulatory documents (Article 10(1)), as well as other documents of potential interest to foreign businesses, such as statistics (Article 10(3)), government procurement projects (Article 10(6)) and approval and implementation of major construction projects (Article 10(8)). It is clear that the focus of the legislation is on matters that are of general interest to the public, and thus there is a focus on rural work policies (Article 12(1)), land acquisition and requisition (Article 12(4)) and information on implementation of family planning policies (Article 12(8)). Information must be disclosed through government publications and newspapers and on websites (Article 15), and reading rooms must be made available to members of the public to read the information (Article 16). Appeals are available to higher authorities (Article 33), although, as is the standard pattern in Chinese administrative law, the appeal is administrative, rather than judicial. However, a person who believes that their lawful rights or interests have been infringed may lodge an administrative lawsuit under Article 33, or apply for administrative reconsideration.

Much of the emphasis in the legislation is on government departments compiling and cataloguing information. Although fees cannot be charged for the provision of information, they may be charged for searching, copying and posting the information. Fees of this kind can in themselves potentially constitute a considerable imposition on the right to obtain information under the legislation, although the fact that the State Council sets the standards for fees (under Article 27) should keep the charges low.

In August 2007, the State Council issued a circular in relation to implementation of the regulations (SCC, 2007b), which urged all government departments to take appropriate steps to prepare for the implementation of the regulations, including formulating a government disclosure catalogue, improving disclosure mechanisms and rules, setting up information disclosure points and utilizing their websites for the purposes of disclosure. The Ministry of Commerce is one ministry that has responded to this. A sub-heading on the Chinese site (Ministry of Commerce Government Information Disclosure Inquiry System) allows for Internet inquiries for specified categories of information (such as laws, planning, internal trade and communications) to be made. A report by the Ministry indicates that in March 2008 (when the regulations had not yet come into force), the Ministry received 186 comments on the Chinese site; 285 postings in the mailbox; 1674 telephone inquiries, of which 1575 were effective record inquiries; and received and responded to 39 Internet inquiries in English. The initiation of the first lawsuit for failure to disclose under the regulations was reported by thebeijingnews.com on 14 May 2008.

The State Environment Protection Agency (now the Ministry of Environmental Protection) also issued the Measures on Disclosure of Environmental Information (Trial) in April 2007, to come into effect on 1 May 2007. The website of the Ministry incorporates a section on 'Government Information Disclosure' in a prominent position and offers a list of available information, with an option to download a form to apply for information.

As noted above, the Administrative Licensing Law and the Regulations of the People's Republic of China on the Disclosure of Government Information are not specifically directed at trade, business or foreign activities in China. They are of general application and it can be expected that Chinese citizens will be the direct beneficiaries of the improvement in information and government processes that these regulatory changes should bring. The significance of this legislation, following on from the Administrative Licensing Law, is that it does demonstrate a commitment at the central government level to the principle of open government. An important purpose is to reduce the level of corruption; another aim is to improve the efficiency of the public service. However, for Chinese and foreigners alike, the increased public availability of information, including, but not limited to, legislation at all levels of government, must be helpful in all levels of activity, whether business or personal. Certainly, the move towards an assumption by government officials that information should be available upon request and away from a more traditional approach that information should, on principle, not be provided marks a major change in the approach of Chinese government officials. The reduction in licensing requirements, ability to acquire information from government departments, and particularly over the Internet, and right to bring administrative action in the event that government departments do not comply with their obligations are helpful to both businesses and individuals. Certainly for foreign businesses, the enormous expansion in available legislative information at all levels of government on the Internet is a major improvement in terms of preparing for projects, providing timely and accurate advice, and reducing overall costs.

The question is, of course, to what degree government departments, and the Chinese government itself, are truly committed to the concept of open government. The exception for 'state secrets' in the Administrative Licensing Law (Article 5) and the Regulations (Article 14) is potentially wide-reaching and could have a chilling effect on the implementation of the legislation. In addition, despite the willingness of the government to make more government information available to its citizens, there are limits on the information that the government is prepared to allow other sources to provide. The latest version of the Foreign Investment Industry Catalogue, which came into effect on 1 December 2007, includes in the list of industries in which foreign participation is prohibited news agencies, publications of books, newspapers and periodicals, news websites and similar restrictions (NDRC and MOFCOM, 2007). This reiterates the prohibition on foreign investment in Internet news information services in China set out in the 2005 Regulations on Administration of Internet Press Information Services.

The United States and the European Union have both initiated consultations with China in relation to the 2006 changes to the system relating to foreign providers of financial information services, requiring them to supply their services through Xinhua News Agency, which, according to the requests for consultation, acts as both regulator and commercial intermediary (through a subsidiary). The United States request argues that this represents a breach of China's obligation to set up separate regulatory agencies, and an adverse change from the position prevailing when China joined the WTO (WTO, 2008c, 2008d). Certainly it is a strong indication of the intention of the Chinese government to control the sources (and hence the content) of news and information. Overall, China's record in relation to the censorship of information, which independent or outside sources may wish to provide to its citizens, is still subject to strong criticism despite its commitments in the lead up to the Olympic games in August 2008.

CONCLUSION

China's record in relation to its WTO obligations and its commitment to transparency is generally mixed. Substantial progress has been made in a number of significant respects, particularly in relation to the publication of laws and the greatly increased availability of government information. The conflict within the segmented structures of the various Chinese governments (resulting in lack of cooperation between different agencies and levels of government and the inconsistent disclosure of information) and the conflict between the move towards open government and the government (and Communist Party's) wish to control information from foreign sources means that the development of additional transparency and openness in government is likely to be incremental, and is likely to experience steps backward as well as progress. We can expect that in the years to come there will be continuing international (and domestic) disputes about the failure to disclose existing rules and regulations, and, probably, the creation of new ones as government departments seek to protect local interests. It is clear, nonetheless, as the preceding discussion shows, that in terms of open government and availability of information, China has made major advances in terms of transparency since it acceded to WTO both in complying with its specific obligations and in attempting to create a more open and transparent government.

NOTES

1. See comments under the heading '(iv) Transparency' in 'Part II, Trade Policy Regime: Framework and Objectives'.
2. Pursuant to Article 101, local people's congresses at and above the county level both elect and have the power to recall presidents of local people's courts and chief procurators at the corresponding level of government.

REFERENCES

Bath, V. (2008), 'Reducing the role of government – the Chinese experiment', *Asian Journal of Comparative Law*, **3** (1), 253–82.

China Foreign Trade and Economic Cooperation Gazette (*China FTEC Gazette*) (2008), 'Announcement No. 13, 2008 of the National Development and Reform Commission of the People's Republic of China', Issue No. 15, http://english. mofcom.gov.cn/policyrelease/policyrelease.html, accessed 30 May 2008.

Communist Party of China (CPC) (2008), 'Opinions Concerning Deepening Reform of Administrative Management Mechanisms', http://news.xinhuanet.com/news center/2008-03/04/content_7717129.htm (Chinese), accessed 25 November 2008.

Department of Foreign Affairs and Trade of Australia (DFAT) (2005), 'Australia-China FTA Negotiations', Subscriber Update, 11 November 2005, 3rd Round of Negotiations, http://www.dfat.gov.au/geo/china/fta/051111_subscriber_update. html, accessed 30 May 2008.

Dong, Dasheng (undated), 'The Practice of the Rule of Law in China', http:// www.cnao.gov.cn/UploadFile/NewFile/2006628152356558.doc, accessed 30 May 2008.

freedominfo.org (2004), 'Shanghai advances the cause of open government information in China', http://www.freedominfo.org/news/20040420.htm#2, accessed 30 May 2008.

Lubman, S. (2006), 'Looking for Law in China', *Columbia Journal of Asian Law*, **20** (1), 1–92.

Ministry of Foreign Trade and Economic Cooperation (MOFTEC) (now Ministry of Commence (MOFCOM)) (2002), 'Interim Enquiry Measures on the Enquiry

Office for the WTO of the Chinese Government', http://www.hrbmzj.gov.cn/mzbk/04/JJF/FLFG/DWMY/1107.htm (Chinese), accessed 4 June 2008.

Ministry of Foreign Affairs and Trade of New Zealand (MFAT) (2008), 'Free Trade Agreement between New Zealand and China', http://chinafta.govt.nz/1-The-agreement/2-Text-of-the-agreement/index.php, accessed 30 May 2008.

National Development and Reform Commission (NDRC) and Ministry of Commerce (MOFCOM) (2007), 'Catalogue for the Guidance of Foreign Investment Industries (amended in 2007)', http://www.fdi.gov.cn/pub/FDI/zcfg/law_ch_info.jsp?docid=88026 (Chinese), accessed 25 November 2008.

National People's Congress of China (NPCC) (2000), 'Law of the People's Republic of China on Legislation', http://news.xinhuanet.com/legal/2003-01/21/content_699610.htm (Chinese), accessed 4 June 2008.

National People's Congress of China (NPCC) (2003), 'Administrative Licensing Law of the People's Republic of China', http://www.fdi.gov.cn/pub/FDI/zcfg/law_ch_info.jsp?docid=47533 (Chinese), accessed 25 November 2008.

National People's Congress of China (NPCC) (2004), 'Constitution of the People's Republic of China', http://news.xinhuanet.com/newscenter/2004-03/15/content_1367387.htm (Chinese), accessed 4 June 2008.

People's Daily Online (2007), 'China's legislature adopts labor contract law', 30 June 2007, http://english.people.com.cn/200706/29/eng20070629_388809.html, accessed 30 May 2008.

State Administration of Foreign Exchange (SAFE) (2006), 'Qualified Foreign Institutional Investors (QFIIs) with Investment Quotas Granted by SAFE', http://www.safe.gov.cn/model_safe_en/glxx_en/glxx_detail_en.jsp?id=3&ID=30500000000000000,3&id=3, accessed 4 June 2008.

State Council of China (SCC) (2007a), 'Regulations of the People's Republic of China on the Disclosure of Government Information', http://www.gov.cn/zwgk/2007-04/24/content_592937.htm (Chinese), accessed 4 June 2008.

State Council of China (SCC) (2007b), 'Circular of the General Office of the State Council on Efforts to Better Address Implementation of Preparation of the "Regulations of the People's Republic of China on the Disclosure of Government Information"', http://www.gov.cn/gongbao/content/2007/content_744156.htm (Chinese), accessed 4 June 2008.

State Food and Drug Administration of the People's Republic of China (SFDA) (2008), 'SFDA solicits opinions on the amendment of Provisions for Medical Device Advertisement Examination', 9 January 2008, http://eng.sfda.gov.cn/cmsweb/webportal/W43879541/A64025694.html, accessed 30 May 2008.

United States Trade Representative (USTR) (2006), 'Report to Congress on China's WTO Compliance', http://www.ustr.gov/assets/Document_Library/Reports_Publications/2006/asset_upload_file688_10223.pdf, accessed 30 May 2008.

United States Trade Representative (USTR) (2007), 'Report to Congress on China's WTO Compliance', http://www.ustr.gov/assets/Document_Library/Reports_Publications/2007/asset_upload_file625_13692.pdf, accessed 29 May 2008.

US-China Business Council (2007), 'China's Implementation of its WTO Commitments: An Assessment', http://www.uschina.org/public/documents/2007/09/uscbc-china-wto-implementation-testimony.pdf, accessed 30 May 2008.

World Trade Organization (2001a), 'China's WTO Accession Protocol', WT/L/432, 23 November 2001, http://www.wto.org/english/thewto_e/acc_e/completeacc_e.htm, accessed 4 June 2008.

World Trade Organization (2001b), 'Report of the Working Party on the Accession of China', WT/ACC/CHN/49, 1 October 2001, http://www.wto.org/English/thewto_e/acc_e/completeacc_e.htm, accessed 4 June 2008.

World Trade Organization (WTO) (2006), 'Trade Policy Review – China 2006', Secretariat report, WT/TPR/S/161, 28 February 2006, http://www.wto.org/english/tratop_e/tpr_e/tp262_e.htm, accessed 4 June 2008.

World Trade Organization (WTO) (2008a), 'Trade Policy Review – China 2008', Secretariat report, WT/TPR/S/199, 16 April 2008, http://www.wto.org/english/tratop_e/tpr_e/tp299_e.htm, accessed 4 June 2008.

World Trade Organization (WTO) (2008b), 'Trade Policy Review – China 2008', Government report, WT/TPR/G/199, 7 May 2008, http://www.wto.org/english/tratop_e/tpr_e/tp299_e.htm, accessed 4 June 2008.

World Trade Organization (WTO) (2008c), 'China – Measures Affecting Financial Information Services and Foreign Financial Information Suppliers', Request for Consultations by the United States, WT/DS373/1, S/L/320, 5 March 2008, http://www.worldtradelaw.net/cr/ds373-1(cr).pdf, accessed 4 June 2008.

World Trade Organization (WTO) (2008d), 'China – Measures Affecting Financial Information Services and Foreign Financial Information Suppliers', Request for Consultations by the European Communities, WT/DS372/1, S/L/319, 5 March 2008, http://www.worldtradelaw.net/cr/ds372-1(cr).pdf, accessed 4 June 2008.

5. What does a Free Trade Area of the Asia-Pacific mean to China?

Tingsong Jiang and Warwick McKibbin

INTRODUCTION

A Free Trade Area of the Asia-Pacific region (FTAAP) has been proposed for many years. As early as in the Bogor Declaration of 1994 the APEC (Asia-Pacific Economic Cooperation) economies committed themselves to the achievement of free trade and investment in the Asia-Pacific region through a three-pronged programme of trade and investment liberalization, trade and investment facilitation and economic and technical cooperation (APEC, 1994). The call for achieving an FTAAP was renewed in recent APEC Economic Leaders' Meetings. In 2006 in Hanoi, it was proposed as a long-term prospect (APEC, 2006), while in Sydney in 2007, the leaders declared, '[t]hrough a range of practical and incremental steps, we will examine the options and prospects for a Free Trade Area of the Asia-Pacific' (APEC, 2007).

While supporting such a call for an FTAAP in general, China has been following other countries in paying more attention to regional trade agreements (RTAs) and free trade agreements (FTAs). China has signed six free trade agreements, with the China-New Zealand FTA being the latest one, and is currently negotiating with six partners for such an agreement. In addition, China is conducting joint feasibility studies with four partners, of which the joint feasibility studies for China-India RTA and China-Norway FTA have concluded (see Table 5.1). Among many proposals of regional economic integration, the East Asian Free Trade Area (EAFTA), which is based on the proposed ASEAN-China-Japan-Korea FTA (ASEAN+3), is particularly favoured by the Chinese leaders, in contrast to the ambiguous idea of an FTAAP (Sheng, 2006b, 2007).

Because the prospect of achieving an FTAAP appears remote and because no detailed proposals have emerged, there are limited studies on evaluating the impact of an FTAAP on the Chinese economy. And most of these studies are from a geo-political and political economic perspective,

Table 5.1   *China's participation in regional trade agreements (RTAs) and free trade agreements (FTAs)*

Partner	Note
Done deal	
Hong Kong	Closer Economic Partnership Arrangement (CEPA) main text signed on 29 June 2003, six Annexes signed on 29 September 2003; Supplements I, II, III and IV to CEPA signed on 27 October 2004, 18 October 2005, 27 June 2006 and 29 June 2007
Macao	CEPA main text and six Annexes signed on 17 October 2003 for implementing in January 2004; Supplements I, II, III and IV to CEPA signed on 29 October 2004, 21 October 2005, 26 June 2006 and 2 July 2007
ASEAN	Agreement on goods signed on 29 November 2004 for implementation in January 2005; Agreement on services signed on 14 January 2007 for implementation in July 2007; Agreement on investment under negotiation
Chile	Agreement on goods signed on 18 November 2005; Agreement on services and investment under negotiation – the 5th round of services trade negotiations held on 14–17 January 2008
Pakistan	Agreement on goods signed on 24 November 2006; Agreement on services under negotiation
New Zealand	Agreement signed on 7 April 2008
Under negotiation	
Australia	The 10th round of negotiations held on 22–26 October 2007
Gulf Cooperation Council	The 3rd round of negotiations held on 17–18 January 2006; the 4th negotiation meeting held on 19–22 July 2006
Iceland	The 3rd round of negotiations held on 17–18 October 2007; the 4th round held in March 2008
Peru	The 2nd round of negotiations held on 3–7 March 2008; the 3rd round held in May 2008
Singapore	The 1st round negotiation held on 26 October 2006
Southern African Customs Union	Negotiation started on 29 June 2004
Feasibility study	
Costa Rica	The 1st Joint Meeting held on 9–11 January 2008
India	The feasibility study on RTA concluded at the 6th meeting on 21–22 October 2007
Norway	Feasibility study concluded on 13 December 2007
South Korea	The 4th Joint Meeting held on 18–20 February 2008

Sources: People's Republic of China Ministry of Commerce news releases, http://english. mofcom.gov.cn/newsrelease/newsrelease.html.

for example, see Scollay (2005), PECC and ABAC (2006), Sheng (2006b, 2007), CTASC (2007) and Chou (2007).

A static general equilibrium model, namely, Global Trade Analysis Project (GTAP), has been used to quantify the economic impact of an FTAAP (Gilbert, Scollay and Bora, 2001; Scollay, 2005). It is found that China benefits more from an FTAAP than from an ASEAN-China FTA (ACFTA) or an EAFTA (Scollay, 2005).[1] However, due to the nature of comparative static analysis, these simulations 'tend to lack in varying degrees the ability to capture all dynamic effects . . . or the full impact of services trade liberalization' (ibid., p. 25).

Moreover, an important drawback of static modelling analyses is their lack of a time profile that makes the dynamic adjustment explicit. In many cases, different outcomes may happen in different time periods. At this stage the ACFTA is a done deal, and the EAFTA, or ASEAN+3, is on track,[2] but the FTAAP has not even entered the picture yet. Therefore, it is somehow misleading to present the impacts that will happen in different time periods without being explicit about the timing of the impacts.

This chapter examines the impact of the FTAAP on the Chinese and the regional economy in a general equilibrium framework. The impact is compared with those of other forms of FTAs such as the ACFTA and EAFTA. It contributes to the existing literature by using a dynamic general equilibrium model of the global economy, APG-Cubed,[3] to examine the impact of not only tariff removals, but also productivity improvement and investment enhancement associated with the FTAAP. It also examines the impact of such an agreement on different regions and different types of households in China by using a general equilibrium model of the Chinese economy with regional dimensions, CERD.

The rest of the chapter is organized as follows. The next section introduces the methodology used in the analysis. The third section discusses the major findings of the analysis. The final section summarizes the results and discusses the direction for future research.

METHODOLOGY

Models

Three general equilibrium models are used in the analysis: a dynamic, multisectoral global model, APG-Cubed; a static global model, GTAP; and a static China model with regional dimensions, CERD. The reason for using three models is that APG-Cubed gives a dynamic story at a moderate degree of disaggregation by country and by sector and GTAP enables this to be expanded to many more sectors. CERD enables the detailed results to be further explored in the context of regions within China.

APG-Cubed

APG-Cubed is the Asia-Pacific version of the G-Cubed model[4] (McKibbin and Wilcoxen, 1992; McKibbin, 1998; McKibbin and Wilcoxen, 1999). G-Cubed is a multicountry, multisector, intertemporal general equilibrium model, which includes detailed real sectors as well as financial sector, international trade and capital flows. Most parameters in G-Cubed are econometrically estimated. It has been used to study a variety of policies in the areas of environmental regulation, tax reform, monetary and fiscal policy, international trade and currency crisis.

Table 5.2   Model coverage of economies

APG-Cubed	GTAP
APEC economies	
Australia	Australia
Canada	Canada
	Chile
China	China
Hong Kong	Hong Kong
Indonesia	Indonesia
Japan	Japan
Korea	Korea
Malaysia	Malaysia
	Mexico
New Zealand	New Zealand
	Peru
Philippines	Philippines
Russia	Russia
Singapore	Singapore
Taiwan	Taiwan
Thailand	Thailand
United Sates	United Sates
	Vietnam
	Rest of Southeast Asia
	Rest of Oceania
Non-APEC economies	
India	
Rest of OECD	European Union
Non-oil developing countries	Rest of the world
Oil exporting developing countries	

Table 5.3   List of sectors in APG-Cubed, GTAP and CERD

Model	Sectors
APG-Cubed	Energy; mining; agriculture; durable manufacturing; non-durable manufacturing; services
GTAP	Agriculture; mining; food manufacturing; textile, clothing and footwear; motor vehicles and parts, transport equipment (MPV); electronics and machinery; other manufacturing; primary energy; secondary energy; services
CERD	Agriculture (12); mining (4); food processing (1); light industry (6); chemical industry (3); motor vehicles and parts (1); machinery and equipment (4); electronics and electrical equipment (3); construction (1); utilities (3); services (13)

Notes: Sectors in CERD are listed at aggregate level to save space. Numbers in parentheses are the number of sectors within each of the aggregated sectors.

The APG-Cubed[5] covers almost every APEC economy (see Table 5.2). As a compromise, its six sectors are highly aggregated (see Table 5.3).

GTAP
Global Trade Analysis Project (GTAP) is also a widely used general equilibrium model (Hertel, 1997). It is a static global model, with detailed sector and country coverage. The GTAP Database Version 6 identifies 87 countries or country groups, and 57 sectors (Dimaranan, 2006). This study uses an aggregated version with 23 country groups (see Table 5.2) and 10 sectors (see Table 5.3).

CERD
The model of Chinese Economy with Regional Dimensions (CERD) is a static, one-country, general equilibrium model (Jiang, 2003, 2004). It identifies three regions in China: the Eastern coastal, Central and Western regions. Several features make the CERD different from other one-country, multiregional, models. First, it uses the 'bottom-up' approach to model the regional economies in China. Each region in CERD is treated as an open economy with its own agents and behavioural functions, which are mainly drawn from that presented in Yang and Huang (1997).

Second, CERD identifies rural and urban households in each region according to their possession of primary factors. This feature is very important, and appropriate, for the analysis of the Chinese economy where rural and urban areas are still separated to some extent.

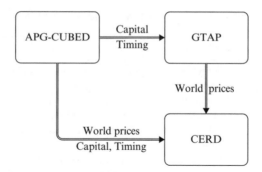

Figure 5.1   Model interactions

Third, CERD treats regional links through a national 'pool' of primary factors and commodities to avoid arbitrary decisions in creating the regional flows.

Finally, CERD has a fairly detailed representation of commodities. There are 51 sectors in the model, among which are 12 agricultural sectors, four mining sectors, 18 manufacturing, one construction sector, three utilities and 13 services sectors (see Table 5.3).

These three models are used interactively due to their distinct features (see Figure 5.1). As a dynamic model with financial sectors, APG-Cubed is able to provide inputs of capital stocks and time profile to the two static, real models. Because CERD is a one-country model, it needs information of world price changes due to FTAs from the other two global models.

Simulations

Three FTAs, an ACFTA, an EAFTA and an FTAAP, are simulated using the above-mentioned models. Each of these three FTAs has three components: trade liberalization on goods, services and investment.

Merchandise trade liberalization is measured by the reduction in import tariffs in participating economies of the relevant FTA. Services liberalization is simulated with productivity improvement in services, as services are usually non-tradable, while investment liberalization is modelled as reducing the uncertainties in investment environment in each of the participating economies.

The APG-Cubed model is able to simulate all of the three components, and provides additional information, mainly the annual changes in capital stock, for the GTAP and CERD models (see Figure 5.1).

Timing

As mentioned above, timing is important in assessing different FTAs. But it is also difficult to predict when a proposed FTA will be actually achieved. The uncertainty increases along with the number of parties involved.

The easiest task is to determine the timing of the ACFTA. China and ASEAN have already signed the goods and services agreements, and the negotiation for an investment agreement is under way. Taking into account past experiences,[6] it is assumed that an investment agreement will come into effect in 2010.

As for the EAFTA, a solid foundation has been established. The proposal for an ASEAN+3 took shape in 2001 when the East Asia Vision Group (EAVG) recommended formation of EAFTA (EAVG, 2001). This was followed by the 2002 report of the East Asia Study Group (EASG), established by the ASEAN+3 leaders on 24 November 2000, which proposed the EAFTA as a mid-term to long-term measure (EASG, 2002). Following the decision of the ASEAN+3 Economic Ministers Meeting in 2004, a Joint Expert Group (JEG) for Feasibility Study on EAFTA was created and submitted its report, '*Towards an East Asia FTA: Modality and Road Map*', in July 2006 (JEG, 2006), recommending the ASEAN+3 framework to launch negotiations in 2009, completion of negotiation by 2011 and completion of EAFTA by 2016 (with 2020 for new ASEAN members, Cambodia, Lao PDR, Myanmar and Vietnam [CLMV]) (ibid.).

It seems that the road map to an EAFTA has been followed closely (see Figure 5.2). Two ASEAN+1 FTAs, that is, ACFTA and AKFTA, have been achieved. Japan has signed agreements separately with six original ASEAN member countries, and the negotiation of an agreement with ASEAN as a whole was concluded in November 2007. The remaining block is the China-Japan-Korea FTA (CJKFTA). On this path, a trilateral joint research project on the economic effects of a possible CJKFTA has been undertaken since 2003 and it recommended CJKFTA as a mid-term goal and inclusion of services (DRC, NIRA and KIEP, 2006).

Therefore, it is assumed that an EAFTA on goods will be achieved by 2015. It is also assumed that the timing of achieving services and investment agreements follows the same profile of the ACFTA, that is, the services and investment agreements will be signed in two years and five years, respectively, after achieving an agreement on goods.

By contrast, there has not been a solid plan for forming an FTAAP. The Bogor Declaration of 1994 set a timeframe of achieving FTAs among developed and developing APEC economies by 2010 and 2020, respectively. But a joint feasibility study for an FTAAP has not been undertaken yet. Diversified development levels and different regional economic

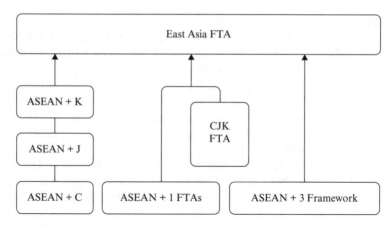

Source: Adapted from Lee (2007).

Figure 5.2   The path to an EAFTA

integration strategies among members have made it rather difficult to achieve an agreement in short time. Considering that it was set as a long-term prospect by APEC Economic Leaders, it is assumed that an FTAAP on goods, services and investment will be formed in 2025, 2027 and 2030, respectively.

Another issue of timing is the phase-out period, which is usually prolonged. For example, the North American Free Trade Agreement (NAFTA) has a phase-out period of 15 years from 1994 to 2008. In the case of ACFTA, the phase-out period for normal items is five years for China and six original ASEAN member countries (ASEAN-6)[7] and 10 years for new ASEAN members (CLMV), while tariffs on the sensitive items will be phased out in 13 years for China and ASEAN-6 and in 15 years for CLMV. In the case of AKFTA, the phase-out period of normal items is slightly shorter for Korea and ASEAN-6 (four years).

Therefore, a five-year phase-out period is assumed for both EAFTA and FTAAP. This assumption is appropriate if combined with the timing of reaching an agreement, although an FTA covering more parties with different levels of development tends to have a longer phase-out period because less-developed economies are usually given a longer phase-out period. For example, under the provisions of ACFTA and AKFTA, the four less-developed ASEAN members (CLMV) will eliminate all tariffs on normal items by 2020, five years after the assumed agreement of the EAFTA.

Figure 5.3 illustrates the timing of the three FTAs and their components.

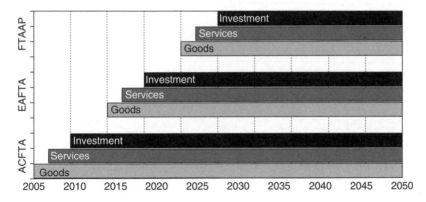

Source: Authors' assumption.

Figure 5.3   Timing of FTAs

Quantifying shocks

For the APG-Cubed, shocks are formulated with a phase-out (for tariff reduction) or phase-in (for productivity improvement) period, usually five years. Reduction in tariffs on goods is mainly drawn from the GTAP database version 6 (see Table 5.4) and the phase-out schedules discussed above. Although the GTAP 6 database does not reflect some new development,[8] it remains the most comprehensive and consistent database for general equilibrium analysis.

Services liberalization cannot be modelled as tariff reductions as in the case of merchandise trade liberalization because services are mainly non-tradable and there are no tariffs data for services in GTAP 6 database. However, the literature shows a link between services policy reform and productivity improvement in services and other sectors, for example, see Rajan and Zingales (1998), Arnold, Javorcik and Mattoo (2006), Eschenbach and Hoekman (2006), Kox and Lejour (2006), and Mattoo, Rathindran and Subramanian (2006). Therefore, services liberalization is modelled by gradual improvement in productivity in the sector with a full impact of 1 per cent increase in five years after a services agreement.

Investment liberalization is modelled by gradual reduction in country risk premium with a full impact of one basis point reduction in five years after an investment agreement. In the study of the Australia-US FTA (TheCIE, 2004), a five basis points shock was used, which was based on the equity risk premium of 120 basis points for Australia relative to the United States (Dimson, Marsh and Staunton, 2003) adjusted by several factors such as the importance of investment rules, the share of the US

Table 5.4 Average tariff rates

Economy	Agriculture	Mining	Food Manufac-turing	Textiles	Metal	MVP	Other Manufac-turing	Electrical Machinery and Equipment	Primary Energy	Secondary Energy
Australia	0.35	0.16	3.38	15.52	3.59	12.93	3.36	2.46	5.52	0.00
Canada	1.17	0.01	13.62	9.02	0.40	0.77	0.59	0.27	0.00	0.27
Chile	6.87	6.55	6.82	6.76	6.72	4.60	6.56	6.73	6.94	6.92
China	41.22	0.66	18.27	19.41	7.47	20.49	12.92	11.52	0.05	8.05
Hong Kong	0.00	0.00	0.00	0.00	0.00	0.00	0.00	0.00	0.00	0.00
Indonesia	1.76	1.49	9.08	7.93	5.92	9.63	4.77	2.75	0.00	3.40
Japan	22.63	0.13	31.36	9.73	0.55	0.00	1.03	0.04	0.00	1.60
Korea	123.91	1.27	26.17	9.51	3.81	3.88	6.61	3.39	4.03	5.57
Malaysia	25.26	0.25	10.11	11.03	8.54	31.67	6.66	1.58	2.15	0.32
Mexico	10.70	5.98	12.15	7.83	4.63	5.41	4.29	3.86	0.88	2.22
New Zealand	0.10	0.01	2.55	6.14	1.36	3.48	1.46	1.78	0.00	0.40
Peru	15.60	10.69	16.10	15.68	9.92	11.96	10.69	12.04	9.66	10.08
Philippines	5.65	2.72	11.08	6.49	3.91	11.51	4.76	0.69	3.27	2.73
Russia	5.24	1.51	16.68	15.80	5.80	12.75	9.77	6.37	0.14	1.06
Singapore	0.00	0.00	0.53	0.00	0.00	0.00	0.00	0.00	0.00	0.00
Taiwan	5.58	0.19	20.21	8.26	3.38	16.07	3.99	1.52	1.95	5.15

Thailand	13.30	2.68	39.11	17.37	9.25	23.95	10.85	6.26	0.04	0.60
US	1.07	0.09	3.22	9.80	1.15	1.09	1.34	0.62	0.00	0.97
Vietnam	10.93	3.84	43.70	28.85	5.06	46.90	8.47	8.21	0.00	9.79
Rest of Southeast Asia	5.58	6.40	22.42	10.32	3.54	24.96	6.81	6.67	1.59	2.49
Rest of Oceania	11.74	1.36	31.18	20.19	5.98	9.52	17.74	7.66	0.00	2.15
EU	3.34	0.00	4.85	2.53	0.70	0.83	0.46	0.38	0.00	0.41
Rest of World	11.10	4.01	20.15	14.57	6.90	9.17	7.87	6.05	4.08	5.04

Source: GTAP 6 database.

Table 5.5   Regional shares in China's total imports

Sector	ASEAN	ASEAN-Japan-Korea	Asia-Pacific
Agriculture	14.21	15.49	67.32
Mining	2.47	4.39	46.69
Food manufacturing	25.72	32.56	73.72
Textiles	32.98	82.74	87.24
Metal	10.72	46.86	74.23
MVP and other transport equipment	2.60	21.53	63.49
Other manufacturing	25.38	58.20	78.37
Electrical machinery and equipment	24.70	61.10	75.12
Primary energy	11.94	11.94	17.89
Secondary energy	24.87	59.47	74.02
Services	46.49	50.30	63.61
Average	25.39	53.35	72.11

Source: GTAP 6 database.

investment in Australia and the share of non-sensitive sectors. In this study, a more conservative measure is taken to reflect the uncertainty of the scope of an investment agreement.

For the two static models, shocks on goods and services trade liberalization are formulated at their full impact level, while the investment liberalization is modelled by increase in capital stocks generated by the APG-Cubed.

As CERD is a one-country model, the reduction in China's tariffs is adjusted according to the shares of involved parties in China's total imports to reflect the fact that FTAs are not unilateral liberalization. On average, imports from the ASEAN, ASEAN-Japan-Korea and the Asia-Pacific regions account for 25.4, 53.4 and 72.1 per cent, respectively, of China's total imports (Table 5.5).

RESULTS

Macro Effects

The macro impact of the three FTAs simulated by the APG-Cubed is summarized in Figure 5.4. These results are presented as percentage deviation from the baseline. There are three lines in each panel, showing the impact of ACFTA (upper bound of the grey area), EAFTA (upper bound of the white area) and FTAAP (upper bound of the black area). It is clear from these diagrams that an FTAAP has the largest impact when it is fully implemented. However, a more meaningful measure would be the net benefit an FTA will bring about, because the three FTAs happen subsequently and a later FTA is built on top of previous ones. Therefore, the net impact of a later FTA should exclude that of previous FTA/FTAs. Graphically, the net impact is the distance between two lines, for example, the net impact of an EAFTA is the height of the white area. One observation from the chart is that these FTAs have a similar, albeit with different magnitude, impact on China.

For China, all three FTAs bring about a positive impact. Both output and welfare (measured by real consumption) increase above the baseline. Real GNP increases more than real GDP does, reflecting the fact that China increases its holdings of foreign assets. Real consumption increases more than output does due to cheaper imports after the commencement of an FTA. Investment also increases above the baseline to support further growth in output.

Both exports and imports increase above the baseline. Because China's exports are higher than imports in the baseline, increases in exports and imports lead to positive impact on the current account. The increase in current account surplus means net capital outflows, which is consistent with the result of higher GNP growth than GDP growth. To facilitate these changes, the real exchange rate depreciates (reflecting the outflow of capital).

Production and welfare gains
The additional production (real GDP and GNP) and welfare (real consumption) gains over 50 years from 2007 to 2056 under the three FTAs are reported in Figure 5.5. Results are presented in net present value terms with a discount rate of 5 per cent, which allows us to place a current value on gains that may not be experienced until some time in the future.

Over 50 years, China gains US$731 billion in real GDP, US$899 billion in real GNP and US$605 billion in consumption. The ACFTA contributes about 36 per cent, the EAFTA more than 40 per cent and the FTAAP about 20 per cent, to the GDP and GNP gains. To the consumption gains, the ACFTA contributes a little more than half, the EAFTA about 36 per cent and the FTAAP about 14 per cent. As noted above, the decomposition is about the net contribution an FTA makes to the total gains. If, however, the FTAAP is formed in 2035 without an EAFTA in place, its contribution would be higher – about 40 per cent of production gains

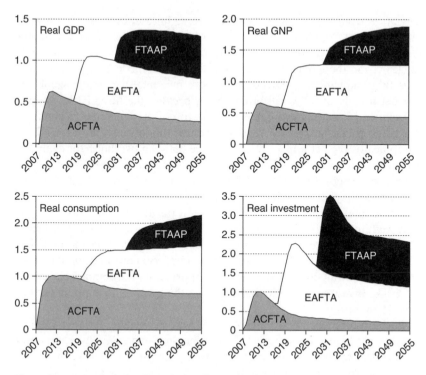

Note: Percentage deviation from the baseline except the current account, which is percentage of baseline GDP deviation.

Figure 5.4   Macro effects of FTAs: China

and 55 per cent of welfare gains, although the total benefits are smaller – US$646 billion, US$799 billion and US$560 billion of gains in real GDP, GNP and consumption, respectively.

These gains could be further increased if the EAFTA or the FTAAP happened earlier. Moving the EAFTA one year earlier would see additional gains of US$7.7 billion in real GDP, US$12.6 billion in real GNP and US$7.7 billion in consumption, over the 50 years period. Similarly, moving the FTAAP one year earlier would see additional gains of US$7.8 billion in real GDP, US$8.9 billion in real GNP and US$4.9 billion in consumption, if the FTAAP is established from an EAFTA. If there is no EAFTA before an FTAAP, one year earlier commencement of the FTAAP would see higher additional benefits – US$15.9 billion, US$21.7 billion and US$12.9 billion additional gains for GDP, GNP and consumption, respectively (Table 5.6).

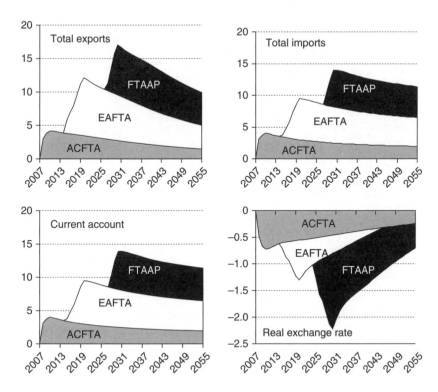

Source: APG-Cubed simulations.

GTAP and CERD simulations reveal similar patterns of total annual gains, that is, China gains the most from an FTAAP, followed by an EAFTA and an ACFTA (Figure 5.6). We should be cautious in making comparison of results from different models. For example, while the APG-Cubed results in Figure 5.6 are for 2055, we are not sure of the timing of the GTAP and CERD results – they are comparative static results and no time is associated with these results. That said, the results generated by the three models are close, especially for the gains in real consumption. The larger discrepancy in GDP gains between APG-Cubed and the two static models is understandable – the latter two do not capture international financial assets, in other words, production gains are fully reflected in domestic products without considering the increase in China's holding of foreign assets. Therefore, it might be more appropriate to compare the GNP numbers from the APG-Cubed with the GDP gains from GTAP

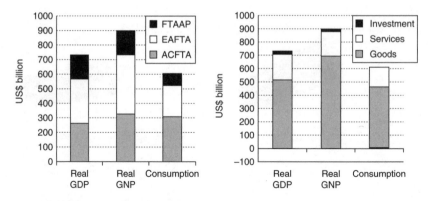

Note: Over 50 years discounted at a 5 per cent real interest rate.

Source: APG-Cubed simulations.

Figure 5.5   Production and welfare gains: China

and CERD. In fact, APG-Cubed simulations show that China's GNP will be 0.4, 1.3 and 1.9 per cent higher than the baseline under ACFTA, EAFTA and FTAAP, respectively, which are much closer to the GDP gains revealed by GTAP and CERD simulations.

Sources of benefits
The sources of these gains are reported in the right panel of Figure 5.5. Over 70 per cent of the gains are from merchandise trade liberalization, and 20–25 per cent of the gains are from services liberalization. Investment liberalization contributes to only 2 to 3 per cent of the production gains, due to our conservative assumption on the reduction in risk premium. It is interesting to note that the investment liberalization brings about a small (about 1 per cent), negative impact on consumption. This is because the reduction in risk premium boosts investment at the expense of consumption initially.

Employment
All the three FTAs have positive impact on employment in China. Figure 5.7 reports the impact on employment (left panel) and real wage rate (right panel). Because wage rate adjusts slowly, in a short time after the commencement of an FTA, employment deviates from the underlying long-term level. The impact on employment peaks in six years after the commencement of an FTA, which is consistent with the assumption of a five-year phase-out period of a goods agreement. The employment could be 0.4 per cent higher than the baseline in 2011 for an ACFTA, 1 per

Table 5.6   Benefit of one year earlier commencement of FTAs

	Unit	EAFTA	FTAAP	
			With EAFTA	Without EAFTA
GDP	US$ billion	7.71	7.84	15.85
GNP	US$ billion	12.56	8.95	21.74
Consumption	US$ billion	7.69	4.93	12.85

Note: Over 50 years discounted at 5 per cent real interest rate.

Source: APG-Cubed simulations.

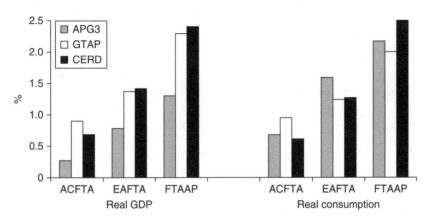

Source: APG-Cubed, GTAP and CERD simulations.

Figure 5.6   Comparison of total annual gains

cent higher in 2021 for an EAFTA and 2 per cent higher in 2031 for an FTAAP. As wages adjust, short-term employment impact dampens down over time, and the employment falls back to its long-term level. The impact transforms to permanent, higher wage rates. The real wage rate could be 5 per cent higher than the baseline level in 50 years.

Sectoral Impact

Figure 5.8 reports the changes in sectoral output under ACFTA, EAFTA and FTAAP, while Table 5.7 reports more detailed sectoral impact under the FTAAP. The textile industry would gain the most from the FTAAP, followed by the services and food manufacturing sectors; while the motor

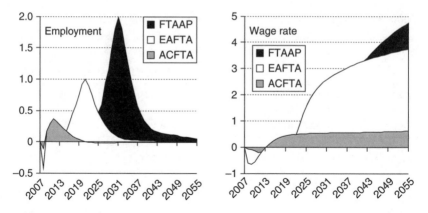

Note: Percentage deviation from the baseline.

Source: APG-Cubed simulations.

Figure 5.7   Impact on employment

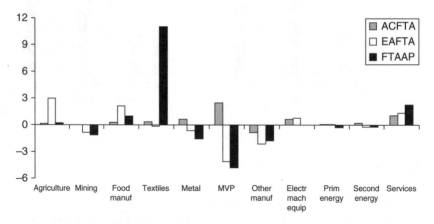

Note: Percentage deviation from the baseline.

Source: GTAP simulations.

Figure 5.8   Sectoral impact of various FTAs

vehicle and parts and other transport equipment (MVP) sector would suffer the most, followed by other manufacturing and metal sectors.

It is interesting to note that some sectors may shift from winner to loser under different FTA arrangements; for example, the MVP sector

Table 5.7   Sectoral impact of an FTAAP

Sector	Output	Employment		Exports	Imports
		Unskilled	Skilled		
Agriculture	0.22	0.23	0.24	85.49	85.57
Mining	−1.12	−1.50	−1.49	1.17	−1.02
Food manufacturing	0.96	−0.36	−0.30	22.65	45.40
Textiles	11.00	9.76	9.83	39.42	75.83
Metal	−1.57	−2.54	−2.47	9.30	17.55
MVP and other transport equipment	−4.82	−6.02	−5.95	17.08	42.83
Other manufacturing	−1.75	−3.00	−2.93	8.17	31.92
Electric machinery and equipment	−0.02	−1.27	−1.21	15.80	23.89
Primary energy	−0.28	−0.72	−0.71	4.00	2.11
Secondary energy	−0.22	−1.93	−1.87	9.16	14.29
Services	2.23	0.16	0.23	−0.73	1.36

Note: Percentage deviation from the baseline.

Source: GTAP simulations.

gains from an ACFTA and loses from an EAFTA and an FTAAP. This is because China has comparative advantage in MVP over ASEAN countries, while it faces much tougher competition from Korea, Japan and/or the United States under an EAFTA or an FTAAP.

Regional Impact

Figures 5.9 and 5.10 report the impact on production, foreign trade and household consumption in China's Eastern coastal, Central and Western regions. All three regions gain from any of the three FTAs. As with the national pattern of impacts, an FTAAP has the highest impact on the regions. Regional exports increase more than imports do.

Rural and urban households in the same region increase their consumption by a similar magnitude under an FTA, although there are significant differences across regions.

The Eastern region gains the most, followed by the Western and Central regions. Regional development level in China follows a gradient pattern, with the Eastern region being the most developed region and the Western the least. The uneven pattern of gains implies that China's regional disparity would become worse under any of the FTAs.

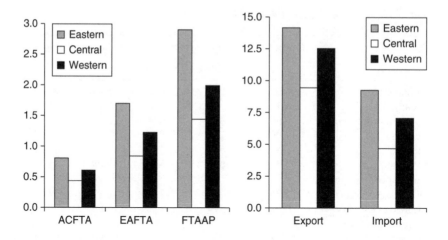

Note: Percentage deviation from baseline. Imports and exports in the right panel are for FTAAP only.

Source: CERD simulations.

Figure 5.9   Changes in regional production, exports and imports

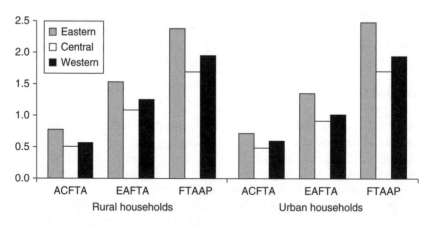

Note: Percentage deviation from baseline.

Source: CERD simulations.

Figure 5.10   Changes in rural and urban household consumption

The result that the Central region gains least may surprise someone who expects a similar gradient pattern of gains across regions from an FTA. However, the result may be justified in the following ways. First, the Western region has the cheapest labour, which helps in the development of labour-intensive sectors.

Second, the Western region has relatively abundant resource endowments, which leads to its comparative advantage in resource-intensive products. In fact, under an FTAAP, the resources sector in the Western region has the highest growth among the three regions.

Finally, the industrial base in the Western region may not be as poor as people think. The Chinese government has made huge investments in the so-called 'third line' programme, which brought about development in some sectors. This can be evidenced by the result that the electrical machinery and equipment sector in the Western region boosts at a similar magnitude to the Eastern region.

Impact on Other Economies

Figure 5.11 reports the equivalent variation (EV), a welfare measure used by GTAP, of major countries or country blocs under different FTA arrangements. It shows that the trade diversion effects dominate when an economy is excluded from an FTA. For example, the United States could gain US$156 billion in EV under an FTAAP, compared with a loss of

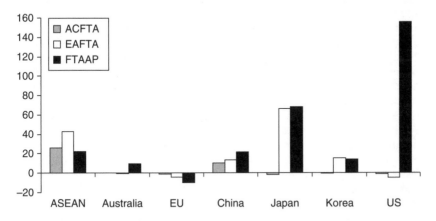

Note: Annual equivalent variation (EV).

Source: GTAP simulations.

Figure 5.11 Impact on other economies

US$4.6 billion under an EAFTA; while the European Union loses under all the three FTAs. The ASEAN as a whole gains less under an FTAAP than under an ACFTA or an EAFTA because it faces more competition and as a result the capital stock increases less under an FTAAP than under the other two FTAs.

China–US bilateral trade
Soaring China trade surplus with the United States is one of the major conflicts between the two giants in the Asia-Pacific region. It is hoped that an 'FTAAP can subsume into a broader and cooperative context, including orderly dispute settlement mechanism, the growing bilateral trade and other economic conflict between the United States and China', and possibly curb or even reduce the US trade deficit with China (Bergsten, 2005).

The results of this study partly support the argument. Table 5.8 reports the simulated impact of FTAAP and EAFTA on China–US bilateral trade by GTAP. Although total US exports to China grow three times more than its imports from China (71 per cent versus 23 per cent) under

Table 5.8   Impact on US–China bilateral trade

Sector	US Export to China		China Export to US	
	FTAAP	EAFTA	FTAAP	EAFTA
Agriculture	480.57	13.97	9.44	−17.42
Mining	2.51	−0.81	0.59	−0.11
Food manufacturing	59.52	−11.72	11.07	−10.10
Textiles	71.21	−43.17	69.93	−5.98
Metal	20.17	−10.73	14.59	0.17
MVP and other transport equipment	−14.79	−40.18	24.43	7.50
Other manufacturing	34.73	−28.61	7.83	−0.37
Electrical machinery and equipment	61.93	−29.38	15.31	6.70
Primary energy	76.07	9.61	−4.81	−1.86
Secondary energy	26.20	−7.27	−2.07	0.21
Services	4.62	−1.33	−2.51	0.66
Total	70.93	−54.32	22.82	−17.73
US trade deficit with China	6.11	9.02		

Note: Percentage deviation from the baseline.

Source: GTAP simulations.

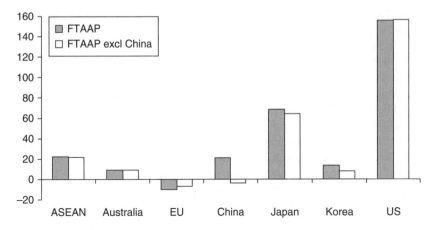

Note: Annual equivalent variation (EV).

Source: GTAP simulations.

Figure 5.12   Impact of an FTAAP without China

an FTAAP, its trade deficit with China increases by more than 6 per cent due to the huge imbalance in the baseline. Of course, an FTAAP puts the United States in a better position than an exclusive EAFTA, which may lead to more than a half reduction in its exports to China and a 9 per cent increase in trade deficit with China.

An FTAAP without China?

It has been proposed that an FTAAP could be launched without China's participation. It is also hoped that the trade diversion effect would induce China to join the FTAAP if it does not do so at the beginning. China should seek to join the FTAAP at the very beginning, as suggested by the quick assessment of an FTAAP without China by the GTAP simulation. China would become a loser by US$4 billion in EV a year by not joining the FTAAP, and would be a winner by US$21.3 billion with a membership of the FTAAP (Figure 5.12).

CONCLUDING REMARKS

This study uses a suite of general equilibrium models to examine the impact of a Free Trade Area of the Asia-Pacific, in conjunction with the possible development in the existing ASEAN-China FTA and a proposed East Asian FTA. It is found that China gains from all three FTAs. When all the effects are fully realized at the end, an FTAAP will bring about the largest gains to China, followed by an EAFTA and the existing ACFTA. However, if considering the difficulty of reaching a future FTA and the sequence of FTAs, an EAFTA would add more net benefits to the existing ACTFA than an FTAAP. Measured by increased consumption, the additional benefit an EAFTA will bring about would be around US$220 billion over a period of 50 years, compared with US$82 billion of net benefit from an FTAAP. It seems that China is using the same calculation to formulate its regional economic integration strategy, which favours an EAFTA.

That said, it is in China's interest to pursue early formation of an FTAAP – one year earlier commencement of the FTAAP would see additional gain of about US$5 billion of increased consumption over 50 years if an EAFTA is in place before an FTAAP. The benefit would be higher if there is no EAFTA in place when the FTAAP commences. Moreover, China should avoid the situation where an FTAAP is formed without China's participation. Huge trade diversion effect brings China a net loss of US$4 billion in EV, compared with a gain of US$21.3 billion under an FTAAP including China.

Another issue China should consider is the worsening trend in regional disparity after the commencement of an FTA. The Eastern region receives most of the gains from an FTA, although other regions gain as well. Moreover, given the fact that large-scale, comprehensive, programmes have been launched to develop the Western region and to restructure the old industrial bases in the Northeast, the government should consider a more sensible strategy of not excluding the Central region, as this region would gain the least from an FTA.

This study could be extended in several directions. First, the databases may be updated to reflect most recent economic development and protection levels in China and major economies, which would be a major undertaking. Second, more FTA options may be considered, such as ASEAN+6 (ASEAN+3 plus Australia, New Zealand and India), and FTAs among China's major partners. It will provide more balanced information for China to consider.

NOTES

1. Using a gravity model, Sheng (2006a) also shows big welfare gains for China if it participates in the FTAAP.
2. In addition to the FTAs on goods and services with China as mentioned in Table 5.1, ASEAN has signed FTAs with Korea on goods (13 December 2005) and services (4

November 2007). ASEAN also signed the Framework for Comprehensive Economic Partnership with Japan on 18 October 2003, a prerequisite for achieving an FTA. Besides, Japan and Korea are negotiating an FTA, while Korea and China are conducting feasibility studies for an FTA.

3. See McKibbin (1998) for the Asia-Pacific version of the G-Cubed model. The G-Cubed model is derived in McKibbin and Wilcoxen (1999).
4. G-Cubed stands for Global General Equilibrium Growth Model.
5. This study uses Version 58 of APG-Cubed.
6. It took three to four years for China and Korea, respectively, to reach an agreement with ASEAN. China and ASEAN signed on 4 November 2002 the Framework Agreement on Comprehensive Economic Cooperation, and signed goods and services agreements on 29 November 2004 and 14 January 2007, respectively.
   Following the ASEAN-Korea Summit in Bali in October 2003, an ASEAN-Korea Experts Group (AKEG) was set up to do the feasibility study of an ASEAN-Korea FTA. Both parties started negotiation after the Joint Declaration on Comprehensive Cooperation Partnership between the ASEAN and Korea on 30 November 2004 adopted the recommendation of forming an ASEAN-Korea FTA by the AKEG. The Framework Agreement was signed on 13 December 2005, and the agreements on goods and services were signed on 13 December 2005 and 24 August 2006, respectively.
   In the case of ASEAN-Japan FTA, the negotiation was launched in April 2005 and concluded in November 2007, taking a little more than two-and-a-half years.
7. The Agreement came into effect on 1 January 2005, and it states that, 'each party shall eliminate all its tariffs for tariff lines placed in the Normal Track not later than 1 January 2010, with flexibility to have tariffs on some tariff lines, not exceeding 150 tariff lines, eliminated not later than 1 January 2012'.
8. The reference year for GTAP Database Version 6 is 2001 (Dimaranan, 2006, p. 3-1). See, for example, Davis, Hanslow and Stockel (2007, Chart 1.3, p. 10), for a comparison of Korean agricultural tariffs between GTAP 6 database and the 2006 Korean tariff schedule.

REFERENCES

APEC (1994), 'APEC Economic Leaders' Declaration of Common Resolve', 1994 Leaders' Declaration, Asia-Pacific Economic Cooperation, Bogor, Indonesia, 15 November.

APEC (2006), '14th APEC Economic Leaders' Meeting Hanoi Declaration', 2006 Leaders' Declaration, Asia-Pacific Economic Cooperation, Hanoi, Vietnam, 18–19 November.

APEC (2007), 'Strengthening Our Community, Building A Sustainable Future', 2007 Leaders' Declaration, Asia-Pacific Economic Cooperation, Sydney, Australia, 9 September.

Arnold, J., B. Javorcik and A. Mattoo (2006), 'The Productivity Effects of Services Liberalization: Evidence from the Czech Republic', Economic Development and Transition Seminar Series (EDTS), 14 September 2006, International Policy Center, University of Michigan, Ann Arbor, MI, http://ipc.umich.edu/edts/pdfs/czech_services_april25.pdf, accessed 16 March 2008.

Bergsten, C. (2005), 'A New Strategy for APEC', Speech at the 16th General Meeting of the Pacific Economic Cooperation Council, 6 September 2005, Seoul, South Korea, http://www.iie.com/publications/papers/bergsten0905apec.pdf, accessed 16 March 2008.

Chou, T. (2007), 'Assessment of FTAAP by APEC', in *Free Trade Area of Asia-Pacific in the Wave of Regional Integration*, edited by Chinese Taipei APEC Study Center (CTASC), Taipei: Taiwan Institute of Economic Research.

CTASC (2007), *Free Trade Area of Asia-Pacific in the Wave of Regional Integration*, APEC Issues Series, Chinese Taipei APEC Study Center (CTASC), Taipei: Taiwan Institute of Economic Research.

Davis, L., K. Hanslow and A. Stockel (2007), 'Impact of KORUS on Australian Agriculture: . . . And What an Australia-Korea FTA Could Mean', Report prepared for the National Farmers' Federation, Centre for International Economics, Canberra, http://www.thecie.com/content/publications/KORUS_report_20_August_2007.pdf, accessed 16 March 2008.

Dimaranan, V. (ed.) (2006), *Global Trade, Assistance, and Production: The GTAP 6 Database*, Center for Global Trade Analysis, Purdue University, West Lafayette, IN.

Dimson, E., P. Marsh and M. Staunton (2003), 'Global Evidence on the Equity Risk Premium', SSRN eLibrary, http://papers.ssrn.com/sol3//papers.cfm?abstract_id=431901, accessed 5 November 2008.

DRC, NIRA and KIEP (2006), 'Joint Report and Policy Recommendations Concerning a Free Trade Agreement among China, Japan and Korea', Trilateral Joint Research conducted by Development Research Center (China), National Institute for Research Advancement (Japan) and Korea Institute for International Economic Policy (Korea), 11 December 2006, http://www.nira.or.jp/past/newse/paper/joint6/houko_E.pdf, accessed 26 March 2008.

EASG (2002), 'Final Report of the East Asia Study Group', Final report submitted to the ASEAN+3 Summit on 4 November 2002, East Asia Study Group, http://www.mofa.go.jp/region/asia-paci/asean/pmv0211/report.pdf, accessed 26 March 2008.

EAVG (2001), 'Towards an East Asian Community: Region of Peace, Prosperity and Progress', East Asia Vision Group Report 2001, East Asia Vision Group, http://www.mofa.go.jp/region/asia-paci/report2001.pdf, accessed 26 March 2008.

Eschenbach, F. and B. Hoekman (2006), 'Services policy reform and economic growth in transition economies', *Review of World Economics*, **142** (4), 746–64.

Gilbert, J., R. Scollay and B. Bora (2001), 'Assessing Regional Trading Arrangements in the Asia-Pacific', *Policy Issues in International Trade and Commodities Study Series No. 15*, United Nations Conference on Trade and Development, New York and Geneva.

Hertel, T. (ed.) (1997), *Global Trade Analysis: Modeling and Application*, Cambridge, UK, New York and Melbourne, Australia: Cambridge University Press.

JEG (2006), 'Towards an East Asia FTA: Modality and Road Map', A Report by Joint Expert Group for Feasibility Study on EAFTA, 22 July 2006, Joint Expert Group for Feasibility Study on EAFTA.

Jiang, T. (2003), 'The impact of China's WTO accession on its regional economies', *Australasian Agribusiness Review*, **11** (9).

Jiang, T. (2004), 'WTO accession and food security in China' (*Guanli Shijie*) *Management World* (3), 82–94.

Kox, H. and A. Lejour (2006), 'Dynamic Effects of European Services Liberalization: More to be Gained', MPRA Paper 3751, University Library of Munich, Germany, http://ideas.repec.org/p/pra/mprapa/3751.html, accessed 16 March 2008.

Lee, C. (2007), 'East Asia FTA: First Step towards an East Asia Community',

Presentation to the 10th Academic Forum on East Asian Economy (the 2nd East Asia-Pacific Forum), 1 March, National Institute for Research Advancement, http://www.nira.or.jp/past/newsj/kanren/180/187/pdf/R_cjlee.pdf, accessed 16 March 2008.

Mattoo, A., R. Rathindran and A. Subramanian (2006), 'Measuring services trade liberalization and its impact on economic growth: an illustration', *Journal of Economic Integration*, **21** (1), 64–98.

McKibbin, W. (1998), 'Regional and Multilateral Trade Liberalization: The Effects on Trade, Investment and Welfare', in P. Drysdale and D. Vines (eds), *Europe, East Asia and APEC: A Shared Global Agenda?*, Cambridge, UK and New York: Cambridge University Press, pp. 195–220.

McKibbin, W. and P. Wilcoxen (1992), 'G-Cubed: A Dynamic Multi-sector General Equilibrium Model of the Global Economy (Quantifying the Costs of Curbing CO_2 Emissions)', Brookings Discussion Paper No. 98, The Brookings Institution, Washington, DC.

McKibbin, W. and P. Wilcoxen (1999), 'The theoretical and empirical structure of the G-Cubed model', *Economic Modelling*, **16** (1), 123–48.

Ministry of Commerce of China, various news releases, http://english.mofcom. gov.cn/newsrelease/newsrelease.html, accessed 30 April 2008.

PECC and ABAC (2006), *An APEC Trade Agenda? The Political Economy of a Free Trade Area of the Asia Pacific*, A Joint Study by PECC and ABAC, the Pacific Economic Cooperation Council and the APEC Business Advisory Council.

Rajan, R. and L. Zingales (1998), 'Financial dependence and growth', *American Economic Review*, **88** (3), 559–86.

Scollay, R. (2005), 'Preliminary Assessment of the Proposal for a Free Trade Area of the Asia-Pacific (FTAAP)', An Issues Paper for the APEC Business Advisory Council (ABAC), June, The Australian APEC Study Centre, Monash University, Melbourne, http://www.apec.org.au/docs/koreapapers2/SX-RS-Paper.pdf, accessed 16 March 2008.

Sheng, B. (2006a), 'APEC Trade Liberalization: A Gravity Model Estimation', Memo, APEC Study Center of Nankai University, Tianjin.

Sheng, B. (2006b), 'The Political Economy of an Asia Pacific Free Trade Area: A China Perspective', in PECC and ABAC (eds), *An APEC Trade Agenda? The Political Economy of a Free Trade Area of the Asia Pacific*, A Joint Study by PECC and ABAC, The Pacific Economic Cooperation Council and the APEC Business Advisory Council, pp. 53–70.

Sheng, B. (2007), 'Political economy of the Asia-Pacific Free Trade Area: a dilemma for China', *China and World Economy*, **15** (5), 38–49.

TheCIE (2004), 'Economic Analysis of AUSFTA: Impact of the Bilateral Free Trade Agreement with the United States', Report prepared for Department of Foreign Affairs and Trade, Centre for International Economics, Canberra and Sydney, http://www.thecie.com/content/publications/CIE-economic_analy sis_ausfta.pdf, accessed 16 March 2008.

Yang, Y. and Y. Huang (1997), 'The Impact of Trade Liberalization on Income Distribution in China', Economics Division Working Papers, China Economy No. 97/1, Research School of Pacific and Asian Studies, Australian National University, Canberra.

PART II

Foreign Direct Investment and Exchange Rate

6. Characteristics of FDI firms in China after WTO accession

Chunlai Chen

INTRODUCTION

After China's accession to the World Trade Organization (WTO), foreign direct investment (FDI) inflows into China have increased rapidly, reaching a peak of US$74.8 billion in 2007, an increase of 60 per cent on those in 2001. The manufacturing sector has been the most attractive sector to FDI. After WTO accession, average annual FDI inflows into the manufacturing sector surged to US$36.44 billion during 2002–06, an increase of 34.86 per cent over those during 1997–2001, and accounting for 68.74 per cent of the total FDI inflows into China.[1]

This chapter provides a brief overview of the trend of FDI inflows into China and into manufacturing, examines the structural changes of FDI firms in the manufacturing sector and compares the firm characteristics between FDI firms and domestic firms in the manufacturing sector after China's WTO accession.

The chapter is structured as follows. The next section presents the general trend and characteristics of FDI inflows into China. The third section discusses the features of the sectoral distribution of FDI inflows into China after WTO accession. The fourth analyses the structural changes of FDI in the manufacturing sector. The fifth section discusses the firm characteristics of FDI firms as compared with domestic firms in the manufacturing sector. The final section concludes the chapter.

INCREASING FDI INFLOWS AFTER WTO ACCESSION

FDI flowed into China in three phases (see Figure 6.1): the experimental phase from 1979 to 1991, the boom phase from 1992 to 2001 and the post-WTO phase from 2002 to 2007.

During the experimental phase, FDI inflows were low, but they grew steadily. The period was characterized by small investment projects, high

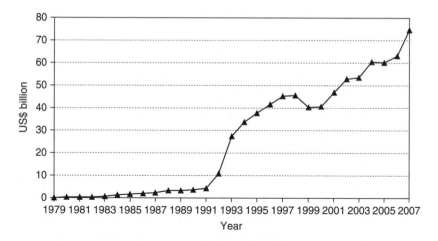

Note: Data include FDI inflows into non-financial sectors only.

Sources: Calculated from National Bureau of Statistics of China (NBS) (various issues), *China Statistical Yearbook*, Beijing: China Statistics Press.

Figure 6.1   FDI inflows into China (at current prices)

investment costs, restrictive price controls, poor infrastructure and lack of legal framework.

In the boom phase, FDI inflows initially increased very rapidly; however, they slowed down after 1997 and declined in 1999 and 2000, followed by a moderate recovery in 2001. The slowdown from 1997 to 2000 could be explained by several factors. First, there has been a slowdown from the surge in transfers of labour-intensive activities from neighbouring Asian economies. In addition, the East Asian financial crisis weakened substantially the ability of outward investment of the East and Southeast Asian economies. As a result, FDI flows into China from those economies have declined substantially since 1997. Second, rates of return to investment in China were not as high as foreign investors expected. In many cases foreign investors' high hopes for China's market were slow to materialize. Informal relationships and corruption hindered many business transactions by foreigners. In addition, inefficient state-owned enterprises continued to dominate many key sectors of the economy, especially the services sector. Restrictions on FDI, such as on ownership shares, modes of FDI entry, business scope and operation and regional and sectoral locations inhibited inflows.

Therefore, China's accession to the WTO in 2001 came at a very critical time, when the country was facing difficulties sustaining a high level of FDI inflows. Could China's accession to the WTO revive the trend of increasing high levels of FDI inflows?

After China's accession to the WTO, FDI inflows entered the third phase. As shown in Figure 6.1, FDI inflows into China increased from US$46.88 billion in 2001 to US$74.8 billion in 2007,[2] at an annual rate of growth of 8.1 per cent. Trade and investment liberalization and reduction in foreign investment barriers as part of China's accession to the WTO accelerated FDI inflows into China.

There has, however, long been an issue of 'round-tripping' of investment in China. Round-tripping is driven by differences in the treatment of foreign and domestic investors, which can motivate investors to channel funds out of, and subsequently into, an economy in the form of FDI. Because the funds originate in the host economy itself, round-tripping inflates actual FDI inflows. In China, because of the preferential treatments offered to foreign investors (mainly through tax incentives), a significant share of FDI inflows are round-tripped, mainly via Hong Kong (UNCTAD, 2007) and, more recently and increasingly, via tax havens such as the Virgin, Cayman and Samoan islands (He, 2006). Official estimates from the Chinese government are not available, but one estimate, made by Harrold and Lall (1993), suggested that round-tripping inward FDI accounted for 25 per cent of China's FDI inflows in 1992. Some experts estimate that round-tripping FDI currently accounts for 33 per cent of China's total FDI inflows (He, 2006).

On 16 March 2007, China passed the new corporate income tax law, unifying the tax rates for foreign and domestic enterprises. The new tax rate for domestic and foreign enterprises will be 25 per cent. The law is due to take effect on 1 January 2008 (Xinhua News Agency, 2007). The new law has unified the two existing tax codes – one for domestic companies, the other for foreign-invested companies – and represents a fundamental change in China's tax policy. Many of the tax incentives and tax holidays that existed in the old code for foreign investors have been changed or eliminated.

The new corporate income tax law and the unification of the tax rate will reduce the incentive for round-tripping. What, however, are the impacts of the new tax law on domestic and foreign-invested companies and on FDI inflows into China?

Although the current nominal income tax rate is set at 33 per cent, the real average income tax burden on China's domestic companies is 25 per cent (ibid.), so on average the new tax law will not reduce the real tax burden on domestic companies.

The current real income tax burden on foreign-invested companies is 15 per cent (ibid.). On average, the new income tax law will increase the tax burden on foreign-invested companies by 10 percentage points. It seems that the new tax law will have a negative impact on foreign-invested companies – especially in the short term on small-scale, labour-intensive, quick profit-earning enterprises from developing economies.

China's proposed unified corporate income tax rate of 25 per cent for domestic and foreign-invested companies will have little effect on foreign investment in China, especially from large multinational enterprises.

First, the average corporate income tax rate for the world's 159 countries and regions who levy corporate income tax is 28.6 per cent, and the average corporate income tax rate for China's 18 neighbouring countries and regions is 26.7 per cent (BBC CHINESE.com, 2007). China's proposed unified tax rate of 25 per cent is below the global average, so it is quite competitive for attracting foreign and domestic investment.

Second, in the past few decades, time-series econometric analyses and numerous surveys of international investors have shown that tax incentives are not the most influential factor for multinationals in selecting investment locations (Morisset, 2003). Foreign investors are, of course, interested in tax rate, but factors such as broad investment climate and domestic market, the cost and availability of labour, basic infrastructure and economic and political stability, carry more weight in decision-making.

Third, China's overall investment environment is quite competitive, with relatively efficient public services, good infrastructure, a large and fast-growing domestic market, abundant and well-educated human resources, low labour costs and macroeconomic and political stability – making China one of the most attractive locations for FDI. According to the '2005 Foreign Direct Investment Confidence Index' (A.T. Kearney Inc., 2007), in 2005 China was the world's most attractive FDI location in the world. China has maintained its lead in the index for the fourth consecutive year. Once again, China is the top FDI location for first-time investors, with more than half (55 per cent) of investors expected to make first-time investments there over the next three years. One in five FDI dollars for first-time investments will be committed to the Chinese market. China has successfully overcome the perceived risk associated with first-time market entry, which is typically the biggest barrier to generating new FDI.

Fourth, the new tax law still has preferential stipulations (but at non-discriminatory base for both domestic and foreign-invested firms): China will continue to offer tax incentives to investment in projects relating to environmental protection, agricultural development, water conservation, energy saving, production safety, high-technology development and public welfare. High-technology enterprises can still enjoy a 15 per cent income tax rate, and small and medium-sized enterprises with slim profits are required to pay income tax at only 20 per cent. Certain tax breaks will also be granted to enterprises in special economic zones and less-developed Western areas of the country (Xinhua News Agency, 2007).

Finally, the new tax law also provides five-year transitional periods to offset the impact on foreign companies. The income tax rate will be increased gradually to 25 per cent during this period, and existing foreign enterprises can still enjoy tax breaks within a regulated time limit (ibid.).

Therefore, the new tax law will bring China's tax laws more in line with international standards. It is a fulfilment of a commitment to the WTO for equal treatment for domestic and overseas investors. The change in the tax law not only proves that the Chinese government is determined to continue its reform and opening-up policies – and work hard to improve the investment climate – it will also help to create a sound investment environment and promote China's industrial restructuring and upgrading.

CONCENTRATION IN THE MANUFACTURING SECTOR

The sectoral distribution of FDI in China has been characterized by the concentration of FDI in the manufacturing sector. As shown in Table 6.1, during the period 1997–2001,[3] the manufacturing sector attracted 60.79 per cent of the total FDI inflows into China. After China's accession into the WTO, FDI inflows continued to be concentrated in the manufacturing sector. As a result, during the period 2002–06, the share of FDI inflows into the manufacturing sector increased to 68.74 per cent as compared with that in the period 1997–2001.

Studies[4] of the impacts of China's accession to the WTO predicted that after the accession to the WTO, China's labour-intensive manufacturing industries, especially textiles and clothing industries, would grow rapidly, led by the large expansion of exports as a result of the reduction of import tariffs and the elimination of import quotas from the developed countries on the imports of China's labour-intensive manufactured goods. However, introduction of foreign capital, technology and advanced equipment to upgrade labour-intensive industries would accelerate this process. Therefore, China's WTO accession provided opportunities to do this.

FDI inflows into the primary sector continued to decline after 2001. Consequently, the share of FDI inflows into the primary sector declined from 3.20 per cent in the period 1997–2001 to only 2.34 per cent in the period 2002–06.

This is not surprising given the declining share of the agricultural sector in China's national economy and the rapid losing of overall comparative

Table 6.1   FDI inflows into China by sectors (US$ billion at 2000 constant prices)

Sector	1997–2001		2002–06	
	Value	(%)	Value	(%)
Primary	7.11	3.20	6.19	2.34
Manufacturing	135.12	60.79	182.19	68.74
Services*	80.03	36.01	76.67	28.93
Total	222.26	100	265.05	100

Note: * Excluding financial services.

Sources: Calculated from National Bureau of Statistics of China (NBS) (various issues), *China Foreign Economic Statistical Yearbook* and *China Statistical Yearbook*, Beijing: China Statistics Press.

advantage in agricultural production in China (Chen, 2006). In addition, China's agricultural land tenure system and the traditional small-scale family-based agricultural production pattern have greatly limited the inflows of agricultural FDI with large-scale production and advanced technology. Therefore, China would not attract large amounts of FDI inflows into its agricultural sector without fundamentally changing its land tenure system and dramatically reforming the traditional family-based small-scale farming pattern.

It is expected that after the accession to the WTO and the opening up of the services sector, more FDI would flow into the services sector. However, evidence has shown that FDI inflows into the services sector have been increasing but at a slower pace. FDI inflows into the services sector increased from US$13.93 billion in 2001 to US$18.86 billion in 2006 with an annual growth rate of 6.23 per cent. Because of the slower growth rate, the share of FDI inflows into the services sector actually declined from 36.01 per cent in the period 1997–2001 to 28.93 per cent in the period 2002–06.

In the services sector, in 2006 FDI inflows mainly concentrated in the following industries: real estate (37.61 per cent), leasing and business services (19.30 per cent), transport, storage and post (9.07 per cent), wholesale and trade (8.18 per cent), power, gas and water production and supply (5.86 per cent), information, computer services and software (4.89 per cent). Together, the above six industries received 84.91 per cent of total FDI inflows into the services sector.

In 2005, China for the first time published the data of FDI inflows into its financial sector. FDI inflows into the financial sector were US$12.1 billion in 2005 and US$6.5 billion in 2006. By the end of 2005, 72 foreign banks from 12 countries and regions have established 254 operational institutions, 117 foreign banks from 40 countries and regions have established 240 representative offices in China, and the total assets of foreign banks have increased to US$87.7 billion. There were 40 foreign invested insurance companies, and their business accounted for 7 per cent of China's total insurance market (Zhang, 2006).

China made substantial commitments to the WTO to open its services sector to international trade and FDI. However, China takes a step by step approach to implement its commitments. In most of the services sectors, especially in telecommunications, banking and insurance, wholesale and retail, storage and transportation, China will fulfil its commitments in three to five years after China's accession to the WTO.

The share of services sector in GDP is around 70 per cent in developed countries, 60 per cent in mid-income countries and 50 per cent in upper low-income countries. However, China's services sector has been underdeveloped in the national economy. The share of services sector in China's GDP has been below 40 per cent. The slow development of the services sector would be a serious 'bottleneck' affecting the overall development of China's national economy.

There are many reasons for the slow development of China's services sector. Among others, two reasons would be the most important. One is closedness and the other is monopoly. Before China's accession to the WTO, China's services sector has been relatively closed to foreign direct participation. The closed nature of the services sector to foreign competition has effectively protected the state monopolies in that sector. At present, China's many services industries are still monopolized by state-owned enterprises, especially in the industries of telecommunications and public utilities.

Opening the services sector has been one of the most important issues in the bilateral negotiations of China's accession to the WTO. China has made some important and concrete commitments to the WTO in opening its services sector to foreign investors. It is expected that with further and full implementation of its commitments to the WTO, China will attract more FDI inflows into the sector.

CHANGING PATTERN OF FDI FIRMS IN MANUFACTURING

As shown in the above section, FDI into China has been overwhelmingly directed to the manufacturing sector. At present, FDI firms have become a major part of China's manufacturing sector. In 2006, FDI firms made up 21.49 per cent of manufacturing enterprises, held 32.95 per cent of manufacturing assets, employed 33.00 per cent of manufacturing labour force and contributed 33.43 per cent of manufacturing value-added.

After China's accession to the WTO, FDI firms in the manufacturing sector have undergone both rapid expansion and structural changes.

Rapid Expansion of FDI Firms in Manufacturing

As Table 6.2 shows, from 2001 to 2006, FDI firms in the manufacturing sector expanded dramatically. The total assets of FDI firms grew from 1386.18 billion yuan in 2001 to 3516.14 billion yuan in 2006, an increase of 153.66 per cent. As compared with domestic firms whose total assets increased by 72.71 per cent during 2001 to 2006, the growth of FDI firms is more than twice the growth of domestic firms.

Among the three industry groups, from 2001 to 2006, the growth in total assets of FDI firms was the highest in capital-intensive industry,[5] increasing 187.07 per cent, which was closely followed by that of FDI firms in technology-intensive industry,[6] increasing 172.98 per cent. FDI firms in labour-intensive industry[7] also had a large expansion and their total assets increased by 109.41 per cent.

Among the industries, as shown in Appendix Table 6A.1, from 2001 to 2006, the expansion of FDI firms is more significant in the following nine industries: furniture manufacturing, chemical materials and products, ferrous metal smelting, non-ferrous metal smelting, general machinery, special machinery, transport equipment, electronics and telecom

Table 6.2   Total assets of FDI firms and domestic firms in the manufacturing sector (billion yuan in 1991 constant prices)

Industry	2001	2006	Change (%)
FDI firms			
Labour-intensive	506.61	1060.89	109.41
Capital-intensive	384.63	1104.15	187.07
Technology-intensive	494.94	1351.10	172.98
Total	1386.18	3516.14	153.66
Domestic firms			
Labour-intensive	1104.88	1973.89	78.65
Capital-intensive	2052.17	3480.09	69.58
Technology-intensive	985.28	1700.29	72.57
Total	4142.33	7154.27	72.71

Sources: Calculated from National Bureau of Statistics of China (NBS) (various issues), *China Statistical Yearbook*, Beijing: China Statistics Press.

Table 6.3   *Employment in FDI firms and domestic firms in the manufacturing sector (million workers)*

Industry	2001	2006	Change (%)
FDI firms			
Labour-intensive	5.25	10.90	107.62
Capital-intensive	1.15	2.55	121.74
Technology-intensive	2.65	7.48	182.26
Total	9.05	20.93	131.27
Domestic firms			
Labour-intensive	15.13	19.69	30.14
Capital-intensive	11.91	12.77	7.22
Technology-intensive	8.06	10.03	24.44
Total	35.11	42.49	21.02

Sources: Calculated from National Bureau of Statistics of China (NBS) (various issues), *China Statistical Yearbook*, Beijing: China Statistics Press.

equipment, and instruments and meters, which had an above-average rate of increase in total assets. It is interesting to note that in the above nine industries, only one is labour-intensive industry (furniture manufacturing) and the other eight are capital-intensive and technology-intensive industries.

In developing countries, where capital is relatively scarce but labour is abundant, foreign companies can be a major source of employment. FDI also indirectly affects employment by raising the growth of the economy and demand for goods from other firms. Research conducted by the International Labour Organization (ILO) suggests the indirect employment effects associated with FDI may be as important, if not more important, than the direct effects (Dunning, 1993).

Together with the rapid expansion in total assets, FDI firms also increased employment substantially. As Table 6.3 shows, the total number of workers employed by FDI firms increased from 9.05 million in 2001 to 20.93 million in 2006, increasing by 131.27 per cent. The increase in employment of domestic firms was only 21.02 per cent during the same period. As a result, by the end of 2006, the share of the labour force employed by FDI firms in the manufacturing sector increased from 20.49 per cent in 2001 to 33.00 per cent in 2006.

The increase in employment of FDI firms is the fastest in technology-intensive industry, increasing 182.26 per cent during the period 2001 to 2006. FDI firms in labour-intensive and capital-intensive industries also increased employment dramatically, increasing over 100 per cent during the same period. As a result, by the end of 2006, 42.73 per cent of the labour force in technology-intensive industry and 35.63 per cent of the labour force in labour-intensive industry were employed by FDI firms.

Changes in the Relative Importance of FDI Firms in Manufacturing

Because of the large increase and higher growth rate in investment, FDI firms have become more and more important in the manufacturing sector. As shown in Table 6.4, in terms of total assets, the share of FDI firms in the manufacturing sector has increased from 25.07 per cent in 2001 to 32.96 per cent in 2006. In other words, one-third of the total assets of the manufacturing sector was held by FDI firms in 2006.

Among the three industry groups, FDI firms in technology-intensive industry gained more share, and therefore, more importance than FDI firms in labour-intensive and capital-intensive industries in the manufacturing sector. By 2006, as shown in Table 6.4 and Figure 6.2, the share of FDI firms in technology-intensive industry reached 44.28 per cent, increasing 10.84 percentage points as compared with that in 2001. The share of FDI firms in labour-intensive industry increased to 34.96 per cent in 2006, rising by 3.52 percentage points on 2001. The share of FDI firms in capital-intensive industry is still relatively low as compared with those in technology-intensive and labour-intensive industries; however, it also increased to 24.09 per cent in 2006, rising by 8.31 percentage points on 2001.

With the rapid growth, FDI firms in some industries have already gained a dominant or significant position in the manufacturing sector. As shown in Appendix Table 6A.2, in the industries of leather and fur products (58.63 per cent), furniture manufacturing (53.03 per cent), cultural, educational and sports goods (64.61 per cent), electronics and telecom equipment (71.24 per cent) and instruments and meters (50.22 per cent),

Table 6.4   Shares of FDI firms in the manufacturing sector by total assets (%)

Industry	2001	2006	Change (percentage points)
Labour-intensive	31.44	34.96	3.52
Capital-intensive	15.78	24.09	8.31
Technology-intensive	33.44	44.28	10.84
Total	25.07	32.95	7.88

Sources: Calculated from National Bureau of Statistics of China (NBS) (various issues), *China Statistical Yearbook*, Beijing: China Statistics Press.

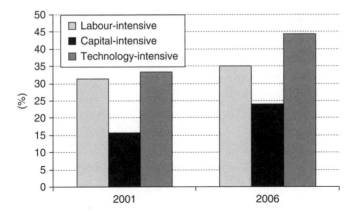

Sources: Calculated from National Bureau of Statistics of China (NBS) (various issues), *China Statistical Yearbook*, Beijing: China Statistics Press.

Figure 6.2   Share of FDI firms in manufacturing (by total assets)

FDI firms have gained the dominant position. In the industries of clothing and other fibre products (48.20 per cent) and paper and paper products (44.63 per cent), rubber products (43.19 per cent), plastic products (47.06 per cent), the shares of FDI firms have reached between 40 and 50 per cent of the industries' total assets.

Changes in the Structure of FDI Firms in Manufacturing

Empirical studies have revealed that multinational enterprises (MNEs), relative to indigenous firms, tend to concentrate their activities in sectors in which the revealed comparative advantage index is greater than 1, or is increasing over time (Dunning, 1993). In other words, FDI firms tend to invest in the industries in which the country has a comparative advantage or the country's comparative advantage is increasing.

For developing countries, because they have a comparative advantage in labour-intensive activities, FDI flows into developing countries mainly aim to make use of the local comparative advantage of cheap labour, and therefore, FDI will usually concentrate in labour-intensive industry. In the case of China, in the early stage of FDI inflows into the manufacturing sector, FDI firms were overwhelmingly concentrated in labour-intensive industry. By the end of 1995, as shown in Table 6.5, in terms of the total assets of FDI firms in the manufacturing sector, 47.19 per cent were in labour-intensive industry while only 25.43 per cent and 27.38 per cent were in capital-intensive and technology-intensive industries.

Table 6.5   Industrial structure of FDI firms in the manufacturing sector by total assets (%)

Industry	1995	2001	2006
Labour-intensive	47.19	36.55	30.17
Capital-intensive	25.43	27.75	31.40
Technology-intensive	27.38	35.71	38.43
Total	100	100	100

Sources: Calculated from National Bureau of Statistics of China (NBS) (various issues), *China Statistical Yearbook*, Beijing: China Statistics Press.

With the fast economic growth, high level of capital accumulation, large improvement in human capital development and technology progress, China's comparative advantage has changed rapidly. Though China still has strong comparative advantage in labour-intensive activities due to its huge population and abundant labour supply, China has greatly increased its comparative advantages in capital-intensive and technology-intensive activities. As a result, FDI flows into China's manufacturing sector have gradually shifted from a high level of concentration in labour-intensive industry toward increasing investment in capital-intensive and technology-intensive industries.

As Table 6.5 shows, by the end of 2001 the structure of FDI firms in the manufacturing sector had changed. In terms of the total assets of FDI firms, the share of labour-intensive industry had fallen to 36.55 per cent, while the shares of capital-intensive and technology-intensive industries had risen to 27.75 per cent and 35.71 per cent respectively.

After China's accession to the WTO, FDI in China's manufacturing sector has made even further and larger structural changes. Though a large amount of FDI still flowed into labour-intensive industry, the share of labour-intensive industry in the total assets of FDI firms has continued to fall, while the shares of capital-intensive and technology-intensive industries in the total assets of FDI firms have been increasing. By the end of 2006, as shown in Table 6.5 and Figure 6.3, the investment structure of FDI firms in China's manufacturing sector has changed fundamentally. Technology-intensive industry has become the most important and the largest sector in receiving FDI, and capital intensive-industry has also surpassed labour-intensive industry in receiving FDI. In terms of the total assets of FDI firms, the shares of technology-intensive industry and capital intensive-industry have increased to 38.43 per cent and 31.40 per cent respectively while the share of labour-intensive industry has fallen to 30.17 per cent.

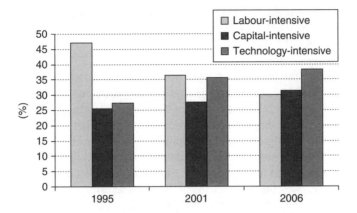

Sources: Calculated from National Bureau of Statistics of China (NBS) (various issues), *China Statistical Yearbook*, Beijing: China Statistics Press.

Figure 6.3   *Structural changes of FDI firms in manufacturing (by total assets)*

As shown in Appendix Table 6A.3, by 2006, electronics and telecom equipment industry attracted the largest amount of FDI, accounting for 20.47 per cent of the total assets of FDI firms, followed by transport equipment (10.19 per cent), chemical materials and products (7.43 per cent), electrical machinery and equipment (6.64 per cent), general machinery (4.78 per cent) and textile industry (4.64 per cent). Together, the above six industries held 54.15 per cent of the total assets of FDI firms. It is worth noting that, except the textiles industry, the other five industries are all capital-intensive and technology-intensive industries.

The above analysis has revealed three important characteristics of FDI inflows into the manufacturing sector after China's accession to the WTO.

First, FDI inflows into the manufacturing sector increased dramatically. The growth rate of investment in total assets of FDI firms was more than twice that of domestic firms.

Second, although FDI inflows into all three industry groups of the manufacturing sector increased dramatically, the growth rate of FDI inflows into technology-intensive industry and capital-intensive industry was much higher than that of FDI inflows into labour-intensive industry.

Third, FDI inflows into the manufacturing sector have gradually changed investment structure, shifting from a high level of concentration in labour-intensive industry toward increasing investment in technology-intensive industry and capital-intensive industry.

China's integration with the global economy

FIRM CHARACTERISTICS – A COMPARISON BETWEEN FDI FIRMS AND DOMESTIC FIRMS IN MANUFACTURING

According to theories about FDI, for a firm to invest overseas it must possess an ownership advantage that confers a degree of market power or cost advantage sufficient to offset the cost of producing abroad. This could be a product or production process to which other firms do not have access, or an intangible asset or capability such as technology, information, managerial, marketing and entrepreneurial skills, organizational systems or access to intermediate or final goods markets.

Therefore, we would expect that FDI firms as compared with domestic firms would be superior in terms of some firm characteristics such as the size of firms, the level of physical capital intensity and the labour productivity.

Size of Firms

Based on total assets, as shown in Table 6.6, the average size of FDI firms increased from 46.83 million yuan in 2001 to 58.70 million yuan in 2006, increasing 25.35 per cent. In contrast, the average size of domestic

Table 6.6   Size of FDI and domestic firms in manufacturing (million yuan of total assets/unit in 1991 constant prices)

Industry	2001	2006	Change (%)
FDI firms			
Labour-intensive	28.74	31.68	10.23
Capital-intensive	81.75	117.40	43.61
Technology-intensive	68.07	79.47	16.75
Total	46.83	58.70	25.35
Domestic firms			
Labour-intensive	17.33	17.47	0.81
Capital-intensive	66.19	66.53	0.51
Technology-intensive	35.00	31.73	−9.34
Total	33.70	32.69	−3.00
FDI firms over domestic firms (index)			
Labour-intensive	1.66	1.81	9.35
Capital-intensive	1.24	1.76	42.87
Technology-intensive	1.94	2.50	28.78
Total	1.39	1.80	29.22

Sources: Calculated from National Bureau of Statistics of China (NBS) (various issues), *China Statistical Yearbook*, Beijing: China Statistics Press.

Table 6.7 Size of FDI and domestic firms in manufacturing (workers/per firm)

Industry	2001	2006	Change (%)
FDI firms			
Labour-intensive	298	325	9.28
Capital-intensive	245	271	10.62
Technology-intensive	365	440	20.58
Total	306	349	14.23
Domestic firms			
Labour-intensive	237	174	−26.58
Capital-intensive	384	244	−36.46
Technology-intensive	286	187	−34.62
Total	286	194	−32.17
FDI firms over domestic firms (index)			
Labour-intensive	1.25	1.87	48.55
Capital-intensive	0.64	1.11	74.08
Technology-intensive	1.27	2.35	84.37
Total	1.07	1.80	68.14

Sources: Calculated from National Bureau of Statistics of China (NBS) (various issues), *China Statistical Yearbook*, Beijing: China Statistics Press.

firms decreased from 33.70 million yuan in 2001 to 32.69 million yuan in 2006, decreasing 3 per cent. As a result, in 2006 FDI firms are on average 1.8 times as large as domestic firms, and two-and-a-half times larger in technology-intensive industries.

In terms of employment, as shown in Table 6.7, the average number of workers employed by FDI firms increased from 306 workers per firm in 2001 to 349 workers per firm in 2006, increasing 14.23 per cent. In contrast, the average number of workers employed by domestic firms decreased from 286 workers per firm in 2001 to 194 workers in 2006, decreasing 32.17 per cent. The decline of the number of workers per firm in domestic firms is mainly due to two reasons. First, millions of workers have been laid off by domestic firms through enterprise reform during the late 1990s and early 2000s. Second, there has been a large increase in the number of domestic firms during the period 2001–06. For example, the total number of domestic firms increased from 0.123 million in 2001 to 0.219 million in 2006, increasing 78.04 per cent, while the total employment of domestic firms increased only 21.02 per cent during the same period. As a result, in 2006 FDI firms on average employed 1.9 times as many workers as domestic firms, and more than twice as many workers in technology-intensive industries.

The above analysis reveals that FDI firms on average are larger than domestic firms both in terms of total assets and in terms of employment, which is particularly apparent in technology-intensive industries. This suggests that FDI firms are more able than domestic firms to capture economies of scale.

Capital Intensity (Capital-to-labour Ratio)

A high level of physical capital intensity (as measured by the capital-to-labour ratio) would suggest that the firm employs technologically advanced production methods. As Table 6.8 shows, in 2001, FDI firms on average had a higher capital-to-labour ratio than did domestic firms in the same industry. However, during the period 2001–06, on average the capital-to-labour ratio of FDI firms increased only marginally by 9.73 per cent while the capital-to-labour ratio of domestic firms increased dramatically by 42.71 per cent. As a result, the gap between FDI firms and domestic firms in terms of capital intensity has been reduced substantially. In particular, for labour-intensive industries, the capital-to-labour ratio of FDI firms has fallen below that of domestic firms. But in capital-intensive and technology-intensive industries the capital-to-labour ratio

Table 6.8   *Capital–labour ratio of FDI and domestic firms in manufacturing (1000 yuan/worker in 1991 constant prices)*

Industry	2001	2006	Change (%)
FDI firms			
Labour-intensive	96.56	97.37	0.84
Capital-intensive	333.82	433.39	29.83
Technology-intensive	186.46	180.53	–3.18
Total	153.11	168.02	9.73
Domestic firms			
Labour-intensive	73.02	100.26	37.30
Capital-intensive	172.28	272.57	58.22
Technology-intensive	122.20	169.50	38.71
Total	117.00	168.39	42.71
FDI firms over domestic firms (index)			
Labour-intensive	1.32	0.97	–26.56
Capital-intensive	1.94	1.59	–17.94
Technology-intensive	1.53	1.07	–30.20
Total	1.30	1.00	–23.11

Sources: Calculated from National Bureau of Statistics of China (NBS) (various issues), *China Statistical Yearbook*, Beijing: China Statistics Press.

of FDI firms is still higher than that of domestic firms, suggesting that foreign firms in capital-intensive and technology-intensive industries do possess superior ownership advantages and that production methods are more advanced.

The closing gap between FDI firms and domestic firms in terms of capital intensity could be attributed to a couple of reasons. First, through enterprise reform and restructuring, domestic firms have improved their structure and production methods by increasing physical capital investment and reducing labour input, which has dramatically increased their capital-to-labour ratio. Second, the fast expansion in employment of FDI firms, especially in labour-intensive and technology-intensive industries, tends to slow down the growth or even reduce the capital-to-labour ratio of FDI firms. These changes indicate that through enterprise reform and competition, domestic firms have been catching up with FDI firms, especially in labour-intensive industries.

Labour Productivity

Due to their ownership advantages, FDI firms in general are expected to have a higher labour productivity than do domestic firms in the same industry. In 2001, labour productivity, as measured by the value-added per worker, on average was more than one-and-a-half times higher in foreign firms than that in domestic firms (Table 6.9).

However, the superiority of FDI firms in labour productivity over domestic firms has been weakening. As shown in Table 6.9, during the period 2001–06, labour productivity in FDI firms on average increased 45.44 per cent while labour productivity in domestic firms on average increased 127.98 per cent. In other words, from 2001 to 2006, labour productivity in domestic firms increased nearly three times the increase in labour productivity of FDI firms.

As a result, in 2006, labour productivity in FDI firms on average was only marginally higher (2 per cent higher) than that in domestic firms. In labour-intensive industries, labour productivity in FDI firms has fallen below that in domestic firms (12 per cent lower). In capital-intensive and technology-intensive industries, although labour productivity in FDI firms was still 52 per cent and 28 per cent higher than that in domestic firms respectively, the gap between FDI firms and domestic firms in labour productivity has been narrowed down substantially.

The above analysis has revealed some interesting findings. First, FDI firms on average are larger than domestic firms both in terms of total assets and in terms of employment, which is particularly apparent in technology-intensive industries. This suggests that FDI firms are more

*Table 6.9　Labour productivity of FDI and domestic firms in manufacturing
(1000 yuan/worker-year in 1991 constant prices)*

Industry	2001	2006	Change (%)
FDI firms			
Labour-intensive	24.78	34.11	37.62
Capital-intensive	73.90	128.90	74.42
Technology-intensive	51.66	64.73	25.31
Total	38.92	56.60	45.44
Domestic firms			
Labour-intensive	17.98	38.98	116.83
Capital-intensive	32.85	84.91	158.44
Technology-intensive	23.76	50.58	112.86
Total	24.35	55.52	127.98
FDI firms over domestic firms (index)			
Labour-intensive	1.38	0.88	−36.53
Capital-intensive	2.25	1.52	−32.51
Technology-intensive	2.17	1.28	−41.13
Total	1.60	1.02	−36.20

Sources: Calculated from National Bureau of Statistics of China (NBS) (various issues),
China Statistical Yearbook, Beijing: China Statistics Press.

able than domestic firms to capture economies of scale. Second, FDI firms
on average have higher physical capital intensity (as measured by capital-
to-labour ratio) than do domestic firms. However, the difference between
FDI firms and domestic firms in terms of physical capital intensity has
been reducing particularly in labour-intensive industries. Third, FDI firms
on average have higher labour productivity than do domestic firms, especially on capital-intensive and technology-intensive industries. However,
the gap between FDI firms and domestic firms in labour productivity has
been closing especially in labour-intensive industries in which the labour
productivity of FDI firms has fallen below that of domestic firms.

CONCLUSION

After China's accession to the WTO, with the implementation of the WTO
commitments and broader and deeper liberalization in trade and investment, FDI inflows into China has presented an increasing trend, rising
from US$46.88 billion in 2001 to US$74.8 billion in 2007, with an annual
growth rate of 8.1 per cent.

FDI inflows into China continued to concentrate in the manufacturing sector. The share of FDI inflows into the manufacturing sector increased from 60.79 per cent in the period 1997–2001 to 68.74 per cent in the period 2002–06. China's manufacturing is very competitive in attracting FDI inflows. China maintained its position as the number one destination for manufacturing and assembly in 2005. Therefore, China's manufacturing sector will continue to attract large FDI inflows.

With the rapid increase in FDI inflows into manufacturing, FDI firms in the manufacturing sector have also undergone some structural changes. Three changes are most important.

First, the growth rate of FDI inflows into technology-intensive industries and capital-intensive industries was much higher than that of FDI inflows into labour-intensive industries. As a result, the relative importance of FDI firms in technology-intensive industries has surpassed the relative importance of FDI firms in labour-intensive industries in China's manufacturing sector. In 2006, FDI firms in technology-intensive industries held 44.28 per cent of the industries' total assets, while FDI firms in labour-intensive industries held 34.96 per cent of the industries' total assets.

Second, the investment pattern of FDI firms in manufacturing has been changing gradually, especially after China's entry into the WTO. FDI inflows into the manufacturing sector have shifted from concentrating in labour-intensive industries toward increasing investment in technology-intensive industries and capital-intensive industries. As a result, technology-intensive industries and capital-intensive industries have become more and more important to FDI, and by 2006 their combined share reached 69.83 per cent of the total assets of FDI firms in the manufacturing sector.

Third, in terms of firm characteristics, FDI firms on average are more advanced and superior than domestic firms in terms of firm size, physical capital intensity and labour productivity. However, the relative superiority of FDI firms over domestic firms in physical capital intensity and labour productivity has been lessening. In labour-intensive industries, both physical capital intensity and labour productivity of FDI firms have fallen below those of domestic firms, though FDI firms still have relatively higher physical capital intensity and labour productivity in capital-intensive and technology-intensive industries than do domestic firms. These changes indicate that through enterprise reform and competition, domestic firms have been catching up with FDI firms, especially in labour-intensive industries.

Several factors could be attributed to the changing structure of FDI in the manufacturing sector. First, China's changing pattern in comparative advantage in its economy might influence the investment pattern of FDI in the sector. After nearly 30 years of economic reform and fast economic growth, China's comparative advantage has changed rapidly. Though China still has strong comparative advantage in labour-intensive activities, China has greatly increased its comparative advantages in capital-intensive and technology-intensive activities. As FDI firms tend to invest in the industries in which the host country has a comparative advantage or the host country's comparative advantage is increasing, it is expected that China's increasing comparative advantage in capital-intensive and technology-intensive activities will increasingly attract more and more FDI inflows into technology-intensive and capital-intensive industries.

Second, through enterprise reform and intense competition, China's domestic firms have greatly improved their competitiveness. In 2006, the labour productivity of domestic firms in labour-intensive industry has surpassed that of FDI firms in the manufacturing sector. The increasing and fierce competition from domestic firms in labour-intensive industry has made FDI gradually lose competitiveness in labour-intensive industry, pushing FDI toward capital-intensive and technology-intensive industries in which FDI has relatively strong competitiveness as compared with domestic firms.

Third, China has greatly improved its business market environment and strengthened intellectual property protection, especially since China's entry into the WTO, which has greatly increased the confidence of foreign investors, encouraging them to bring more capital and technology through their investments.

The fourth factor is China's increasing per capita income and growing domestic market demand for high-quality goods, which attract more and more capital-intensive and technology-intensive MNEs to flow into China.

NOTES

1. The average annual FDI inflows into the manufacturing sector are calculated at the 2000 constant US dollar prices.
2. The data are FDI inflows into non-financial sectors only.
3. Data for actual FDI inflows by sectors are not available before 1997.
4. For example, McKibben and Wilcoxen, 1998; Walmsley and Hertel, 2000; UNCTAD, 2000; Chen, 2002.
5. Capital-intensive industry includes beverage manufacturing, tobacco processing, paper and paper products, petroleum refining and coking, chemical materials and products, chemical fibres, ferrous metal smelting, non-ferrous metal smelting and transport equipment.
6. Technology-intensive industry includes medical and pharmaceutical products, general machinery, special machinery, electrical machinery and equipment, electronics and telecom equipment and instruments and meters.
7. Labour-intensive industry includes food processing, food manufacturing, textiles, clothing and other fibre products, leather and fur products, timber processing, furniture

manufacturing, printing, cultural, educational and sports goods, rubber products, plastic products, non-metal mineral products, metal products and others.

REFERENCES

A.T. Kearney Inc. (2007), '2005 Foreign Direct Investment Confidence Index', http://www.atkearney.com/main.taf?p=5,3,1,140,10, accessed 5 June 2007.

BBC CHINESE.com (2007), 'China's corporate income tax will be unified to 25%', 8 March, http://news.bbc.co.uk/chinese/simp/hi/newsid_6420000/newsid_6429200/6429275.stm, accessed 25 November 2008.

Chen, C. (2002), 'Foreign Direct Investment: Prospects and Policies', in *China in the World Economy: The Domestic Policy Challenges*, Paris: OECD, pp. 321–58.

Chen, C. (2006), 'Changing Patterns in China's Agricultural Trade after WTO Accession', in Ross Garnaut and Ligang Song (eds), *The Turning Point in China's Economic Development*, Australian National University, Canberra: Asia Pacific Press, pp. 197–224.

Dunning, J. (1993), *Multinational Enterprises and the Global Economy*, Wokingham, UK: Addison-Wesley.

Harrold, P. and R. Lall (1993), 'China Reform and Development in 1992–93', World Bank Discussion Paper, No. 215, Washington, DC: The World Bank.

He, Q. (2006), 'China's FDI policy is undergoing important changes', My China News Digest, 12 November, http://www.cnd.org/my/modules/wfsection/article.php%3Farticleid (in Chinese) accessed 13 November 2006.

McKibben, W. and P. Wilcoxen (1998), 'The Global Impacts of Trade and Financial Reform in China', Asia Pacific School of Economics and Management, Working Paper No. 98-3, the Australian National University.

Morisset, J. (2003), 'Tax Incentives: Using Tax Incentives to Attract Foreign Direct Investment', Public Policy for the Private Sector, the World Bank Group, Private Sector and Infrastructure Network, Note No. 253.

National Bureau of Statistics of China (various issues), *China Foreign Economic Statistical Yearbook*, Beijing: China Statistics Press.

National Bureau of Statistics of China (various issues), *China Statistical Yearbook*, Beijing: China Statistics Press.

United Nations Conference on Trade and Development (UNCTAD) (2000), *World Investment Report, Cross-border Mergers and Acquisitions and Development*, United Nations, New York and Geneva: United Nations Publication.

United Nations Conference on Trade and Development (UNCTAD) (2007), 'Rising FDI into China: The Facts Behind the Numbers', UNCTAD Investment Brief, No. 2, the Investment Issues Analysis Branch.

Walmsley, T. and T. Hertel (2000), 'China's Accession to the WTO: Timing is Everything', Center for Global Trade Analysis, Purdue University.

Xinhua News Agency (2007), 'Parliament adopts corporate income tax', 16 March, http://news.xinhuanet.com/english/2007-03/16/content_5854950.htm, accessed 4 June 2007.

Zhang, Y. (2006), 'China's Economic Progress and its Role in Strengthening Cooperation between East and South Asia', Paper prepared for the ADB Research Project on Strengthening East and South Asia Economic Relations.

APPENDIX

Table 6A.1   Total assets of FDI firms and domestic firms in manufacturing (billion yuan in 1991 constant prices)

Industry	2001	2006	Change (%)
FDI firms			
Food processing	40.26	101.88	153.06
Food manufacturing	38.05	70.45	85.15
Beverage manufacturing	42.70	72.12	68.91
Tobacco processing	0.97	0.81	−16.27
Textiles	73.80	163.07	120.96
Clothing and other fibre products	45.99	93.32	102.92
Leather and fur products	29.16	64.93	122.68
Timber processing	15.04	21.54	43.23
Furniture manufacturing	10.51	34.51	228.40
Paper and paper products	52.84	117.13	121.67
Printing	21.31	31.00	45.48
Cultural, educational and sports goods	18.58	37.34	100.96
Petroleum refining and coking	22.41	49.59	121.28
Chemical materials and products	85.25	261.08	206.25
Medical and pharmaceutical products	31.88	66.66	109.11
Chemical fibres	18.28	43.14	136.02
Rubber products	24.14	47.90	98.42
Plastic products	57.42	119.35	107.86
Non-metal mineral products	71.01	130.84	84.25
Ferrous metal smelting	27.75	135.21	387.25
Non-ferrous metal smelting	16.93	66.87	294.97
Metal products	61.34	109.83	79.04
General machinery	56.79	167.91	195.67
Special machinery	25.26	96.68	282.74
Transport equipment	117.50	358.19	204.84
Electrical machinery and equipment	96.69	233.62	141.62
Electronics and telecom equipment	263.76	719.84	172.91
Instruments and meters	20.57	66.38	222.71
By industry group			
Labour-intensive	506.61	1060.89	109.41
Capital-intensive	384.63	1104.15	187.07

Table 6A.1 (continued)

Industry	2001	2006	Change (%)
Technology-intensive	494.94	1351.10	172.98
Total	1386.18	3516.14	153.66
Domestic firms			
Labour-intensive	1104.88	1973.89	78.65
Capital-intensive	2052.17	3480.09	69.58
Technology-intensive	985.28	1700.29	72.57
Total	4142.33	7154.27	72.71

Sources: Calculated from National Bureau of Statistics of China (NBS) (various issues), *China Statistical Yearbook*, Beijing: China Statistics Press.

China's integration with the global economy

Table 6A.2   Shares of FDI firms in the manufacturing sector by total assets (%)

Industry	2001	2006	Change (percentage points)
Food processing	23.42	29.85	6.43
Food manufacturing	38.50	38.75	0.24
Beverage manufacturing	27.24	35.93	8.69
Tobacco processing	0.72	0.47	−0.25
Textiles	21.68	28.02	6.34
Clothing and other fibre products	43.92	48.20	4.28
Leather and fur products	52.75	58.63	5.88
Timber processing	36.11	27.03	−9.06
Furniture manufacturing	48.08	53.03	4.95
Paper and paper products	35.49	44.63	9.14
Printing	34.08	31.87	−2.21
Cultural, educational and sports goods	61.30	64.61	3.31
Petroleum refining and coking	10.35	13.27	2.92
Chemical materials and products	17.16	28.66	11.50
Medical and pharmaceutical products	17.69	22.04	4.35
Chemical fibres	21.73	31.99	10.26
Rubber products	37.84	43.19	5.35
Plastic products	46.12	47.06	0.94
Non-metal mineral products	20.52	22.24	1.72
Ferrous metal smelting	5.16	11.86	6.71
Non-ferrous metal smelting	9.72	15.84	6.12
Metal products	40.66	37.78	−2.88
General machinery	20.56	29.12	8.56
Special machinery	13.84	25.57	11.73
Transport equipment	24.14	37.07	12.93
Electrical machinery and equipment	30.53	35.85	5.32
Electronics and telecom equipment	56.68	71.24	14.56
Instruments and meters	34.76	50.22	15.46
By industry group			
Labour-intensive	31.44	34.96	3.51
Capital-intensive	15.78	24.09	8.31
Technology-intensive	33.44	44.28	10.84
Total	25.07	32.95	7.88

Sources: Calculated from National Bureau of Statistics of China (NBS) (various issues), *China Statistical Yearbook*, Beijing: China Statistics Press.

Table 6A.3 Structure of FDI firms in manufacturing by total assets (%)

Industry	1995	2001	2006
Food processing	4.64	2.90	2.90
Food manufacturing	3.34	2.75	2.00
Beverage manufacturing	3.73	3.08	2.05
Tobacco processing	0.10	0.07	0.02
Textiles	8.76	5.32	4.64
Clothing and other fibre products	5.11	3.32	2.65
Leather and fur products	3.41	2.10	1.85
Timber processing	1.32	1.09	0.61
Furniture manufacturing	0.78	0.76	0.98
Paper and paper products	2.25	3.81	3.33
Printing	1.16	1.54	0.88
Cultural, educational and sports goods	1.35	1.34	1.06
Petroleum refining and coking	0.27	1.62	1.41
Chemical materials and products	5.48	6.15	7.43
Medical and pharmaceutical products	2.34	2.30	1.90
Chemical fibres	1.60	1.32	1.23
Rubber products	1.62	1.74	1.36
Plastic products	4.14	4.14	3.39
Non-metal mineral products	6.68	5.12	3.72
Ferrous metal smelting	2.58	2.00	3.85
Non-ferrous metal smelting	1.64	1.22	1.90
Metal products	4.87	4.43	3.12
General machinery	4.11	4.10	4.78
Special machinery	1.81	1.82	2.75
Transport equipment	7.77	8.48	10.19
Electrical machinery and equipment	6.16	6.98	6.64
Electronics and telecom equipment	11.51	19.03	20.47
Instruments and meters	1.46	1.48	1.89
By industry group			
Labour-intensive	47.19	36.55	30.17
Capital-intensive	25.43	27.75	31.40
Technology-intensive	27.38	35.71	38.43
Total	100	100	100

Sources: Calculated from National Bureau of Statistics of China (NBS) (various issues), *China Statistical Yearbook*, Beijing: China Statistics Press.

7. Foreign banks in China: market segmentation and expanded presence in the post-WTO environment

Lilai Xu

INTRODUCTION

Theoretically, openness to foreign banks has both positive and negative impacts on the banking sector in a developing country: (1) local banks will be exposed to fierce competition and existing bank–customer relationships can be destroyed, resulting in market instability; (2) the spillover effect of foreign banks' technology and quality service will enhance the efficiency of local banks, thereby improving the provision of financial services and capital.

Studies by Goldberg and Saunders (1981), Walter (1981, 1985, 1988), Gray and Gray (1981) and many others have found that easing restrictions on the entry of foreign banks has potential benefits for the domestic market in terms of resource allocation and efficiency. Lavine (1996) asserts that foreign banks promote financial development directly by providing high-quality services, and indirectly by three means: (1) by spurring domestic banks to improve service quality and to cut costs; (2) by encouraging the upgrading of accounting, auditing and rating institutions; and (3) by creating domestic pressures to harmonize bank regulatory and supervisory procedures, and to bring standards in line with those of developed countries. However, when a country gains the benefits of financial development from relaxing foreign bank entry, and product and market controls, the costs and risks involved can also be substantial (Stigliz, 1993). Seth, Nolle and Mohanty (1998) report that the motivation to 'follow their customers' has not been the sole reason for foreign banks to enter the US market over the past few decades. There seems to be a trend among foreign banks to steer away from lending to companies from their home countries in recent times, and foreign banks seem gradually to be entering the market of domestic banks. On the contrary, a study by Buch and Golder (2001) finds that in Germany, while the degree of international capital mobility has increased in recent decades, domestic banks have remained the dominant suppliers of financial services on the domestic market, with foreign financial institutions accounting for a relatively stable 3–5 per cent of retail banking activities. This raises the issue of whether foreign banks are actually able to penetrate the markets of domestic banks or whether their activities are confined to certain niche markets.

In the context of China, have foreign banks penetrated the market of domestic banks? Will the entire market be dominated sooner or later by foreign banks? Or is it more accurate to say that foreign banks only service different market segments from those of domestic banks, and thus play a supplementary role in China's financial system?

PRESENCE OF FOREIGN BANKS IN CHINA

On 11 December 2001 when China became the 143rd member of the World Trade Organization (WTO), the Chinese government announced a gradual removal of geographic and customer restrictions on foreign banks engaging in RMB business. In the following years, the RMB business activities of foreign banks gradually expanded from the initial four cities of Shanghai, Shenzhen, Tianjin and Dalian to the entire nation, and their RMB business clients were allowed to expand from foreign enterprises and individuals to China's domestic ones.

On 11 November 2006, to honour China's WTO commitments, the Regulations on the Administration of Foreign Invested Banks (the 'New Regulations') were promulgated by the State Council, with implementing rules issued by the China Banking Regulatory Commission (CBRC) on 24 November 2006. The New Regulations apply to the following forms of foreign invested banks established within China: (1) locally incorporated wholly foreign-funded banks; (2) Chinese–foreign joint venture banks; (3) foreign bank branches; and (4) representative offices of foreign banks. The institutions listed in (1), (2) and (3) are collectively treated as operational foreign banking entities.

As of the end of December 2006, there were 200 branches and 79 sub-branches in 25 Chinese cities established by 74 banks from 22 countries/regions. In addition, there were 14 subsidiaries (or locally incorporated wholly foreign-owned banks as defined by the Chinese authorities) and joint venture banks, which opened 19 branches and sub-branches. Of all the operational foreign banking entities, about two-thirds were established by banks from Hong Kong (99), the United States (26), the United Kingdom (21), Japan (19), Singapore (17) and France (15). There were a further 242 representative offices in 24 cities, representing 186 foreign banks from 41 countries/regions. In terms of the geographical coverage, 100 operational entities were located in Shanghai, making up 32 per cent of the total number, 40 in Shenzhen (13 per cent), 37 in Beijing (12 per cent), 28 in Guangzhou (9 per cent), 17 in Tianjin (5 per cent), 16 in Xiamen (5 per cent), and the rest in other cities (24 per cent). Foreign banks have accelerated their pace in entering the Western regions of China, where 30 (10 per cent) operational entities had been set up by the end of 2006 (CBRC, 2007).

According to CBRC figures, in May 2007 foreign banks altogether owned RMB581.9 billion in foreign exchange assets and RMB407.7 billion in RMB assets, an increase of 77 per cent and 743 per cent respectively compared with the end of 2001. Over the same period, total outstanding deposits with foreign banks increased by 427 per cent, while total outstanding loans by foreign banks increased by 239 per cent. Foreign banks account for less than 2 per cent of total assets of the banking sector in China.

MARKET SEGMENTATION: THE CASE OF SHANGHAI

There are numerous studies to test the hypothesis of integration of banking markets in countries like the United States (DeYong and Nolle, 1996; Amel and Hannan, 1999; Centeno and Mello, 1999) or, in contrast, the hypothesis of market segmentation as seen in Germany (Buch and Golder, 2001). Data limitation impedes a rigorous statistical analysis of foreign banks in China. However, a close examination of the bank account holders is good enough to identify the different types of customers targeted by foreign banks, and thus helps to identify to what extent foreign banks in China are integrated with or segmented from the traditional market of domestic banks.

It is estimated that in China's financial centre Shanghai, foreign banks owned combined assets of RMB509.4 billion by the end of 2006, roughly 14 per cent of the total assets of the banking sector in Shanghai. The outstanding RMB deposits with, and loans from, foreign banks were RMB99.9 billion and RMB138.97 billion respectively, or 3.97 per cent and 8.11 per cent of the Shanghai market (Shanghai Finance Office, 2007). According to the PBC 2006 statistics, foreign banks in Shanghai had a total of 9701 enterprise settlement account (ESA) (referred to as business transaction account in Western countries) holders, of which 16.84 per cent were large or extra-large enterprises.[1] Domestic banks in Shanghai had 1.12 million ESA holders, but only 3.28 per cent of their account holders

Table 7.1 Breakdown of ESA holders in Shanghai by industrial sector, 2005

	Primary (%)	Secondary (%)	Tertiary (%)	Total (%)	Large-business Customers* Within the Group (%)
FB+DB	0.82	31.54	67.64	100	
FB	0.13	41.66	58.21	100	16.84
DB					3.28
Policy	3.19	18.95	77.86	100	
Shareholding	0.33	25.76	73.91	100	
State	0.59	33.76	65.65	100	
Local	1.58	30.13	68.29	100	

Note: * Registered capital >CNY50 billion; FB: foreign banks; DB: domestic banks.

Source: PBC Research Team (2006).

were large or extra-large enterprises. Foreign banks constituted only 0.86 per cent of the Shanghai market, but secured 3.87 per cent of large enterprises and 4.6 per cent of extra-large enterprises as their loyal customers.

Interestingly, as shown in Table 7.1, market segmentation or client bias also exists among domestic banks. There are four types of domestic banks in China: policy banks, shareholding commercial banks, state-owned commercial banks and local commercial banks. Policy banks target large and extra-large state-owned enterprises involved in infrastructure projects or projects of national security. Shareholding and state commercial banks are more interested in well-established large enterprises and export- or real-estate-oriented private enterprises, while local commercial banks normally prefer local small- and medium-sized enterprises.

In terms of industrial sectors, it is found that 67.64 per cent of the ESA holders in Shanghai are from the tertiary industry, 31.54 per cent from the secondary industry and only 0.82 per cent from the primary industry. Primary industry customers are more satisfied with local commercial banks and state-owned commercial banks, with these banks accounting for 93.31 per cent of this industry in Shanghai.

State-owned commercial banks and local commercial banks together have a lion's share of the secondary industry market, accounting for 85.90 per cent of the city's total. However, a closer look at the data reveals that out of the foreign bank ESA holders, 41.66 per cent are from the secondary industry, compared with 33.76 per cent for state-owned commercial banks, 30.13 per cent for local commercial banks, 25.76 per cent for shareholding

Table 7.2   *Breakdown of ESA holders with foreign and domestic banks in Shanghai, 2005*

	Foreign Banks	Domestic Banks
Total	9 701 (100%)	1 119 131 (100%)
Foreign firms	7 719 (79.6%)	61 943 (5.5%)
Domestic firms	1 982 (20.4%)	1 047 188 (94.5%)
Manufacturing, leasing & business services	7 828 (80.7%)	637 904 (57.0%)

Source: PBC Research Team (2006).

commercial banks, and 18.95 per cent for policy banks. Foreign banks assign more importance (10.20 per cent higher than domestic banks' average) to the secondary industry, reflecting a traditional segment for FDI in developing countries, driven by the 'follow the customers' strategy (PBC Research Team, 2006).

With regard to the tertiary industry customers, state-owned commercial banks and local commercial banks have recorded nearly the same high level as seen in the secondary industry, making up a combined 81.90 per cent of the total. The proportion of ESA holders from the tertiary industry within the total for policy banks is 77.86 per cent, followed by shareholding commercial banks (73.91 per cent), local commercial banks (68.29 per cent), state-owned commercial banks (65.65 per cent), and foreign banks (58.21 per cent).

Table 7.2 further indicates that foreign banks, although very small in terms of the number of ESA holders, assign significantly larger weight to foreign-funded enterprises (79.6 per cent) than domestic banks (5.5 per cent). Foreign banks also attach more importance to the manufacturing and service sectors (80.7 per cent) than domestic banks (57.0 per cent). Moreover, foreign banks' customers are mainly capital- and technology-intensive companies rather than labour-intensive businesses (PBC Research Team, 2006).

Xiao and Lu (2006) and Huang and Xiong (2005) provide further evidence by revealing the proportions of loans granted by foreign banks to China-based companies, global companies and home country companies. Xiao and Lu (2006) also indicate that in the foreign currency loan market, the correlation coefficient of the value of FDI against the foreign bank loans received by foreign-funded companies in Shanghai was as high as 0.8673 over the past ten years, while the correlation coefficient between the value of FDI and domestic bank loans received by foreign-funded companies was only 0.4215. As expected, a high correlation coefficient of 0.8056 was also captured for local companies' exports against their deposits with domestic banks over the same period.

Two surveys conducted by PricewaterhouseCoopers (2005, 2007) also show that Asian banks mainly follow their customers from home countries, while European and US banks target home country and multinational companies. It has been found that foreign banks as a group have had a very low level of success in penetrating the loan markets of domestic banks despite their combined assets in Shanghai remaining a two-digit percentage of the city's total – well above the average for developing economies. It appears that foreign banks' activities are still confined to certain market niches. The Shanghai case thus lends, at least partially, support to the market segmentation hypothesis.

A possible explanation of this dichotomy is foreign banks' cost disadvantages. Handling credit applications, assessing business conditions and obtaining information on policy changes in China are all costly matters. If these costs, or switching costs as defined by Thompson and Cats-Baril (2002), are positively related to the 'institutional proximity' of a bank and customer, foreign banks will then service different market niches and deal mainly with foreign-funded companies. The entry of foreign banks into the market segment traditionally serviced by domestic banks will occur only if deregulation has a sufficiently large impact on relative cost structures (Buch and Golder, 2000). Other factors contributing to market segmentation as cited by many academics and practitioners include: (1) the introduction of a range of regulations hindering foreign banks' market entry and expansion (Siackhachanh, 2006); and (2) multilayered regulations, which often lack a 'clarity of coordination' (PricewaterhouseCoopers, 2007).

EXPANSION IN THE NEW POST-WTO ENVIRONMENT

As a result of the wide opening up of China's banking market in 2007, rapid expansion of foreign banks has been witnessed in the overall banking landscape. Their strategies are becoming more defined in the new post-WTO environment.

Before 11 December 2006, the Chinese banking sector had seen an influx of foreign institutions buying into domestic commercial banks in advance of the new WTO measures (see Appendix Table 7A.1). This reflects foreign banks' preference to acquire equities in Chinese banks rather than to embark on the relatively slow branch network expansion. The benefit of equity acquisition is immediate access to market information and the established customer relationships of domestic banks. To domestic banks, foreign equity participation brings about new sources of capital and, most importantly, the management expertise required for market development. Under the current regulations, total foreign bank ownership of up to 25 per cent in a domestic bank is permitted, with an individual foreign bank being allowed to own 20 per cent. Where the combined equity of foreign investors in a non-listed domestic bank exceeds 25 per cent, this domestic bank will be treated as a joint-venture bank by the regulatory authorities.

Local Incorporation

In the post-WTO environment, the most popular strategic option for expansion in China remains organic growth; however, creating a new financial entity rather than partnership with a domestic bank has increased in attractiveness. The most frequently cited change now is foreign banks' moving to local incorporation. The New Regulations require a foreign bank to establish a subsidiary bank with corporate status in order to operate the full range of RMB business in China (see Appendix Table 7A.2). To set up foreign bank subsidiaries in China, a minimum of RMB500 million of total capital is required.[2] The newly incorporated foreign banks are subject to the same regulations as domestic banks and are able to compete on equal terms with domestic banks. Otherwise, a foreign bank branch is neither permitted to issue bank cards nor to accept term deposits of less than 1 million yuan (see Table 7.3).

Retail Banking

The impact of the local incorporation of foreign banks has far-reaching implications. In retail banking, the market has become more competitive and the products more diversified and innovative. While Citibank has initiated debit cards and continued to issue credit cards through its local partners, many newly incorporated foreign banks, or foreign bank subsidiaries, are busy formulating their plans to launch local cards, yuan-denominated mortgages, wealth management products and various deposit and loan services.

As a matter of fact, the first four banks to incorporate locally have already offered yuan-denominated mortgages and wealth management products for high-net-worth local customers. According to HSBC Premier Centre's publicity pamphlets, customers with deposits exceeding US$50 000 can enjoy for free the HSBC Premier Financing Service. The Centre provides customers with such services as savings deposits of up to eight different currencies, one-on-one manager service and round-the-clock telephone

Table 7.3 Foreign banks: capital requirement and business scope

	Locally Incorporated Wholly Foreign-owned Bank	Joint-venture Bank	Foreign Bank Branch
Registered capital	RMB1 billion	RMB1 billion	N.A.
Working capital	RMB100 million	RMB100 million	RMB200 million
Deposits by local residents	No limit	No limit	Minimum: RMB1 million term deposit
Bank card business	Yes	Yes	No

Source: State Council of China (2006).

service. Customers can also conveniently book tickets for sporting events, entertainment productions and golf course facilities. They can even make flight reservations, book accommodation and get emergency assistance in case of theft of their personal documents, passports or luggage.

Individual financing services provided by domestic banks are still in the embryonic stages, with many remaining at the basic level of selling bonds and funds (Tan and Ding, 2005; LHZQ, 2007). Unlike domestic bank free individual services, foreign bank individual services are offered at fixed but rather high prices. For instance, HSBC charges 300 yuan a month for value-added premium services to customers with balances below 500 000 yuan (PricewaterhouseCoopers, 2007). Profits in China's wealth management market stood at US$31 billion in 2002 and US$57 billion in 2006 (Li, 2006). The wealth management business is developing rapidly throughout the world, while it is still in its infancy in China.

It is estimated that about 20 per cent of the Chinese population holds 80 per cent of China's financial assets, and more than 10 million households have family assets outstripping 1 million yuan. A survey by McKinsey & Company shows that there are 30 million middle- and high-income households in China, with annual incomes exceeding US$4300. Four per cent of them, or 1.2 million households, have deposits of more than US$100 000 (ibid.). It is predicted that by the year 2010 three product categories, which are closely related to wealth management, will experience rapid growth: credit cards, investment products and mortgages (PricewaterhouseCoopers, 2007).

Apart from moving to local incorporation as discussed above, the expanded market presence of foreign banks in retail banking is also to be observed in the launch of a wide range of mature and market-tested products on the Internet. Compared with Chinese banks, foreign banks have far fewer branches; and it is impractical for them to open large numbers of outlets. However, their Internet services can help to remedy this disadvantage, because of its fast speed, low cost and multiregional services. It is noted that the average cost of a traditional bank service is 1.07 yuan, of a telephone service, 0.45 yuan, and for an ATM service, 0.2 yuan, while that of an Internet service is only 0.01 yuan (Tan and Ding, 2005).

Wholesale Banking

On the wholesale banking side, foreign banks are already active in core areas such as trade finance, corporate banking and treasury/FX/money markets. With the growth of the Chinese economy, enterprises in China will need a whole range of financial products and services including risk hedging, custodian and local or overseas investments. Foreign banks are looking forward to expanding their activities by taking advantage of their risk management skills, capabilities and expertise, as well as their financial stability. The RMB-denominated product areas expected to grow by 2010 are interest and cross-currency swaps, structured products and debt capital markets (PricewaterhouseCoopers, 2007; Liu, 2008).

Structured products are new financial instruments introduced by foreign banks and non-banking financial institutions in China. They give the investor the flexibility to have an investment structure tailored to their needs by taking into account such factors as goals, risk tolerance and time horizons. These products have returns that can be linked to the performance of an underlying benchmark such as interest rates, equity/foreign exchange markets or commodities.

It is reported that foreign banks as a group have been consistently successful in their chosen market segments. The non-performing loans (NPL) ratio of the foreign banks, according to official statistics, was recorded to be 0.54 per cent in 2007, compared with 6.91 per cent for domestic commercial banks. In a survey conducted by PricewaterhouseCoopers (2007), 14 out of 37 responding foreign banks envisage their annual growth to be 50 per cent or greater; and only four banks forecast their growth rate at below 20 per cent by the year 2010. The target markets of greatest importance for foreign banks over the coming years, as identified by many of the foreign bank CEOs in China, will be the Top 100 and global corporations, trade finance, foreign exchange, retail deposits, high-net-worth individuals and the SME sector. It appears that the primary influences on foreign banks' strategies continue to be the pace and direction of changes in regulations, followed by product changes and increasing customer demands.

CONSTRAINED SOURCES OF RMB FUNDS

Foreign banks in all developed and developing countries find it difficult to attract market shares in the retail deposit market because they often lack access to a well-established branch network. Foreign banks in China are further disadvantaged in their efforts to increase bank liabilities due to the fact that (1) local currency is not fully convertible; (2) every foreign bank has a foreign debt quota, and once reached the borrower has to pay a 5 per cent business tax; (3) there are limits on offshore funding; and (4) foreign bank branches are not allowed to accept term deposits of less than 1 million yuan.

It has been observed that in China, interest rate spread remains large, for example, benchmark rates in March 2007 were 2.79 per cent and 6.39 per cent respectively. This reflects the inefficiency of the banking sector, yet, on the other hand, a larger difference between the interest rate charges on a bank loan and the lender's cost of funds enables foreign banks to offset part of the switching cost. Clearly, foreign banks in China could have dozens of branches, but the licensing process is slow – effectively one city per year – with permission to open sub-branches in these cities taking even longer. Table 7.4 gives an indication of the sources of funds before the New Regulations became effective. Over the period 2002 through 2005, an average of 91 per cent of foreign banks' RMB funds came from deposits. Since foreign banks do not have widespread branch networks, they cannot mobilize enough deposits to satisfy the increasing demand for both retail and wholesale banking services in the post-WTO environment, thereby relying on borrowing from the inter-bank market, local securities market or international markets.

Moreover, despite the progress of banking sector reforms, foreign banks often have difficulties with the regulatory and supervisory requirements for the following reasons:

Table 7.4   Foreign banks: sources of RMB funds (in RMB billion)

	2000		2001 (end of June)		2002		2003		2004		2005	
	Balance	%	Balance	%	Balance	%	Balance	%	Balance	%	Balance	%
Deposits	64.7	23.0	60.4	21.5	215.1	84.6	388.7	91.2	557.4	92.9	891.3	94.1
Inter-bank borrowing	217.5	77.0	220.1	78.5	33.9	13.4	32.8	7.7	30.9	5.1	44.1	4.6
Securities	0	0	0	0	5	2.0	4.7	1.1	11.6	2.0	12	1.3

Source: National Bureau of Statistics of China (NBS) (2006), *China Statistical Yearbook 2006*.

- The authorities rely on direct administrative controls due to the lack of effective supervisory frameworks or the capacity to assess, evaluate and monitor both foreign and domestic banks.
- Anything that is not explicitly allowed can be implicitly prohibited. As a result, there are numerous steps required for approval of new financial products and new business activities.
- Some provincial authorities impose additional requirements on foreign banks, undermining the reform efforts of the central government. For example, SOEs in some provinces are not allowed to open bank accounts outside that province. Such a requirement has virtually forbidden foreign banks with no branches in that province to conduct the deemed no-geographical-restriction business (Siackhachanh, 2006).

Given the fact that the opening up of the Chinese banking sector is in line with the overall economic opening-up strategy, and is instrumental in helping China build up a socialist market economy, some suggestions might well be outlined as follows:

- Restrictions on foreign debt quotas should be lifted because such currency restriction has a negative effect on the growth of foreign banks, and can give rise to credit risk in the banking sector.
- The policy of directing foreign banks to expand in the inland provinces needs further clarification; the waiting period for foreign banks to obtain approval for opening a branch or sub-branch should be reduced.
- An RMB swap market between foreign and domestic banks, and between foreign banks and Chinese multinational companies, should be effectively facilitated.
- Foreign banks should be allowed to raise RMB funds in the local bill and bond (either secured/listed or unsecured) markets; new financial instruments and products including securitization of residential mortgages should be further encouraged.
- There is a need to benchmark the effectiveness and transparency of supervisory and regulatory practices with international standards.

CONCLUDING REMARKS

Foreign banks in China initially try to exploit market niches where they have had competitive success in other countries; eventually they may attempt to compete more broadly as they gain experience within that domestic market.

Along with the opening up of China's banking market at the end of 2006, profound changes have been and will surely continue to be witnessed in the market competition and overall banking landscape. China will, on the pre-condition of national financial safety, introduce supervisory tools and risk control measures in accordance with prudential principles and international best practices, thereby ensuring the sustainable development of the banking industry. As long as an adequate supervisory and regulatory system is in place to ensure the safety, soundness and transparency of the financial system, there is a need to speed up reform in the area of foreign exchange control, and to facilitate financial innovations if China wants to benefit more from the presence of foreign banks in its domestic market, where foreign banks currently play a very small role in the financial system.

NOTES

1. An enterprise with registered capital of less than RMB10 million is regarded as a small enterprise; if registered capital is between RMB50 million and RMB100 million, or above RMB100 million, this enterprise will be regarded as a large or extra-large enterprise.
2. This requirement is more than 10 times the amount for Chinese banks to set up subsidiaries in Europe.

REFERENCES

Amel, D. and T. Hannan (1999), 'Establishing banking market definitions through estimation of residual deposit supply equations', *Journal of Banking and Finance*, **23** (1), 1667–90.

Buch, C. and S. Golder (2000), 'Domestic and Foreign Banks in Germany: Do They Differ?', Kiel Working Paper No. 986, pp. 10–12.

Buch, C. and S. Golder (2001), 'Foreign versus domestic banks in Germany and the U.S.: a tale of two markets', *Journal of Multinational Financial Management*, **11** (1), 341–61.

CBRC (2007), 'Report on the Opening-up of the Chinese Banking Sector', http://chinapaymentsnews.com/2007/03/report-on-the-opening-up-of-the-chinese-banking-sector.html, accessed 30 May 2008.

Centeno, M. and A. Mello (1999), 'How integrated are the money market and the bank loans market within the European Union?', *Journal of International Money and Finance*, **18** (1), 75–106.

DeYong, R. and D. Nolle (1996), 'Foreign-owned banks in the United States: earning market share or buying it?', *Journal of Money, Credit and Banking*, **28** (4), 622–36.

Goldberg, L. and A. Saunders (1981), 'The determinants of foreign banking activity in the United States', *Journal of Banking and Finance*, **5** (1), 17–32.

Gray, J. and H. Gray (1981), 'The multinational bank: a financial MNC?', *Journal of Banking and Finance*, **5** (1), 33–63.

138   *China's integration with the global economy*

Huang, X. and F. Xiong (2005), 'Motivation and strategies of foreign banks in China', *Finance Research*, **2** (1), 12–13.

Lavine, R. (1996), *Foreign Banks, Financial Development and Economic Growth*, Washington, DC: AEI Press.

LHZQ (2007), 'Foreign Banks' Retail Business Competition Strategy', http://www.lhzq.com/index.jsp?pageAlias=news_cont&newsid=1258126 (Chinese) accessed 30 March 2008.

Li, Z. (2006), 'Banks Scramble for Wealth Management Pie', http://www.bjreview.cn/EN/En-2005/05-15-e/bus-2.htm, accessed 30 March 2008.

Liu, Z. (2008), 'Opening-up of the banking sector and newly corporate foreign banks in China', *Finance and Insurance* (Beijing) (2), 5–9.

National Bureau of Statistics of China (2006), *China Statistical Yearbook 2006*, Beijing: China Statistics Press.

PBC Research Team (2006), 'Foreign banks in Shanghai: an analysis of the structure of corporate customers', *Shanghai Finance* (Shanghai) (8), 9–13.

PricewaterhouseCoopers (2005), *Foreign Banks in China 2005*, Report researched and written by Brian Metcalfe.

PricewaterhouseCoopers (2007), *Foreign Banks in China 2007*, Report researched and written by Brian Metcalfe.

R&D Department, Bank of Communications (2008), *China Macro-economy and Finance Outlook 2008*, Shanghai: Shanghai Far East Press.

Seth, R., D. Nolle and S. Mohanty (1998), 'Do banks follow their customers around?', *Financial Markets, Institutions & Instruments*, **7** (4), 1–25.

Shanghai Finance Office (2007), 'Shanghai Financial Service Industry Performance Report 2006', http://image2.sina.com.cn/cj/pc/2007-05-30/32/U1251P31T32D32647F1539DT20070530183532.pdf (Chinese), accessed 28 November 2008.

Siackhachanh, N. (2006), 'How the PRC Opens up for Foreign Banks', Seminar given at the East and Central Asia Department, Asian Development Bank.

State Council of China (2006), 'Regulations of the People's Republic of China on the Administration of Foreign-invested Banks', Order of the State Council of the People's Republic of China, No. 478, http://www.fdi.gov.cn/pub/FDI_EN/Laws/GeneralLawsandRegulations/AdministrativeRegulations/P020070118611973433071.pdf, accessed 21 July 2008.

Stigliz, J. (1993), 'The Role of the State in Financial Markets', *Proceedings of the World Bank Annual Conference on Development Economy*, pp. 299–326.

Tan, R. and G. Ding (2005), 'The effect of foreign banks' entry into Chinese market', *Journal of Foreign Economics and Management* (Shanghai), **27** (5), 16–18.

Thompson, R. and W. Cats-Baril (2002), *Information Technology and Management*, Boston, MA.: McGraw-Hill/Irwin.

Walter, I. (1981), 'Country risk, portfolio decisions, and regulation in international bank lending', *Journal of Banking and Finance*, **5** (1), 77–92.

Walter, I. (1985), *Barriers to Trade in Banking and Financial Services*, Thames Lectures, Trade Policy Research Centre, London.

Walter, I. (1988), *Global Competition in Financial Services: Market Structure, Protection, and Trade Liberalization*, Cambridge, MA: AEI Press and Ballinger.

Xiao, H. and D. Lu (2006), 'Influence of foreign banks in the bank industry in Shanghai', *Finance Research* (Beijing), **11** (1), 141–7.

APPENDIX

Table 7A.1   Foreign ownership in domestic banks

Date	Domestic Bank	Foreign Financial Institution	% of Ownership
09/1999	Bank of Shanghai	International Finance Corporation	5
11/2001	Bank of Nanjing	International Finance Corporation	15
12/2001	Bank of Shanghai	HSBC	8
12/2001	Bank of Shanghai	Shanghai Commercial Bank (HK)	3
03/2002	Bank of Shanghai	International Finance Corporation	7
09/2002	Xi'an City Commercial Bank	Bank of Nova Scotia	2.50
09/2002	Xi'an City Commercial Bank	International Finance Corporation	2.50
12/2002	Shanghai Pudong Development Bank	Citibank	5
10/2003	China Minsheng Bank	International Finance Corporation	1.22
12/2003	Industrial Bank	Government of Singapore Investment Corporation	5
12/2003	Industrial Bank	International Finance Corporation	4
12/2003	Industrial Bank	Hang Seng Bank	15.98
06/2004	Shenzhen Development Bank	Newbridge Capital	17.89
08/2004	Bank of Communications	HSBC	19.90
11/2004	China Bohai Bank	Standard Chartered Bank	19.99
12/2004	Chinese Mercantile Bank	ICBC (Asia)	n.a.
12/2004	Jinan City Commercial Bank	Commonwealth Bank of Australia	10.68
01/2005	China Minsheng Bank	Temasek (a Singapore government firm)	4.55
03/2005	Bank of Beijing	ING/Deutsche Bank	19.90
06/2005	China Construction Bank	Bank of America	8.52
07/2005	China Construction Bank	Temasek	5.88
08/2005	Bank of China	RBS	10
08/2005	Bank of China	Temasek	5
09/2005	Bank of Nanjing	BNP Paribas	19.2
09/2005	ICBC	Goldman Sachs, American Express, Allianz	6.05
10/2005	Bank of Beijing	International Finance Corporation	5

Table 7A.1 (continued)

Date	Domestic Bank	Foreign Financial Institution	% of Ownership
10/2005	Bank of Beijing	ING Group	n.a.
10/2005	Tianjin Rural Coop Bank	Rabobank	n.a.
12/2005	Bank of Tianjin	ANZ Bank	20
01/2006	Bank of China	UBS	1.61
01/2006	URCB Hangzhou	Rabobank	19.92
04/2006	Huaxia Bank	Deutsche Bank and Sal Oppenheim	7.02
07/2006	Hangzhou City Commercial Bank	Commonwealth Bank of Australia	19.92
11/2006	Guangdong Development Bank	Citibank, IBM, China Life, State Grid	20
03/2007	Bank of Dalian	Bank of Nova Scotia	n.a.
04/2007	Huishang Bank	ABN AMRO and UCBH	n.a.

Source: PricewaterhouseCoopers (2007) and R&D Department, Bank of Communications (2008).

Table 7A.2 Foreign bank subsidiaries in China

Name of Bank	Locality of Registered Office	Registration Date
HSBC	Shanghai	02/04/2007
Standard Chartered Bank	Shanghai	02/04/2007
Bank of East Asia	Shanghai	02/04/2007
National City Bank	Shanghai	02/04/2007
Hang Seng Bank	Shanghai	28/05/2007
DBS	Shanghai	28/05/2007
Mizuho Corporate Bank	Shanghai	01/06/2007
Bank of Tokyo-Mitsubishi UFJ Ltd	Shanghai	02/07/2007
ABN AMRO Holding	Shanghai	03/07/2007
OCBC Bank	Shanghai	01/08/2007
J.P. Morgan Chase Bank	Beijing	11/10/2007
Hana Bank	Beijing	Pending
Shinhan Bank	Beijing	Pending
Woori Bank	Beijing	12/11/2007
Deutsche Bank	Beijing	Pending
Société Générale	Beijing	Pending
Wing Hang Bank	Shenzhen	01/06/2007

Source: R&D Department, Bank of Communications (2008).

8. The impact of the RMB revaluation on China and the world economy

James Xiaohe Zhang

INTRODUCTION

Since China ended a peg of its currency to the US dollar in July 2005, the Renminbi (RMB) has appreciated, with an accumulated rate of more than 18 per cent during a period of two-and-a-half years up to the time when this chapter was written in June 2008. However, the issues on whether, how and to what extent will the nominal rate of the RMB be further revaluated remain unsolved.

Although the pressures on RMB revaluation from the United States, Japan and the European Union intensified over the last two years, the Chinese authority is still reluctant to appreciate the RMB further. One of the reasons for this reluctance is that the Chinese banking system and financial institutions are still too vulnerable to manage international currency shocks for a full convertible RMB in the foreseeable future. Another concern is massive unemployment resulting from a considerable fall in exports when the appreciation accelerates. According to a report released by the Ministry of Labor and Social Security recently, the appreciation will mainly bring negative impact on China's employment. Industrial sectors that are most affected by the appreciation are textiles, clothing, shoemaking, toys, motorcycles and agricultural sectors. When the RMB appreciates by 5–10 per cent, about 3.5 million workers in the non-agricultural sectors lose their jobs. Meanwhile, millions of farmers could be also affected adversely (China.com, 2007).

The Chinese official position is shared not only by most of the academia and business people in China, but also by some Western scholars including Robert Mundell and Joseph Stiglitz, two Nobel laureates in economics. Mundell (2006) maintains that a big change of its exchange rate will cut down China's growth rate from 9 per cent now to perhaps half of that. Other adverse economic impacts include falls in exports and corporate profitability, increase in unemployment and capital flight. Stiglitz (2005) also argues that the RMB revaluation will have little effect on the trade deficit in the United States because the Chinese imports in the US market could be easily replaced by imports from other developing countries.

Based on this background, this chapter has two objectives. First, it attempts to examine the so-called Mundell–Stiglitz conjecture that a considerable revaluation of RMB will affect the Chinese economy adversely, yet have little impact on the balance of payment in the United States. Second, it attempts to examine the sectoral impact of the RMB revaluation on the world economy in general, and on the Chinese economy in particular. The results of simulations employed on a multicountry computable general equilibrium model (the GTAP model) for a considerable revaluation of the RMB by 20 per cent support the Mundell–Stiglitz conjecture conditionally. The results also indicate that when most of the labour-intensive exporting industries, particularly food and textiles, contract, exports from capital-intensive sectors such as machinery and utilities are more likely to increase in China.

The rest of the chapter is organized as follows. The next two sections review briefly the reforms in China's exchange rate regime in its post-reform era and the debates of RMB revaluation. The simulation results on some hypothetical perspectives of a 20 per cent revaluation of the RMB are reported in the fourth and fifth section. Concluding remarks and policy implications are summarized in the final section.

REFORMS IN THE RMB EXCHANGE RATE REGIME

China's road toward a full convertibility of its currency has involved a number of important reforms that have been implemented in a step-by-step manner. When China assumed its seat on the Executive Board of the International Monetary Fund (IMF) in 1980, the official rate was about 1.50 RMB yuan per US dollar. Since then, although the Chinese authority has termed the currency regime as 'managed float', in reality the exchange rate had been pegged with the US dollar until July 2005.

At the beginning of 1981, an internal settlement rate was introduced, at which all purchases of foreign exchange had to take place. Between 1986 and 1994 three different rates were effective at the same time: the 'official' rate (an-oft-adjusted peg to the US dollar); the 'swap' market rates (unofficial floating rates that the central bank occasionally adjusted through market intervention) and the 'effective' exchange rates actually faced by exporters (weighted averages of official and unofficial rates; see Roberts and Tyers, 2001). The apparent overvaluation of the official exchange rate during the 1980s, at least relative to the market-based exchange rates, was a source of concern to policy-makers who recognized it as a tax on exports.

Committed to improving the trade balance, the authorities intervened in the swap market and repeatedly devalued the official rate from 3.45 RMB yuan per US dollar in 1986 to about 5.76 RMB yuan per US dollar in 1993, and eventually unified the official and swap market exchange rates at the prevailing swap price of 8.62 RMB yuan per US dollar in 1994. The RMB rate was revaluated to 8.27 RMB yuan per US dollar in 1998 and stabilized at this level for seven years until July 2005 when the People's Bank of China announced a revaluation of the RMB by 2.1 per cent.

The current exchange rate regime is categorized as administrable floating (Lu, 2004). The People's Bank of China publishes daily the median rate of RMB against the US dollar according to the transaction price prevailing in the inter-bank foreign exchange market the previous day. On the basis of this, the designated banks will then list their own exchange rates (ibid.). The reforms have achieved a substantial breakthrough and the currency started to appreciate gradually from the second half of 2005. Along with the widening range of fluctuations, the Chinese authority also announced that the RMB rate is linked to a basket of currencies including the US dollar, the euro, the Japanese yen and the Korean won weighted by their importance in China's external transactions. In addition, China has loosened its controls on the offshore investment projects of domestic companies and started to encourage individual portfolio investment in foreign markets, with an aim of releasing some of the pressures in RMB appreciation.

Despite these measures, the accumulated appreciation of more than 18 per cent is considered too little and too late by most of the Western governments. This prolonged appreciation, along with deflation occurring in China in the beginning of this decade, might have made the RMB rate even more undervalued. Table 8.1 presents both the nominal exchange rate and the real exchange rate of the RMB against the US dollar between 1994 when the two-tier exchange rates were merged and 2005 when the RMB was revaluated after an almost fixed rate for seven years. The real exchange rate is calculated as a product of the nominal rate and the ratio of consumer price indexes between the two countries.

The figures in Table 8.1 show that as compared with 1994, the RMB rate appreciated by less than 5 per cent in nominal terms but depreciated by more than 50 per cent in real terms by the end of 2005. The divergence between the nominal rate and the real rate enlarged as the two rates moved in opposite directions, as a result of different movement in consumer price indexes between China and the United States. This de facto depreciation might have helped China increase its exports in the world market and accumulation of foreign exchange reserves significantly over the last decade. Table 8.2 presents a comparison in the value of international trade and the current account balance for the two countries.

Table 8.1   Change in the real RMB exchange rate (1993–2007)

Year	1	2	3	4	5
	Nominal Exchange Rate	China Consumer Price Index	US Consumer Price Index	Real RMB Exchange Rate (1)*(3/2)	Change of Real RMB Exchange Rate
	100 US$	(1994=100)	(1994=100)	100 US$	% change of (4)
1993	576.2				
1994	861.87	100	100	861.87	
1995	835.1	94.36	102.83	910.06	5.59
1996	831.42	87.27	105.87	1008.62	10.83
1997	828.98	82.84	108.3	1083.76	7.45
1998	827.91	79.94	109.99	1139.13	5.11
1999	827.83	79.13	112.42	1176.10	3.25
2000	827.84	80.9	116.19	1188.96	1.09
2001	827.70	81.14	119.5	1219.01	2.53
2002	827.70	79.94	121.39	1256.87	3.11
2003	827.70	81.55	123.94	1257.94	0.08
2004	827.70	83.72	127.29	1258.46	0.04
2005	819.17	82.03	131.61	1314.29	4.44
2006	797.18	81.79	136.03	1325.86	0.88
2007	730.00				

Sources: Data for China are obtained from National Bureau of Statistics (2006), *China Statistical Yearbook 2006*, http://www.stats.gov.cn/english/statisticaldata/yearlydata/, and for the United States are obtained from the US Census Bureau, 'The 2007 Statistical Abstract', http://www.census.gov/compendia/statab/brief.html.

THE DEBATES ON RMB VALUATION

There are several approaches that have been used to estimate the 'equilibrium' real exchange rate. These include absolute and relative purchasing power parity (PPP) calculations, balance of payment method and simulation exercises employing multicountry general equilibrium models. The results of different estimations, nevertheless, have been mixed by a wide margin ranging from undervaluation of somewhere between 15 per cent to 40 per cent (Chang and Shao, 2004; Goldstein, 2004, 2007; Zhang and Pan, 2004; Frankel, 2005; Goldstein and Lardy, 2006), no significant undervaluation (Bosworth, 2004; Tyers et al., 2007), to overvaluation (Wang, 2004, 2005; Funke and Rahn, 2005; Sinnakkannu and Nassir, 2006).[1]

Table 8.2   Exports, imports and trade balances, China and the United States (US$ billion)

Year	China			US		
	Exports	Imports	Balance	Exports	Imports	Balance
1978	9.75	10.89	−1.14	178.43	208.19	−29.76
1980	18.12	20.02	−1.9	271.83	291.24	−19.41
1985	27.35	42.25	−14.9	289.10	410.92	−121.82
1989	52.54	59.14	−6.6	487.00	580.14	−93.14
1990	62.09	53.35	8.74	525.23	616.09	−90.86
1991	71.91	63.79	8.12	578.34	609.48	−31.14
1992	84.94	80.59	4.35	616.55	653.00	−36.45
1993	91.74	103.96	−12.22	642.89	711.68	−68.79
1994	121.01	115.61	5.4	703.90	800.57	−96.67
1995	148.78	132.08	16.7	794.39	890.77	−96.38
1996	151.05	138.83	12.22	851.60	955.67	−104.07
1997	182.79	142.37	40.42	934.17	1042.73	−108.56
1998	183.71	140.24	43.47	933.17	1099.31	−166.14
1999	194.93	165.7	29.23	965.89	1230.97	−265.08
2000	249.2	225.09	24.11	1070.60	1450.43	−379.83
2001	266.1	243.55	22.55	1004.90	1370.02	−365.12
2002	325.6	295.17	30.43	974.72	1398.45	−423.73
2003	438.23	412.76	25.47	1017.57	1514.67	−497.1
2004	593.32	561.23	32.09	1157.25	1769.34	−612.09
2005	761.95	659.95	102	1283.07	1997.44	−714.37
2006	969.1	791.6	177.5	1445.70	2204.22	−758.52
2007	1218	955.8	262.2			

Sources: Same as Table 8.1.

Based on the absolute PPP approach, some economists believe that the RMB was significantly undervalued in the first half of the 2000s. For instance, Zhang and Pan (2004) estimate that the RMB would have appreciated by 15–22 per cent in 2003 compared with 1996, if there had been no government intervention. Nevertheless, scholars using the relative PPP methods (Bosworth, 2004; Sinnakkannu and Nassir, 2006) seem to perceive that the RMB rate was just about at the right level. As argued by Bosworth (2004) and Woo and Xiao (2007), even if the RMB is undervalued on an absolute PPP basis, the PPP standard itself provides very weak guidance to the appropriateness of exchange rate for low-income economies.

Economists using the balance of payment approach are more likely to believe that the RMB was significantly undervalued. Goldstein (2004,

2007) argues that the undervaluation lies somewhere between 15 per cent and 30 per cent in 2004. However, it seems well perceived that the equilibrium exchange rate and balance of payment are not linearly correlated, that is, a surplus in current account does not guarantee a currency appreciation. For instance, the Japanese yen has been weakening for years despite the tremendous trade surplus that Japan has maintained. In the case of the RMB, because China is notable for its extremely high saving rate of more than 40 per cent of GDP, so long as this characteristic persists, there is little basis for suggesting that it could or should have a current account deficit in the near future (Golley and Tyers, 2007; Woo and Xiao, 2007).

The dynamic general equilibrium modelling approach provides some long-term prospects for the RMB change. Tyers et al. (2007) and Golley and Tyers (2007) link long-term growth shocks with the Chinese real exchange rate and argue that, in the short run, when the dominant force is financial capital inflows, the RMB is more likely to appreciate, but in the long run, when demographic force is weak relative to skill transformation and productivity growth in the service sector, the RMB will depreciate. While financial capital inflows driven by expected appreciation may be self-fulfilling in the short run, these studies indicate that the fundamental forces are more likely to lead to a trend of real depreciation in the long run.

Given these mixed results of estimations on the value of the RMB, the answers to the practical issues on how, when and to what extent should the RMB be further revalued also differ. The law-makers in most of the developed countries including the United States, the European Union, Japan and some international institutions such as the IMF and WTO all present a particularly strong argument in favour of a considerable revaluation. Among economists, while Goldstein (2004, 2007) maintains that an adjustment of 15 per cent to 20 per cent with an enlarged transactional margin of 5 per cent to 7 per cent on either side around the new peg is preferable, Tung and Baker (2004) argue that a considerable revaluation of roughly 15 per cent against the US dollar to a new fixed rate is optimal for China.

However, when the majority seems in favour of a considerable revaluation, a case against the revaluation has also emerged, particularly from the Chinese side. The Chinese authorities have argued that, first, the increase of foreign reserves is largely a result of the 'hot money', inflows of foreign capital hoping to instantaneously capitalize on a rapid RMB revaluation, rather than long-term foreign direct investment in capital projects. Second, while China's trade surplus with the United States increases, China runs trade deficits with most other countries it trades with. Should the RMB be significantly appreciated, China would face stronger competition from its Asian neighbours in the markets of labour-intensive goods in North America, Europe and Japan, as well as in these economies themselves.

Ironically, the views presented by some US economists, including Stiglitz (2005) and Mundell (2006), are similar to the Chinese authorities. They believe that preconditions for a full convertibility of the RMB have not yet been met. Mundell in his online discussion on 13 February 2006 pointed out that a too sharp revaluation of RMB would even cause a financial crisis because the revaluation will lead to a fall in import price and deflation, which bring more pressures on the RMB. Other adverse impacts include possible falls in foreign direct investments, shrinkage in profit margin in Chinese exports and increase in unemployment. According to Mundell (2006), a floating exchange rate system is not suitable for China, and abandoning the fixed exchange rate system will bring long-term adverse impact to the country. He thus suggests a fixed rate of 8 RMB per US dollar.

In reference to the conflict over trade balance between the United States and China, Stiglitz (2005) pointed out that whether:

> a succession of revaluations eliminates China's trade surplus will have little effect on the more important problem of global trade imbalances, and particularly on the US trade deficit. China's recent gains in textile sales . . . largely came at the expense of other developing countries. America will once again be buying from them, so that their total imports will be largely unchanged. . . . Unless domestic investment goes down or domestic savings go up, the trade deficit will persist, unabated.

The Mundell–Stiglitz conjecture that a considerable revaluation of the RMB will have adverse impact on China and will have virtually no effect on the trade deficits in the United States is an empirical question that cannot be answered without some quantitative assessment over the interaction and feedback effects among many countries in a general equilibrium setting of the world economy. This task is usually carried out through simulation exercises on computable general equilibrium models. Given the fact that empirical studies on this issue are still very limited,[2] this chapter attempts to fill the gap.

MODEL, SCENARIO AND HYPOTHESES

Following the exercises of Zhang et al. (2006) and Zhang (2008), this chapter tackles the issue of the impact of a considerable RMB revaluation on the world economy by simulating a scenario on a computable multicountry general equilibrium model (the GTAP model).

The Model

The GTAP model is based on the Global Trade Analysis Project, which is coordinated by the Center for Global Trade Analysis at Purdue University in the United States. The newly released GTAP dataset includes 87 regions and 57 sectors. Version 6 of the GTAP dataset, which is based on the 2001 data is used for simulations. The world economy is aggregated into 10 regions and 10 sectors to capture the regional and sectoral impact of the RMB revaluation. The method of the aggregation is detailed in Appendix Tables 8A.1 and 8A.2.

There are several ways in which macroeconomic shocks are introduced into applied general equilibrium models. One way of doing this is to impose the shocks exogenously by changing the real prices of investment flows or primary factors of production (Tec, 2000). Another approach is to build explicitly dynamic models (Golley and Tyers, 2007; Tyers et al., 2007). In this chapter, a third approach is experimented with. To approximate the revaluation of the RMB by 20 per cent, a corresponding change in relative price for all traded goods (imports and exports) between China and the rest of the world is projected. To capture the regional and sectoral impact of the change, the world economy is divided into 10 regions and 10 sectors. Particular attentions are paid to the changes in the balance of payment between China and its major trade partners including the United States, the EU, Japan and the East Asian newly industrializing economies (NIEs, including Korea, Hong Kong and Taiwan), and the ASEAN countries.

The Scenario

There are a number of variables in the GTAP model that could be shocked as approximate relative price change after a real exchange rate revaluation. One possible way of doing this is to increase the actual tariff rate of the Chinese exports in all other regions by a given proportion (say 100 per cent) and decrease the actual tariff rate of imports from all other regions into China by an equal proportion (say also 100 per cent). In this chapter, a combined shock of removing the tariffs for imports from all other regions into China and doubling of the tariffs for the Chinese exports in all other regions is used as an approximation of 20 per cent revaluation of the RMB. This is consistent with the macroeconomic consequence of a real exchange rate revaluation since the ultimate adjustment entails changes in the relative prices of the traded goods. In other words, it is assumed that an equi-proportionate change in the relative prices of the traded goods is equivalent to an appreciation of the real exchange rate by the same proportion. Thus, in this chapter, the RMB revaluation is interpreted as relative price changes in all traded goods that China imported from and exported into all other regions.[3]

The Hypotheses

The first hypothesis conjectured by Mundell and Stiglitz is that a considerable revaluation of the RMB will have adverse impact on the Chinese economy and will have virtually little effect on the US trade deficit.

The second hypothesis is based on the export orientation and labour-abundant nature of the Chinese economy. As the fourth-largest exporting nation in the world, more than 30 per cent of China's GDP is created by exports. A considerable revaluation of the RMB will therefore mainly hurt the most labour-intensive industries such as textiles and clothing, and help the other industries, which could be more capital-intensive, to expand.

These two hypotheses are tested through simulations of the GTAP model.

THE RESULTS

Changes in GDP and International Trade

Table 8.3 summarizes the changes of some aggregate macroeconomic variables in the world economy after a revaluation of the RMB by approximately 20 per cent. There are several interesting points that need to be highlighted.

First, the results show a significant decrease in GDP growth and a considerable fall in trade surplus in China, and corresponding increases in GDP and improvements in trade balance elsewhere in the rest of the world. The fall in growth rate in China (7.2 per cent) is so large that it would remove the double-digit economic growth rate by more than two-thirds. This approximates the hard landing consequence that Japan has experienced for a decade. This fall in China's GDP growth rate is also far beyond what Mundell (2006) has conjectured. While the growth rate in China falls significantly, the changes in growth rate in all other regions vary from negative in the rest of the world (ROW), slightly more than zero in the rest of Europe, 0.12 per cent in the United States and Europe, 0.28 per cent in Australia and New Zealand (ANZ), 0.35 per cent in the rest of Asia and 0.51 per cent in the six original ASEAN countries, to 0.59 per cent in Japan and the NIEs.

Second, the changes in the balance of payment show a similar pattern to the changes in GDP. A revaluation of the RMB by 20 per cent would

Table 8.3   Changes in value of regional GDP and international trade

Regions	GDP Growth (%)	Exports (%)	Imports (%)	Change in Trade Balance (US$ million)	Change in Trade Balance (%)
ANZ	0.28	0.18	−0.23	372	8.76
China	−7.20	6.98	17.79	−22912	−21.38
Japan and NIEs	0.59	1.11	0.98	2243	2.09
US	0.12	0.70	0	6349	1.61
EU-15	0.12	0.27	0.03	6556	11.98
ASEAN-6	0.51	−0.09	−0.34	886	1.25
Rest of Asia	0.35	0.13	−0.56	747	26.94
Rest of America	0.23	0.06	−0.32	2473	9.85
Rest of Europe	0.03	0.03	−0.28	1576	8.49
ROW	−0.14	−0.07	−0.51	1711	21.13

Source: Author's simulation results.

cut China's trade surplus by more than 21 per cent, but it would not have any significant impact on the balance of payment in the United States. The drop of less than 2 per cent in the US trade deficit is too trivial to make a difference of any degree. This seems to support Stiglitz's (2005) contention that the elimination of China's trade surplus will have little impact on the US trade deficit.

Another implication of Table 8.3 is that when the improvement in the trade deficit is negligible for the United States, the improvement in the current account in the rest of Asia is significant. The overall trade deficit reduces greatly by more than 26 per cent. This seems to underpin Stiglitz's contention that the vacancy created by the falls of the Chinese exports in the US market could be easily filled by the increases of exports from other developing countries, particularly in Asia.

Changes in Exports and Imports at Industry Level

To examine the impact of the RMB revaluation on different industries, the 57 sectors in the GTAP dataset are further aggregated into 10 industries for each of the 10 regions. Table 8.4 presents the changes in exports and imports in these industries for the major six regions. Significant falls in exports of food (38 per cent) and textiles (17 per cent) appear in China. This change deserves some attention by the policy-makers because the export of food is the major source of foreign exchange earnings in the rural sector, and the fall in textile exports may create massive unemployment of

Table 8.4   *Changes in exports and imports in China and its major trade partners (%)*

	ANZ	China	Japan and NIEs	US	EU-15	ASEAN
Value of exports						
Food	1.74	−37.52	−0.15	10.86	0.74	−0.78
Other primary goods	−3.36	15.05	12.58	1.19	−0.13	−0.94
Textiles	4.06	−17.11	15.23	4.69	3.79	3.85
Petroleum and coal	1.68	4.62	2.22	0.44	0	9.84
Metals	3.85	4.64	1.48	−0.19	0.16	−0.48
Machinery	−0.52	25.39	−0.21	−0.45	0.11	−2.02
Utilities	−0.80	22.21	−5.52	−0.30	−0.15	−0.12
Construction	−0.64	14.70	−1.66	−0.36	−0.42	−0.87
Other manufactures	−1.29	11.84	3.21	0.13	−0.63	−2.63
Services	−0.28	12.88	−1.03	0.11	0.22	−0.22
Value of imports						
Food	0.54	80.87	−1.62	0.36	0.05	−0.29
Other primary goods	−0.64	−0.19	0.65	0.29	0.02	2.70
Textiles	−5.04	32.51	−0.33	−2.60	−0.16	0.31
Petroleum and coal	0.21	16.17	1.15	0.03	0.11	1.28
Metals	0.11	11.90	1.09	−0.23	−0.08	−0.95
Machinery	−0.10	21.53	1.86	0.18	−0.02	−1.34
Utilities	0.64	−12.10	3.54	0.04	0.16	1.55
Construction	0.17	−6.62	0.94	−0.23	−0.15	0.25
Other manufactures	0.11	19.24	2.98	1.27	0.03	−0.60
Services	0.39	−8.04	0.90	0.13	0.14	0.35

Source: Author's simulation results.

unskilled workers in China. As a result, the contracting effect in these two sectors may significantly hurt the rural economy because textiles and food are the two key industries that underpin the rural economy in China.

Along with the contracting of exports in the labour-intensive textile and land-intensive food industries, there is a significant increase in exports from other industries including machinery (25 per cent), utilities (22 per cent), other primary goods (15 per cent) and construction (15 per cent) in China. Since these industries are generally more capital-intensive than the textile and food industries, the changes may result in inefficient resource allocation in the world economy. On the import side, significant increases in food (81 per cent) and textiles (33 per cent), alongside modest increases in machinery (22 per cent), other manufactures (19 per cent) and petroleum and coal (16 per cent) result. These combined effects will lead to significant contracting of 7 per cent and 11 per cent in the food and textile industries in China respectively.

Table 8.4 also shows some changes in exports and imports in the rest of the world, particularly of the major trading partners of China. Despite the fact that trade may increase in these countries, the change may not necessarily mean welfare improvement for the world as a whole. In the United States, for instance, while the increase in the exports of food (11 per cent) can be considered as trade-creating and welfare-improving if one believes comparative advantage exists in the food industry of the United States, the increase in the exports of textiles (5 per cent) will produce trade diversion and therefore reduce welfare because textiles production is conventionally considered labour-intensive. A similar change can be found for Japan and the NIEs, and the ASEAN countries where the exports of textiles increase by 15 per cent and 4 per cent respectively. This seems to suggest that Japan and the NIEs, along with the ASEAN countries will replace China to fill the vacancies in exporting textiles to the United States, should a considerable revaluation of the RMB be carried out.

In reference to the two hypotheses, the results presented in Tables 8.3 and 8.4 seem to support the Mundell–Stiglitz conjecture. Specifically, when there is a considerable revaluation of the RMB by more than 20 per cent, China's double-digit growth rate would be reduced significantly by more than two-thirds. However, the revaluation would have little impact on the huge trade deficits in the United States. For the second hypothesis, it is shown in Table 8.4 that when the labour-intensive exports, including food and textiles, contract, the exports of other goods, including capital-intensive machinery and utilities, expand in China. The consequential improvement in trade deficits in the United States would be easily removed when exports from Japan, the NIEs and the ASEAN countries increase. This may not, nevertheless, represent a welfare-improving allocation of resources in the world economy.

CONCLUSION AND IMPLICATIONS

This chapter attempts to assess the economic impacts of a considerable revaluation of the RMB on China and the rest of the world. From the experimental results derived from a simple computable general equilibrium model (the GTAP model), the Mundell–Stiglitz conjecture that a considerable revaluation of the RMB brings mainly adverse impact to the Chinese economy yet has little impact on the current account deficit in the United States is accepted. According to the results of the simulation, a considerable revaluation would not be appealing to the Chinese. Specifically it would remove more than two-thirds of its growth rate, reduce exports of labour-intensive products and switch more economic resources into some relatively more capital-intensive activities such as machinery and utility production, and create massive unemployment in China. Given the dual nature of the Chinese economy, the rural sector, which produces mainly land-intensive food and labour-intensive textiles, would be particularly damaged, which in turn, would enlarge the income gaps between the rural and urban sectors in China (Zhang and Harvie, 2002). Aware of this, some additional policies may need to be implemented to remove these adverse impacts.

Despite the robustness of the result, the conclusion generated from the experiment should not be fully accepted without a certain degree of caution. This is because the simulation results could be improved if the model is modified to incorporate some dynamic variables, or the dataset is updated to reflect some recent changes or more appropriate variables are used as better approximations of the real exchange rate change. Further research is therefore needed to be carried out to increase the degree of accuracy in projections.

Despite the fact that this study rejects a sharp once and for all revaluation of the RMB, it does not exclude the feasibility of a gradual and moderate appreciation of less than 20 per cent in a period of four years, or 4 per cent per year over a decade (Frankel, 2005), if the Chinese authorities have determined to make the RMB a convertible currency in the future.

NOTES

1. Using the relative purchasing power parity theory to measure the competitiveness of China's domestic industries against foreign industries and the International Fisher Effect to measure the under- or overvaluation of the RMB against the US dollar, Sinnakkannu and Nassir (2006) concluded that the RMB was actually overvalued before 21 July 2005. The findings are consistent with the findings of Funke and Rahn (2005).
2. Using a computational general equilibrium model, Zhang, Fung and Kummer (2006) analysed the impacts of Chinese real exchange rate appreciation on the trade balance of China and the United States on various industries of both countries. They used several scenarios with 2.1, 6 and 12 per cent real exchange rate appreciations for their simulation analysis. Their results indicate that China's exchange rate appreciation might not help to reduce the enlarging current account deficits of the United States. Chinese outputs in both primary and manufacturing sectors will increase, whereas the outputs of energy and services sectors will be adversely affected. The price of value-added products declines in light of the RMB appreciation. Zhang (2008), through simulating experiments on a multicountry macroeconometric model (the Fair model, see Fair, 2004), also concludes that the significant once and for all revaluation would not be appealing to the Chinese. To some extent it would cut the economic growth rate so significantly that a recession may result, yet will have little impact on the external trade imbalances between China and the rest of the world. The revaluations, nevertheless, do have significant impact on lowering the rate of inflation in China.
3. The GTAP Version 6 dataset that this chapter uses corresponds to the global economy

in 2001 when the nominal exchange rate of the RMB was the same as in 2005 when the official rate started to appreciate. In the GTAP Version 6 dataset, it is found that the average tariff rate for imports into China was about 11 per cent and the average tariff rate that China faced for its exports in other regions was about 9 per cent. Based on this, the removing of all import tariffs in China and a doubling of the tariffs imposed on the Chinese exports in all other regions are approximate to a revaluation of the RMB by 20 per cent.

REFERENCES

Bosworth, B. (2004), 'Valuing the RMB', Tokyo Club Research Meeting, 9 February, http://www.brookings.edu/views/papers/bosworth/2004 0209_bosworth.htm, accessed 29 December 2007.

Chang, H. and Q. Shao (2004), 'How much is the Chinese currency undervalued? A quantitative estimation', *China Economic Review*, **15** (3), 366–71.

China.com (2007), 'RMB appreciation process becomes quicker', *Chinanews*, 11 May, http://english.china.com/zh_cn/business/news/11021613/20070511/1408 9547.html, accessed 29 December 2007.

Fair, R. (2004), 'Estimating how the macro-economy works', http://fairmodel. econ.yale.edu, accessed 29 December 2007.

Frankel. J. (2005), 'On the Renminbi: The Choice Between Adjustment under a Fixed Exchange Rate and Adjustment under a Flexible Rate,' NBER Working Paper No. 11274, http://papers.ssrn.com/sol3/papers.cfm?abstract_id=711854, accessed 22 July 2008.

Funke, M. and J. Rahn (2005), 'Just how undervalued is the Chinese renminbi?', *The World Economy*, **28** (4), 465–87.

Goldstein, M. (2004), 'Adjusting China's Exchange Rate Policies', Paper presented at the International Monetary Fund's seminar on China's Foreign Exchange System, Dalian, China, 26–27 May 2004.

Goldstein, M. (2007), 'Assessing Progress on China's Exchange Rate Policies', Testimony to the Hearing on Risks and Reform: The Role of Currency in the US–China Relationship, Committee on Finance, US Senate, 28 March 2007, Washington, DC.

Goldstein, M. and N. Lardy (2006), 'China's exchange rate policy dilemma', *American Economic Review*, **96** (2), 422–6.

Golley, J. and R. Tyers (2007), 'China's Real Exchange Rate', in Ross Garnaut and Ligang Song (eds), *China: Linking Markets for Growth*, Australian National University, Canberra: Asia Pacific Press, pp. 316–43.

Lu, D. (2004), 'China's capability to control its exchange rates', *China Economic Review*, **15** (3), 343–7.

Mundell, R. (2006), 'Fast growth in economy, but not RMB appreciation', *People's Daily* Online, 14 February, http://english.people.com.cn/200602/14/ eng20060214_242688.html, accessed 30 December 2007.

National Bureau of Statistics (NBS) (2006), *China Statistical Yearbook 2006*, Beijing: China Statistics Press.

Roberts, I. and R. Tyers (2001), 'China's Exchange Rate Policy: The Case For Greater Flexibility', Working Papers in Economics and Econometrics No. 389, the Australian National University.

Stiglitz, J. (2005), 'Stiglitz on China and Why U.S. Economic Advice is Discounted', *Economists View*, 26 July, http://economistsview.typepad.com/economistsview/2005/07/stiglitz_on_chi.html, accessed 30 December 2007.

Sinnakkannu, J. and A. Nassir (2006), 'A study on the effect of de-pegging of the renminbi against the US dollar on China's international trade competitiveness', *International Research Journal of Finance and Economics*, **1** (5), 64–77.

Tec, R. (2000), 'The effect of a RMB devaluation on ASEAN countries: an applied general equilibrium approach', ASEAN Secretariat, the WTO, http://unpan1.un.org/intradoc/groups/public/documents/APCITY/UNPAN010329.pdf, accessed 30 December 2007.

The US Census Bureau (2007), 'The 2007 Statistical Abstract', http://www.census.gov/compendia/statab/brief.html, accessed 22 July 2008.

Tung, C. and S. Baker (2004), 'RMB revaluation will serve China's self-interest', *China Economic Review*, **15** (3), 331–5.

Tyers, R., J. Golley, Y. Bu and I. Bain (2007), 'China's Economic Growth and its Real Exchange Rate', Paper presented at the 10th Annual Conference on Global Economic Analysis, Purdue University, 7–9 June 2007.

Wang, T. (2004), 'Exchange Rate Dynamics', in E. Prasad (ed.), *China's Growth and Integration into the World Economy: Prospects and Challenges*, IMF Occasional Paper No. 232, Washington, DC, pp. 21–8.

Wang, T. (2005), 'Sources of real exchange rate fluctuations in China', *Journal of Comparative Economics*, **33** (4), 753–71.

Woo, W. and G. Xiao (2007), 'Facing Protectionism Generated by Trade Disputes: China's Post-WTO Blues', in Ross Garnaut and Ligang Song (eds), *China: Linking Markets for Growth*, the Australian National University, Canberra: Asia Pacific Press, pp. 45–70.

Zhang, F. and Z. Pan (2004), 'Determination of China's long-run nominal exchange rate and official intervention', *China Economic Review*, **15** (3), 360–65.

Zhang, J., H. Fung and D. Kummer (2006), 'Can renminbi appreciation reduce the US trade deficit?', *China and the World Economy*, **14** (1), 44–56.

Zhang, X. (2008), 'How Does RMB Appreciation Affect China and the World Economy?', Paper presented at the CES Annual Conference, Nankai University, Tianjin, China, 17–20 April 2008.

Zhang, X. and C. Harvie (2002), 'Income Inequality among Different Regions in China's Post Reform Era', in Amnon Levy and Joao Faria (eds), *Economic Growth, Inequality and Migration: National and International Perspectives*, Cheltenham, UK and Northampton, MA, USA: Edward Elgar, pp. 68–88.

APPENDIX

Table 8A.1   The aggregation of the 10 regions

No.	Region Code	Comprising Economies	Description
1	ANZ	Australia, New Zealand	Australia, New Zealand
2	China	China	China
3	Japan & NIEs	Japan, Korea, Hong Kong, Taiwan	Japan plus East Asian newly industrialized economies (NIEs)
4	US	US	US
5	EU-15	Austria, Belgium, Netherlands, Luxembourg, France, Italy, Germany, UK, Ireland, Denmark, Greece, Spain, Portugal, Sweden, Finland	The 15 member countries of European Union in 2001
6	ASEAN	Singapore, Malaysia, Indonesia, Philippines, Thailand, Brunei	ASEAN members in 2001
7	The rest of Asia	India, Pakistan, Bangladesh and the rest of Asia	India, Pakistan, Bangladesh and the rest of Asia
8	The rest of America	All countries in America except the US	All countries in America except the US
9	The rest of Europe	Hungry, Poland, the rest of Central European Association, former Soviet Union, Turkey	The rest of Europe
10	ROW	Rest of the world	All countries not included in the other nine groups

Table 8A.2 The aggregation of the 10 sectors

No.	Sector Code	Comprising Industries	Description
1	Food	Paddy rice, wheat, cereal grain, vegetables, fruits, nuts, oil seeds, sugar cane, sugar, beet, crops, cattle, sheep, goats, horses, animal products, raw milk, fishing, meat, dairy products, beverages and tobacco	Primary production, land and resource-intensive goods
2	Other primary goods	Plant-based fibres, wool, silk-worm cocoons, forestry, coal, oil, gas, minerals	Primary production, land and resource-intensive goods
3	Textiles	Textiles, apparel, leather	Labour-intensive goods
4	Petroleum and coal	Petroleum and coal, chemicals, rubber, minerals	Resource-based and capital-intensive goods
5	Metals	Ferrous metals, metal products	Resource-based and capital-intensive goods
6	Machinery	Motor vehicles and parts, transportation equipment, electronic equipment, machinery equipment	Capital- or labour-intensive goods
7	Utility	Electricity, gas distribution, water	Capital-intensive
8	Construction	Construction, dwelling	Labour-intensive
9	Other manufactures	Shoe polish, and other manufactures	Labour-intensive
10	Services	Trade, transport (sea, air, road), communication, financial service, insurance, recreation, public administration, education	Labour-intensive

PART III

Agricultural Trade and Energy Demand

9. China's grain TRQs: five years since WTO accession

Zhangyue Zhou and Xia Kang

INTRODUCTION

In December 2001, China was accepted to the World Trade Organization (WTO). Many anticipated that, following China's accession to the WTO, its grain imports would increase rapidly. To mitigate the likely strong shock on Chinese grain producers' income and its grains industry, China was allowed a 'transition period' of a few years. During this transition period, China's grain imports would be managed under a TRQ (tariff-rate quota) arrangement. That is, if the imports are within the quota, a lower in-quota tariff will be charged; otherwise, a much higher out-quota tariff applies. The higher above-quota tariff would discourage imports and thus would provide protection to Chinese farmers and its grains industry.

Five years have passed since China became a member of the WTO. Then, what has happened to China's grain trade under the TRQ arrangement? How did China implement the grains TRQ? Were China's TRQ practices in alignment with WTO rules? Such questions have continuously drawn much interest from grain traders and many international observers. Australia, as a major grain exporter, has also paid much attention to looking for answers to such questions.[1] So far, however, little effort has been made to examine China's grain TRQ implementation and management. This study attempts to fill this gap.

In the next section, we first provide an overview over the developments in China's grain trade and its trade policies in the past five years. This is important because an understanding of China's grain TRQ practice must be placed in the broader context of issues that affect China's grain imports and grain trade policies. In the third section, we examine China's grain TRQ implementation and management. The fourth section discusses the prospects of China's grain TRQ practices as well as the likely trade policy developments. The last section concludes the chapter.

DEVELOPMENTS OF CHINA'S GRAIN TRADE AND TRADE POLICIES SINCE 2001

Grain Trade

Since 2001, China's grain trade (not including soybean) followed no clear pattern.[2] The amount of imports, exports as well as net imports changed between years, and often abruptly (see Table 9.1). If soybean is included, total grain imports show a trend of increasing while total grain exports tend to change between years. However, China's net imports are increasing.

At the crop level, while the level of soybean export has been stagnant, its import has increased rapidly in the past few years (see Parts A and B of Table 9.1). Soybean imports account for a major proportion of China's total grain imports; around 80–90 per cent. China's barley trade is one way: it imports a relatively large amount of high-quality barley chiefly for brewing purposes. China was able to net export a significant amount of corn even after joining the WTO. However, the level of export has declined rapidly in recent years. China has been a net rice exporter but its export level has dramatically dropped since 2003 (see Part C of Table 9.1). Over the past five years, China's wheat trade has been most erratic. In 2002, the first year after China's joining the WTO, China was a net wheat exporter although the volume was small. The net wheat export in the following year, 2003, however, was significant, being over 2 million tonnes. This was followed by a dramatic net wheat import increase in 2004 to about 6.5 million tonnes. It dropped to about 3 million tonnes in 2005. In 2006, China was again net-exporting wheat to the world market (Part C of Table 9.1).

Compared with the trade level before WTO accession, China's total grain trade (both imports and exports) since 2001 has increased (see Figure 9.1). During 1990–2006, the annual growth rate of the grain trade was 4.1 per cent. Prior to the accession, namely, 1990–2001, the growth rate was 2.8 per cent with an annual average trade volume being 22 million tonnes. Since 2001, the growth rate has jumped to about 7 per cent with an annual average trade volume being 38.7 million tonnes.

There have also been noticeable changes in the composition of grain imports after WTO accession. Excluding soybean, the proportion of wheat import has increased sharply, from 22 per cent in 1999–2001 to 58 per cent in 2004–06 (Figure 9.2). On the other hand, the proportion of barley import out of total grain imports has declined from 71 per cent to 31 per cent. The changes in the proportion of rice and corn are relatively small. The three-year average annual grain import (not including soybean, 2004–06) has more than doubled that of 1999–2001.

Table 9.1   China's grain trade, 1990–2006 ('000 tonnes)

Part A: Imports

	Imports by Crops					Total Imports	
	Wheat	Rice	Barley	Corn	Soybean	Without soybean	With soybean
1990	12527	59	652	369	31	13693	13724
1991	12370	140	764	1	1	13449	13450
1992	10581	104	829	0	121	11625	11746
1993	6420	100	774	0	99	7422	7521
1994	7300	520	1318	1	52	9148	9200
1995	11590	2000	1274	5181	1744	20516	22260
1996	8250	760	1308	440	2988	11122	14110
1997	1860	359	1800	3	6260	4170	10430
1998	1490	240	1520	250	3200	3880	7080
1999	450	170	2270	0	4890	3390	8280
2000	880	240	1970	0	10930	3150	14080
2001	690	270	2370	0	13990	3440	17430
2002	600	240	1910	8	11321	2849	14170
2003	430	371	1360	1	20742	2191	22933
2004	7260	770	1710	0	20230	9750	29980
2005	3538	522	2179	4	26591	6272	32863
2006	613	730	2140	65	28270	3548	31818

Part B: Exports

	Exports by Crops					Total Exports	
	Wheat	Rice	Barley	Corn	Soybean	Without soybean	With soybean
1990	7	326	0	3404	940	5311	6251
1991	0	690	0	7780	1196	10860	12056
1992	3	953	1	10314	658	12983	13641
1993	291	1430	0	11100	730	14620	15350
1994	268	1520	0	8740	1980	13050	15030
1995	225	50	0	115	298	1842	2140
1996	565	270	0	160	260	1790	2050
1997	458	940	0	6610	210	8920	9130
1998	270	3750	0	4690	170	9360	9530
1999	164	2710	10	4310	200	8190	8390
2000	188	2950	0	10470	210	14350	14560
2001	713	1860	0	6000	250	9480	9730
2002	699	1990	0	11670	280	15680	15960
2003	2514	2610	0	16391	270	24103	24373

Table 9.1   (continued)

Part B: Exports

	Exports by Crops					Total Exports	
	Wheat	Rice	Barley	Corn	Soybean	Without soybean	With soybean
2004	1089	910	0	2320	330	4730	5060
2005	605	686	4	8642	413	9761	10175
2006	1509	1253	6	3099	395	5867	6262

Part C: Net imports

	Net Imports by Crops					Total Net Imports	
	Wheat	Rice	Barley	Corn	Soybean	Without soybean	With soybean
1990	12520	−267	652	−3035	−909	8382	7473
1991	12370	−550	764	−7779	−1195	2589	2590
1992	10578	−849	828	−10314	−537	−1358	−1895
1993	6129	−1330	774	−11100	−631	−7198	−7829
1994	7032	−1000	1318	−8739	−1928	−3902	−5830
1995	11365	1950	1274	5066	1446	18674	20120
1996	7685	490	1308	280	2728	9332	12060
1997	1402	−581	1800	−6607	6050	−4750	1300
1998	1220	−3510	1520	−4440	3030	−5480	−2450
1999	286	−2540	2260	−4310	4690	−4800	−110
2000	692	−2710	1970	−10470	10720	−11200	−480
2001	−23	−1590	2370	−6000	13740	−6040	7700
2002	−99	−1750	1910	−11662	11041	−12831	−1790
2003	−2084	−2239	1360	−16390	20472	−21912	−1440
2004	6171	−140	1710	−2320	19900	5020	24920
2005	2934	−164	2176	−8638	26177	−3489	22688
2006	−896	−523	2134	−3034	27875	−2319	25556

Source: Ministry of Commerce, 'Monthly Bulletin of Chinese Agricultural Import and Export Statistics'.

The above discussion shows that China's total grain trade and grain net imports have increased after WTO accession. Thus, to some extent, China's accession to the WTO may have led to increased grain trade between China and the rest of the world. However, five years is a relatively short time and to what extent China's increased grain trade and net imports can be attributed to WTO accession requires further research. In

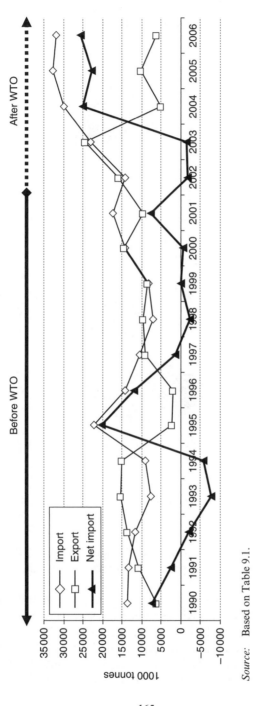

Source: Based on Table 9.1.

Figure 9.1 Changes in the level of China's grain trade before and after WTO accession

165

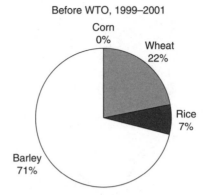

Average import is 3.1 million tonnes from 1999 to 2001.

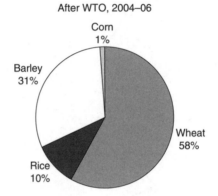

Average import is 6.5 million tonnes from 2004 to 2006.

Source: Based on Table 9.1.

Figure 9.2   Changes in the composition of China's grain trade (excluding soybean)

this regard, two issues are worth particular mention: the sharp increase in soybean import and China's pragmatic approach to grain trade. A brief account on each follows.

Table 9.1 clearly shows that China's recent grain imports are mainly due to the fast increase in soybean imports. On average, soybean imports account for 82 per cent of total grain imports during 2002–06. Excluding soybean, China's total grain imports are relatively small (compared with its domestic total consumption) and in fact, four out of the five years, China was a net grain exporter (Parts A and C, Table 9.1). Given that soybean import is no longer subject to TRQ restrictions, in the rest of the chapter our discussion will focus on other grains, major cereals – wheat, rice and corn.[3]

China follows a very pragmatic approach to its grain trade, attaching much weight to protecting producers' income and ensuring national food security. China exports or imports grains when such a need arises. A quick review of what China has done since the early 1990s will explain this. In the mid-1990s, China's grain supply was believed to be in shortage. The government decided to import grains in large volumes and also took measures to promote grain production. Consequently, domestic grain output increased, and by the late 1990s and early 2000s, China had accumulated large volumes of grains. As part of the response to declining domestic prices, the government encouraged grain export (mainly corn, see Part B, Table 9.1) and China's net grain export increased during 2002–03. Following grain price increases in late 2003 and early 2004, the government reduced incentives for grain exports and facilitated grain imports. In 2004, China became a net grain importer. During 2004–05 the government also took various measures to boost grain production. China's domestic production increased and in 2005, China again became a net grain exporter. This tends to suggest that China's grain trade is to a greater extent dependent upon China's domestic demand and supply situations and on China's needs for grain security but to a lesser extent influenced by WTO accession; at least this has been the case for the past few years. As such, it is valuable to look into policy issues that affect China's grain demand and supply conditions, which in turn affect China's grain trade practices.

Grain Trade Policy

Our discussion on China's grain trade policy developments in the past five years is mainly focused on the following three aspects: market access, export subsidy and domestic support.

Market access
After WTO accession, TRQs are applied to imports of some agricultural products such as grains (wheat, corn and rice), cotton, cooking oil, sugar and wool. The imports of some other agricultural products such as soybean, barley, horticultural products and animal products are subject to a single tariff rate only. Reduced import tariff rates improved the access of foreign agricultural products to the Chinese market. In addition to the tariff rate reduction, China also made changes to import procedures of some key agricultural products that made exports of such products to China easier. For example, in 2004, wool imports were no longer confined to those designated

agents but any traders could import wool. Prior to 2006, a fixed proportion of cooking oil had to be imported only by state trading enterprises (STEs). On 1 January 2006, this proportion was abolished. Thus, it can be seen that TRQs are the only means used by China to influence the access of a small number of foreign agricultural products, including grains, to the Chinese market. As far as grain exports to China are concerned, one can export as much grain as one wishes up to the quota to enjoy the very low level of in-quota tariff rates. When the quota is fulfilled, one can still export grains to China as long as one is prepared to bear the higher out-quota tariff rates. It is interesting to note, however, that the utilization of the grain TRQs in the past five years has been low. In 2004, grain import was the highest since WTO accession, being 8.02 million tonnes. Yet total grain imports accounted for only 36 per cent of the total quota. Details about the TRQ utilization and why the utilization is low are given later in this chapter.

Export subsidy
China agreed to abolish all export subsidies at the time of WTO accession. Since 2002, two measures were introduced that have had impact on China's grain exports: tax rebates on grain exports and exemption of railway construction levies for grain transportation.

Tax rebates on grain exports   On 1 January 2002, the State Council approved that a zero value-added tax (VAT) would be applied to rice, wheat and corn exports, and sales tax imposed on these grains exported would be fully refunded (Ministry of Finance and State Taxation Bureau, 2002). In 2003, the rate of rebates for processed products out of wheat, corn and so on was further increased, from 5 per cent to 13 per cent (Ministry of Finance and State Taxation Bureau, 2003). It is noted that the use of tax rebates is allowed by WTO rules (Chen and Liu, 2002). Such rebates increase China's grain export competitiveness in the world market.

Exemption of railway construction levies for grain transportation   Starting from 1 April 2002, paddy and rice, wheat and wheat flour, corn and soybean were exempted from railway construction levies (State Development and Planning Commission, 2002).[4] This exemption was to be terminated by the end of 2005. However, this policy measure is currently still in use and is expected to continue into the foreseeable future. This measure significantly reduced the transportation cost of grains. According to Wu (2006), the railway construction levy accounts for about 30–40 per cent of total transportation costs of grains. Its exemption, on average, would have reduced rail transportation cost of corn by 40 per cent. This also explains partly why China's corn exports were high in the early years of this decade.

Domestic support
To become a member of the WTO, China committed that its domestic support to agricultural products would not exceed 8.5 per cent of the value of total agricultural production.[5] China used to milk the agricultural sector and gave negative support to agricultural production (Tian, Zhang and Zhou, 2002). Consequently, there is much room for China to increase its domestic support level. Nonetheless, its current support level was merely 0.6 per cent and was far below the level agreed at the WTO accession (Wu, 2006). Despite the still very low level of domestic support, China did indeed initiate or continue some measures that would directly or indirectly increase its domestic support to agricultural production.

'Abolishment of two taxes' and changes in 'three agricultural subsidies'   The two taxes abolished are 'agricultural tax' and 'taxes on special agricultural products' (excluding tobacco). Three subsidies are 'direct subsidy to grain production', 'subsidy to the adoption of improved seeds', and 'subsidy to the acquisition of farm machinery'. At the beginning of 2006, farmers nationwide were free from paying agricultural tax.[6] Since 2002, China's 'three agricultural subsidies' have increased significantly, from 0.1 billion yuan in 2002 to over 30 billion yuan in 2006 (see Table 9.2). Such subsidies provided incentives to farmers to produce grains and also enhanced China's grain production capacity.

Continuation of grain procurement under minimum support prices   In the early 1990s, China introduced a minimum support price (MSP) scheme for grain procurement. After WTO accession, in order to protect the income of farmers in major grain-producing regions, this MSP measure was continued, mainly for paddy and wheat. In 2005, the MSP was effective for rice. In 2006, the government also procured wheat under MSP. MSP provides assurance to grain producers and encourages farmers to produce grains.

Table 9.2   Agricultural subsidy in China, 2002–06 (billion yuan)

	2002	2003	2004	2005	2006
Direct subsidy	–	–	11.60	18.70	29.70
Improved seeds subsidy	0.10	0.30	2.85	3.87	4.07
Farm machine subsidy	–	0.04	0.07	0.30	0.60
Total	0.10	0.34	14.52	22.87	34.37

Note: – = Data do not exist or are not available.

Source: Calculated by authors from publications by the Ministry of Finance (2006).

Assistance to agricultural insurance In June 2006, agricultural insurance was included as part of China's broad agricultural support system. It was made clear that subsidies would be provided to farmers, insurance companies and agricultural reinsurance efforts. The funds would come from both the central and local governments. Through the insurance assistance, the government provides indirect support and protection to the farmers. Subsidy to agricultural insurance falls into the 'Green Box' as allowed by the WTO. Many developed countries also make use of such a subsidy as a means to provide support to their agricultural production.

CHINA'S GRAIN TRQS: IMPLEMENTATION AND MANAGEMENT

Imports of three major grains, that is, wheat, rice and corn, are subject to TRQs after China's WTO accession. The tariff rates for in-quota imports are low, being 1 per cent for raw grains, and less than 10 per cent for processed grain products. Tariff rates for out-quota imports are much higher. The Chinese government promised to make reforms and adjustments to the grain trade over the following years after the accession in 2001. More specifically, proposed major changes include: (1) reduce the out-quota tariff rates for grains subject to TRQs (from 74 per cent in 2001 to 65 per cent in 2004); (2) increase TRQs (for wheat, corn and rice, from 8.468 million tonnes, 5.85 million tonnes and 3.99 million tonnes in 2002 to 9.636 million tonnes, 7.2 million tonnes and 5.32 million tonnes in 2004, respectively); and (3) reduce the proportion of corn imports designated to STEs and increase the proportion to be traded by other participants. Details of proposed changes in out-quota tariff rates and the proportion designated to STEs can be found in Table 9.3.

Grain TRQ Allocation[7]

In China, the management of agricultural import TRQs is carried out by different government departments according to their administrative roles. For example, grain TRQs are managed by the National Development and Reform Commission (NDRC), which also manages cotton TRQs. TRQs of vegetable cooking oils, sugar and wool are managed by the Ministry of Commerce. Highlighted below are general management issues concerning the application, allocation and redistribution of grain TRQs.

The NDRC predicts the amount of imports required in a calendar year and submits a request to the State Council. After the approval by the

Table 9.3   *STE trading proportions and in-quota and out-quota tariff rates*

Grain	Share Designated to STEs (%)	Description	HS Code	Tariff Rate (%)		
				Out-quota		In-quota
				At the time of accession (2001)	Final rate (2004)	
Wheat	90%	Durum wheat	10011000	74	65	1
		Seed	10019010	74	65	1
		Other	10019090	74	65	1
		Wheat or meslin flour	11010000	74	65	6
		Groats and meal	11031100	74	65	9
		Pellets	11032100	74	65	10
Corn	71% in 2001	Seed	10051000	32	20	1
	68% in 2002	Other	10059000	74	65	1
	64% in 2003	Flour	11022000	64	40	9
	60% in 2004	Groats and meal	11031300	74	65	9
		Cereal grains otherwise worked	11042300	74	65	10
Paddy and rice	50%	Seed	10061010	74	65	1
		Other	10061090	74	65	
		Husked (brown) rice	10062000	74	65	1
		Semi-milled or wholly milled rice, whether or not polished or glazed	10063000	74	65	1
		Broken rice	10064000	74	65	1
		Flour	11023000	64	40	9
		Groats and meal	11031400	28	10	9

Source: Based on WTO (2001), 'Agreement of Accession of the People's Republic of China'.

State Council, the NDRC is in a position to distribute the import quotas among traders including STEs. China's WTO agreement allows China's STEs to import grains under the TRQ arrangement at a predetermined proportion. Currently the STE that is designated to handle TRQ imports of grain is COFCO Limited. It has the privilege to be allocated a certain portion of the total grain import TRQs from the NDRC. The remaining TRQs are distributed to other traders according to the following general

172 *China's integration with the global economy*

principle and approach: (1) if the remaining amount of TRQs is greater than the amount requested, all traders eligible for applying for a TRQ are allocated the amount they applied for; (2) if the amount is smaller than the total amount requested, then those who have grain import experience are allocated the TRQs first. The leftover is then distributed among those who have not previously imported grains.

Non-STE traders need to apply to the agents of the NRDC scattered in various provinces between 15 and 30 October each year for an import quota for the next calendar year. The NRDC then determines the amount to be granted based on the approach described above (that is, trader's past import performance, trader's grain processing capacities, with reference to various other commercial considerations). After the amount is determined, the NDRC, through its agents, issues an 'agricultural import TRQ permit' to a trader no later than 31 December of the current year for imports in the next calendar year. The TRQs must be utilized by the traders within a calendar year. If the imports have departed the origin port before 31 December but can only arrive at a port in China sometime in the next calendar year, the trader must apply for an extension. The extension, however, is generally not beyond the end of February of the next calendar year.

If a trader cannot utilize all the allocated TRQs, the unused TRQs must be returned to the NDRC before 15 September. The returned TRQs will be redistributed. Application for redistributed TRQs takes place between 1 and 15 September. Returned TRQs are redistributed to traders according to the order of their applications. Before 1 October, the NDRC informs the traders of the results of their application for extra TRQs through redistribution.

Hence, the initial procedure used by China to distribute the grain TRQs after its WTO accession may be shown as below in Figure 9.3. This procedure is troublesome for traders. If a trader managed to secure a contract with a foreign supplier but then the TRQ import permit is not granted or not granted in full for the amount specified in the contract, the traders cannot make the purchase, leaving both the trader and supplier in a difficult situation. In 2003, modifications were made to make the procedure simpler and take less time to obtain a permit. The simplified procedure is shown below in Figure 9.4 and it has made it much easier for traders to conduct their businesses.

It is noted, however, that the quota granted to private traders tends to be too small in many cases. This makes it less commercially worthwhile for private traders to make use of the quota. Such small amounts of quotas are often returned for reallocation, which in turn often falls into the hands of STEs.

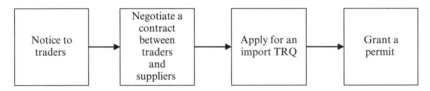

Figure 9.3   Initial TRQ allocation procedures

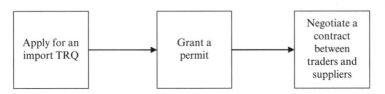

Figure 9.4   Simplified TRQ allocation procedures

Grain TRQ Utilization

China's grain TRQ utilization has been low since its WTO accession although its utilization of the TRQs for some other agricultural products has increased and has reached a relatively high level. For example, during 2002–05, the TRQ usage of sugar, soybean oil and wool exceeded 60 per cent (Han, 2005). According to official statistics, the actual imports of palm oil more than doubled the TRQ amount. The imports of cotton were also 1.6 times of the TRQ amount. On the other hand, the grain TRQ utilization has been relatively low, being about 15 per cent. At the product level, the utilization of wheat TRQ is slightly higher, being 30 per cent, while that of rice and corn is 9 per cent and 0.05 per cent, respectively.[8] In 2006, the TRQ usage remained low. Table 9.4 below provides details of the TRQ usage during 2002–06.

Table 9.5 shows the sources of grains imported under the TRQ arrangement. Canada, Australia, France and the United States are the major sources of wheat imports. Corn chiefly comes from the United States and Laos. Thailand is the major source of rice imports. Apart from those designated STEs, those who imported grains are mainly some large grain processors or traders located in cities along China's southeast coast. In terms of the usage of imported grains, higher protein wheat imported from Canada and the United States is chiefly used for bread production while wheat with lower protein content from Australia is primarily used to produce biscuits and other processed foods. Rice and corn are also used for industrial purposes or food processing.

Table 9.4　Grain tariff-rate quotas and actual imports, 2002–06 ('000 tonnes)

		Wheat	Corn	Rice	Total or Average
2002	TRQ	8468	5850	3990	18308
	Import	605	6	236	847
	Usage (%)	7.1	0.1	5.9	4.6
2003	TRQ	9052	6525	4655	20232
	Import	424	0.0	257	681
	Usage (%)	4.7	0.0	5.5	3.4
2004	TRQ	9636	7200	5320	22156
	Import	7258	2	766	8026
	Usage (%)	75.3	0.0	14.4	36.2
2005	TRQ	9636	7200	5320	22156
	Import	3539	4	522	4065
	Usage (%)	36.7	0.1	9.8	18.3
2006	TRQ	9636	7200	5320	22156
	Import	613	65	730	1408
	Usage (%)	6.4	0.9	13.7	6.4

Sources:　Based on WTO (2001), 'Agreement of Accession of the People's Republic of China', and MOA (2007), Statistical Information.

Table 9.5　Major sources of grain imports (%), 2004–06

	2004	2005	2006
Wheat	61.0	85.5	96.6
Canada	34.9	41.0	15.5
Australia	24.6	28.6	50.2
France	1.4	15.9	
US			30.9
Corn	25.7	67.0	98.1
US	25.7	17.8	90.5
Laos		47.1	7.5
India		1.1	0.1
Rice	96.5	99.9	99.9
Thailand	96.1	91.9	94.5
Vietnam	0.4	8.0	4.9
Burma		0.1	
Laos			0.6

Source:　Ministry of Commerce, 'Monthly Bulletin of Chinese Agricultural Import and Export Statistics'.

Factors Affecting Grain TRQ Utilization

According to Table 9.4, the utilization of the grain TRQs has been relatively low in the past five years. The rates of utilization also differ significantly among the three major grains, namely, wheat, rice and corn. In principle, restrictions imposed by TRQs on imports depend on the out-quote tariff rates specified. If trading parties are willing to trade at the out-quota tariff rates, then imports are not restricted by TRQs. Since the out-quota tariff rates are generally very high, under normal circumstances, trading generally does not take place at the out-quota tariff rates. However, in the past five years there was no need for China to import grains at the out-quota tariff rates, since a large portion of the grain TRQs had not been utilized. Then, what are the major factors that led to China's low utilization of grain TRQs?

Price differentials directly affect the demand for imported grains It is widely accepted that imported foodgrains are generally higher quality. However, imported grains have to bear extra transaction costs, including, for example, transportation, in-quota tariff, VAT. Higher costs translate into higher prices, leading to reduced demand for imported grains. It is noted that China collects a 13 per cent VAT on import. Hence, even if the nominal tariff rates are reduced to zero, this import VAT can still effectively dampen down the price competitiveness of imported grains.

Increased support for domestic grain production reduces the need for imports To a great extent, domestic grain demand and supply situations dictate a country's grain trade. Increased incentives to farmers for greater production improved China's domestic supply, which in turn has led to reduced need for imports. Discussion in the earlier section clearly shows that China's domestic support to grain production has been on the increase since its WTO accession, particularly after 2003 when China experienced another major reduction in grain output and the subsequent price increases in the grain market.

TRQ allocation and implementation to some extent limits grain imports Grain TRQs are first divided between STEs and non-STE traders. A large portion of the TRQs is assigned to STEs. If STEs cannot use up all the assigned TRQs, with the approval by the NDRC, the unused TRQs will be allocated to non-STE traders who have a right to import and export. Procedures to allocate the TRQs to private traders also had impeded grain imports. As pointed out earlier in this section, the allocation and redistribution of TRQs to non-STE traders, though largely reasonable, could indeed sometime lead to difficulties in grain imports. Recently, the government has made efforts to improve the TRQ administration.

Higher-quality grains produced domestically substitute imports   In the past, small-scale farm production coupled with inadequate grain marketing facilities made it very difficult for China to produce grains of the desired quality at the desired quantity for specific usages (Zhou and Tian, 2006). First, the quality of grains varies from farm to farm. Second, grains of better quality are often not handled separately, due to either lack of facilities or the small quantity. As a result, China often imports grains, especially wheat, of high quality for some special usages. Recently, more attention has been given to the production of higher-quality grains through some innovative arrangements between food-processing firms and farms (such as *'ding dan nong ye'* – a kind of contract farming; under such arrangements firms usually provide farmers with technical assistance to produce wheat with desired attributes) (Ministry of Agriculture [MOA] 2003).

Grain export incentives encouraged corn export   As pointed out earlier, after WTO accession, grain exports attract a zero value-added tax and sales tax on grains exported would be fully refunded. Further, no railway construction levies would be imposed on grain transported, which can reduce rail transportation cost by about 40 per cent. The combination of such incentives made it still worthwhile for China to export corn at the world market price. China exported a large amount of corn during 2002–06 (over 42 million tonnes) and its corn TRQ usage is almost zero (see Table 9.4).

According to the above, China's very low-level usage of the grain TRQs is chiefly due to its domestic supply–demand situations. Its grain production and subsidy policies encouraged domestic production and also industrial adjustments to produce grains to meet market demand. Export incentives encouraged grain exports while the implementation of grain TRQs was not always conducive to grain imports. Will China be able to maintain such a low level of grain imports into the near future? This largely depends upon its domestic grain supply–demand situations and the outcomes of its bilateral and multilateral trade negotiations.

CHINA'S GRAIN TRADE AND POLICY PROSPECTS

China's fast economic growth in the past three decades has led to the rapid expansion of non-agricultural sectors, resulting in a continuous decline in the proportion of agricultural GDP out of total GDP. In 1978, when China's economic reform started, agricultural GDP accounted for 28.2 per cent of total GDP. This proportion, however, had dropped to 15.2 per cent by 2001 and has further dropped to 11.8 per cent by 2006 (NBS, 2007). Many agricultural activities are likely to lose their comparative advantage further as the economic returns of non-agricultural activities continue to improve. Declining comparative advantages in agriculture lead to resources deviated to non-agricultural uses, such as water and land. Without the advent of significant technological breakthrough (such as effective yield-augmenting measures), it will be difficult for China's agricultural sector to further increase its output. On the other hand, with improved purchasing power, consumers' demand for agricultural products, especially higher-quality products, has been increasing and will continue to do so into the future.

As far as grain is concerned, grain production is land-intensive. The production of some grain crops is rapidly losing its comparative advantages (for example, rice production in southeast coastal regions). As a result, farmers shift their resources to other economic activities (Zhou and Tian, 2006). For example, total area sown to grain crops declined from 106.1 million hectares in 2001 to 99.4 million hectares in 2003; the area increased to 105.5 million hectares by 2006 due to strong government incentives to grow grain (NBS, 2007). However, China's demand for grains is still increasing – although direct consumption has declined, indirect consumption of grains has been increasing due to increased demand for animal products and for processed food. According to Zhou and Tian (2003), China's demand for feedgrains has been increasing and will become the major component of China's total grain demand. Any future increase in total grain demand in China will be mainly caused by an increasing demand for feedgrains. On the other hand, many believe that China will not be able to meet the increased demand for grains in general and feedgrains in particular with its domestic supply (Garnaut and Ma, 1992; RGCFDS, 1993; Crook and Colby, 1996; Findlay, 1998; Tian and Chudleigh, 1999; Chen, 2004; and Zhou and Tian, 2005). There are two broad approaches China can use to increase its total grain supply: (1) to further increase domestic supply; and (2) to increase grain imports.

The potential of the first option is limited as has been pointed out due to the declining comparative advantage of grain production. Likely future changes in resource allocation and pricing (for example, deviation of land, labour force and water away from agriculture, and possible charges on water use) will further erode China's comparative advantage in grain production. Should China insist on increasing grain supply from domestic production to meet the increasing demand, the cost, both economically and environmentally, can be large. Hence, increasing grain imports is likely to be the chief method for China to increase its total grain supply to match the rising demand.

Although China's future grain imports are expected to increase (Chen, 2004; Zhou and Tian, 2005), policies regarding market access are unlikely to have significant changes in the immediate future. As a result of the failure of the Doha Round, it is to China's advantage to maintain the current market access policies unchanged unless China needs to significantly increase its grain imports. Any major changes in market access policies will also depend upon the progress and outcomes of multilateral and bilateral trade negotiations. In regard to multilateral negotiations, the recent WTO Delhi meeting is unlikely to significantly revive the negotiation process. When negotiations do get restarted, WTO members with major grain exports may press China to further open its grain market. They are likely to pay more attention to the allocation and management of the grain TRQs if the grain TRQs are continued.

China has become increasingly engaged in bilateral trade negotiations in recent years, for example, with ASEAN, Chile, Australia, New Zealand and Pakistan. The negotiations with ASEAN and Chile have been concluded. China-ASEAN FTA was put into practice on 20 July 2005 while the implementation of China-Chile FTA was started on 1 October 2006. Cereal exports to China from these countries will enjoy reduced tariffs. It seems that it is a very wise strategic choice, through bilateral FTAs, for China to maintain close economic and trade relationships with some key grain-exporting countries. This will enable China to secure a relatively diverse source of grain suppliers and will help China to establish a stable source of grain supply. This can be a very important strategy that will help China to achieve its long-term national grain security.

However, some argued that increased trade liberalization does not necessarily ensure China's rural development and increase farmers' income (Shui, 2006). Currently, raising farmers' income, protecting rural employment and reducing rural poverty are major challenges faced by the Chinese government. Grain production remains a major source of income for many small Chinese farms and China may have to rely on this industry to provide the livelihood for many Chinese farmers for years to come. Thus, it may be anticipated that China will be very sensitive in regard to the level of access for imported grains to the Chinese market. Nonetheless, in future negotiations, trading partners are most likely to ask China to open its grain market further. In addition, there is the need for China to import more grains. Consequently, the Chinese government may at times adjust its grain trade policies, either voluntarily or passively. However, any such major adjustments would be still based chiefly on changes in China's domestic grain demand and supply situations.

CONCLUSIONS AND IMPLICATIONS

Five years since China's WTO accession, there have been some notable adjustments in China's grain trade policies. Domestic subsidy has evolved from providing chiefly price support to both price and income support. Such support has increased rapidly in the past five years in order to promote domestic grain production. China also increased its support for grain exports with increased emphasis given to encourage the export of processed grain products. In terms of market access, China has done well to honour its WTO accession commitments and TRQ is the only means used by China to influence the access of grain imports to the Chinese market.

A relatively high proportion of the grain TRQs is traded by STEs and the management of the non-STE portion of the TRQs is still not very transparent, though the government has tried to make improvements. Hence, the use of grain TRQs has to some extent limited the imports of grains to China. However, TRQ administration is only one of the several major factors that have contributed to the low usage of the grain TRQs. Other major factors include: higher prices of imported grains; increased domestic grain production support and improved availability of higher-quality grains produced domestically.

Although it was low in the past five years, TRQ usage is likely to increase in the future. It is generally held that China's increased grain imports will become unavoidable. In future trade negotiations China may agree to further open up its grain market but may attach conditions such as asking for further opening up of labour-intensive product markets by its trading partners. China may also relate its grain and other agricultural product markets opening up to the international movement of production factors such as capital, technology and labour.

However, in the near future, it is unlikely that the Chinese government will bring significant changes to the current grain trade policies, unless there is drastic progress with the WTO multilateral trade negotiations or large unexpected changes in domestic grain supply. Government support to encourage grain production is expected to continue and is likely to increase further. It is not anticipated that export support will increase unless there is a temporary glut in domestic production and China badly needs to export. Whether foreign grains will have improved access to the Chinese market will depend on China's domestic supply and demand;

however, trading partners having a bilateral FTA with China are expected to have improved access to the Chinese grain market. TRQs will continue to be used by China as its only major means to control grain imports to China. Any changes in the amount of TRQs, the management of TRQs and the out-quota tariff rates, will be primarily influenced by China's domestic grain supply and also to a great extent by the progress and outcomes of multilateral and bilateral trade negotiations.

NOTES

1. For example, Australian Wheat Board (AWB) and Grains Research and Development Corporation (GRDC) commissioned researchers at the Australian National University (ANU) to look into the dynamics of China's wheat market and trade soon after its WTO accession and the report emphasized the importance of understanding China's grain TRQ issues (AWB and GRDC, 2005).
2. Grain in China includes cereals (rice, wheat, corn, sorghum, millet and other miscellaneous grains), tuber crops (sweet potatoes and potatoes only, not including taro and cassava), as well as pulses (including mainly soybean, red bean and mung bean). The output of tuber crops (sweet potatoes and potatoes) was converted on a 4:1 ratio, that is, 4 kilograms of fresh tubers were equivalent to 1 kilogram of grain, up to 1963. Since 1964, the ratio has been 5:1. The output of beans refers to dry beans without pods. The term 'grain' generally includes all these 'grains' unless otherwise indicated.
3. Soybean has been one of the major grains in China's international grain trade. As early as in 1996, China started to apply a tariff-rate quota to soybean imports, with an in-quote tariff being 3 per cent, a preferential tariff 40 per cent and an ordinary tariff 180 per cent. During the WTO entry negotiations, China agreed to remove soybean import TRQ and also to reduce soybean import tariffs significantly to be 3 per cent only. For soybean powder, the tariff is 5 per cent. China also agreed that by 2006 soybean oil import TRQ would be removed and the import would be only subject to a 9 per cent tariff.
4. In 2003, State Development and Planning Commission (SDPC) was renamed National Development and Reform Commission (NDRC).
5. Currently developed countries are allowed a minimal amount of Amber Box support ('de minimis'). For support that is not given to specific products, this is defined as 5 per cent of the value of total agricultural production. For support given to a specific product, the limit is 5 per cent of production of that product. Developing countries are allowed up to 10 per cent of these. The framework says de minimis will be reduced by an amount to be negotiated, with special treatment for developing countries, which will be exempt if they 'allocate almost all de minimis support for subsistence and resource-poor farmers' (WTO, 2007).
6. In March 2004, China's Premier, Wen Jiabao, pointed out that the agricultural tax rate would be gradually reduced and agricultural tax should be completely phased out within five years (Wen, 2004). By early 2006, agricultural tax disappeared nationwide. This enabled farmers to retain extra income, which has an important impact on production and livelihood of farmers in poorer regions.
7. Much of the discussion in this section is based on a joint notice by the Ministry of Commerce and the National Development and Reform Commission (2003), 'Temporary Management Procedures of Agricultural Import TRQs', Notice No. 34, 2003, and descriptions in WTO (2001), 'Agreement of Accession of the People's Republic of China'.

8. As a result of price changes in domestic grain market in 2003 and 2004, the utilization rate of wheat TRQ increased in 2004, reaching 75.3 per cent. Rice TRQ usage was also higher, being 14.4 per cent in 2004.

REFERENCES

Australian Wheat Board (AWB) and Grains Research and Development Corporation (GRDC) (2005), 'China: Wheat Market Study', Summary report, AWB and GRDC, August.

Chen, J. and J. Liu (2002), 'WTO accession and impacts on China's fiscal incomes and expenditures', Journal of Contemporary Finance and Accounting (8), 12–14.

Chen, Y. (2004), *China's Food: Demand, Supply and Projections*, Beijing: China Agricultural Press.

Crook, F. and W. Colby (1996), 'The Future of China's Grain Market', USDA *Agriculture Information Bulletin* No. 730, Washington, DC.

Findlay, C. (ed.) (1998), 'Grain Market Reform in China: Global Implications', ACIAR Technical Report No. 43, Australian Centre for International Agricultural Research, Canberra.

Garnaut, R. and G. Ma (1992), *Grain in China*, East Asia Analytical Unit, Department of Foreign Affairs and Trade, Canberra.

Han, Y. (2005), 'Research on TRQ', www.agri.gov.cn, accessed 7 June 2006.

Ministry of Agriculture (MOA) (2003), *China Agricultural Development Report 2003*, Beijing: China Agricultural Press.

Ministry of Agriculture (MOA) (2007), Statistical Information, www.agri.gov.cn/ sjzl/baipsh/2007.htm (Chinese), accessed 11 March 2007.

Ministry of Commerce, 'Monthly Bulletin of Chinese Agricultural Import and Export Statistics', www.mofcom.gov.cn, accessed 15 December 2007.

Ministry of Commerce and National Development and Reform Commission (2003), 'Temporary Management Procedures of Agricultural Import TRQs', Notice No. 34, 2003.

Ministry of Finance (2006), 'Central Government Increases Financial Input of the "Three Nong" (Countryside, Agriculture and Farmer)', http://www.mof.gov.cn, accessed 8 December 2007.

Ministry of Finance and State Taxation Bureau (2002), 'Notice on Zero Value-added Tax to Rice, Wheat and Corn Exports', 28 March, www.chinatax.gov.cn, accessed 1 April 2006.

Ministry of Finance and State Taxation Bureau (2003), 'Notice on Adjustments of Tax Rebates of Exports', 13 October, www.ahhpcpa.com.cn (Chinese) accessed 5 July 2006.

National Bureau of Statistics of China (NBS) (2007), *Highlights of China Statistics*, Beijing: China Statistics Press.

RGCFDS (Research Group for China's Medium- and Long-term Food Development Strategies) (1993), *China's Medium- and Long-term Food Development Strategies*, Beijing: China Agricultural Press.

Shui, S. (2006), 'Agricultural trade and its efficient change after WTO', *China Agricultural Economy Review*, **4** (2), 183–94.

State Development and Planning Commission (SDPC) (2002), 'Notice on Exemption of Railway Construction Levies for Grains, Cotton and Other

Bulky Agricultural Products', 26 March, www.sdpc.gov.cn (Chinese) accessed 1 November 2006.

Tian, W. and J. Chudleigh (1999), 'China's feedgrain market: development and prospects', *Agribusiness*, **15** (3), 393–409.

Tian, W., L. Zhang and Z. Zhou (2002), 'Experiences and Issues in Measuring the Level of Support in China', in OECD (eds), *Agricultural Policies in China After WTO Accession*, Paris: OECD, pp. 284–300.

Wen, J. (2004), 'Government Work Report', 5 March, http://www.gov.cn/test/2006-02/16/content_201193.htm (Chinese) accessed 8 September 2006.

World Trade Organization (WTO) (2001), 'Agreement of Accession of the People's Republic of China', www.wto.org/English/thewto_e/acc_e/china_schedule.zip, accessed 12 October 2007.

World Trade Organization (WTO) (2007), 'Agriculture Negotiations: Backgrounder', http://www.wto.org/english/tratop_e/agric_e/negs_bkgrnd27_boxesframework_e.htm, accessed 16 June 2007.

Wu, L. (2006), 'China's grain trade policies and their impacts', *China Food Industry* (4), 58–9.

Zhou, Z. and W. Tian (2003), *China's Regional Feedgrain Markets: Developments and Prospects*, Canberra: Grains Research and Development Corporation.

Zhou, Z. and W. Tian (eds) (2005), *Grains in China: Foodgrain, Feedgrain and World Trade*, Aldershot, UK: Ashgate.

Zhou, Z. and W. Tian (2006), 'Evolving trends of grain production in China', *Australasian Agribusiness Review*, **14**, Paper 10, http://www.agrifood.info/review/2006/, accessed 16 June 2007.

10. The impact of the ASEAN-China Free Trade Area on China's economy and regional agricultural development

Jun Yang, Huanguang Qiu and Chunlai Chen

INTRODUCTION

China is very active in both multilateral and bilateral trade liberalization. Many studies have demonstrated that a free trade area can improve members' production efficiency, stimulate foreign investment, accelerate domestic reforms and promote economic growth (Fukase and Winters, 2003; Yang, Zhang and Huang, 2005). Because of the slow progress in multilateral trade negotiations, especially the Doha Round, China, like other countries, has actively engaged in negotiating and establishing bilateral free trade areas. By the end of 2006, China has signed free trade agreements with Hong Kong, Macao, the Association of Southeast Asian Nations (ASEAN), Chile and Pakistan. Negotiations with New Zealand, Australia, the Gulf Cooperation Council and southern countries of Africa are in progress, and four free trade areas are at the feasibility study stage.

The ASEAN-China Free Trade Agreement (ACFTA) is a milestone in the cooperation between China and ASEAN. The Framework Agreement on Comprehensive Economic Cooperation, signed in November 2002, provided for the establishment of an ACFTA for goods trade by 2010 for the older ASEAN members, including Brunei, Indonesia, Malaysia, the Philippines, Singapore and Thailand, and by 2015 for the newer ASEAN member states, Vietnam, Laos, Cambodia and Myanmar. The Early Harvest Program (EHP), implemented on 1 January 2004, specifies that China and all older member countries of ASEAN should phase out mutual import tariffs on almost all agricultural goods; newer ASEAN members have until 2015 to eliminate tariffs on these commodities. The enforcement of the Agreement on Trade in Goods of July 2005 signals the operational phase of the ACFTA.

ACFTA is one of the largest free trade areas in terms of population, gross economic output and trade volumes. By the end of 2005, the gross domestic product (GDP) of ACFTA reached US$2971 billion, and the total value of imports and exports reached US$1395 billion.[1] The development of the ACFTA will have significant impacts on the economies of China and ASEAN, as well as far-reaching implications for the economic and trade structure of the whole world.

Many studies have analysed these impacts and reached two general conclusions. First, most studies have predicted that ACFTA will stimulate the economies of member countries through reducing trade barriers and transaction costs, thus promoting the development of bilateral trade. For example, Chirathivat (2002), using a computable general equilibrium (CGE) model, found that the establishment of ACFTA will increase the GDP growth of China by 0.36 per cent and ASEAN by 0.38 per cent, representing US$298.6 billion and US$178.7 billion gains, respectively. However, some scholars have found that ASEAN countries will lose from this bilateral agreement because of lower labour costs in China. They argued that China's cheaper products will have negative impacts on the total welfare of ASEAN countries, or at least on some important sectors in ASEAN countries (Holst and Weiss, 2004; Tongzon, 2005).

The second research conclusion concerns ACFTA's impacts on the rest of the world. Since ACFTA is a regional and relatively close-knit organization, its benefits are mostly exclusive to those countries that belong. Mutual tariff reductions between member countries can make imports of products of non-member countries less competitive, with negative impacts on those countries' total trade volumes and economic welfare (Ahearne et al., 2006).

Many studies have analysed the impacts of ACFTA on China's agricultural sectors at the national level; however, few have examined the impacts of ACFTA on China's agricultural development by regions. Interestingly, results of studies focusing on the national level differ notably. Lu (2006), in a comparison of the agricultural products of China and ASEAN, concluded that most agricultural products of the two sides are complementary, so ACFTA will promote the export of most of China's agricultural products, except for vegetables and fish. However, Rong and Yang (2006) found that agricultural products of the two sides are more competitive than complementary, which has become more apparent in the last few years. Based on these observations, they concluded that ACFTA will have negative impacts on China's agricultural development.

The inconsistency of the above research results may arise for several reasons. First, ACFTA is a large economic community and its members have complex agricultural production structures and trade patterns, making quantitative analysis of economic impacts difficult. Second, these studies did not pay particular attention to the agricultural production conditions of the 11 member countries. Taking China as an example, it has vast geographic diversity and its agricultural production patterns vary significantly across regions. Given the large spatial diversity in its production structure, biased or even misleading conclusions could be drawn by studies that are less attentive to regional differences.

This chapter tries to analyse the impacts of ACFTA on China's agricultural trade and agricultural development at both national and regional levels, using the Global Trade Analysis Project (GTAP) and the China Agricultural Decision Support System (CHINAGRO). The chapter is organized as follows. The next section summarizes the structure and development of agricultural trade between China and ASEAN. The third section outlines the methodology and scenarios of the analysis. Major simulation results and the underlying economic reasoning are presented and discussed in the fourth section. The last section concludes the chapter.

DEVELOPMENT OF CHINA–ASEAN AGRICULTURAL TRADE

Since the late 1990s, agricultural trade between China and ASEAN has expanded rapidly.[2] The market interdependency between the two economies has steadily increased in the past decade. The annual growth rate of exports of agricultural products from ASEAN to China was 17.3 per cent over the period 1999 to 2001, and 27.3 per cent during 2002–05. In 2005, China's total imports of agricultural products from ASEAN reached US$5 billion. As ASEAN's agricultural exports to China grew faster than its total agricultural exports, the share of ASEAN's agricultural exports to China in its total agricultural exports has increased from 4.8 per cent in 1999 to 10.2 per cent in 2005. Compared with the rapid growth of agricultural imports from ASEAN, China's exports of agricultural products to ASEAN grew at only a moderate pace, with an annual growth rate of 17 per cent from 2001 to 2005. In recent years, China has maintained a trade deficit in agricultural trade with ASEAN. Moreover, the deficit has become even larger with the fast growth of ASEAN's agricultural exports to China.

The agricultural import and export structures of China and ASEAN show clear differences (see Table 10.1). The main agricultural products exported from China to ASEAN are fruits and vegetables, processed food and fish, accounting for 77 per cent of the total value of agricultural products exported to ASEAN. On the other side, vegetable oils, rubber and

Table 10.1   *Structure of agricultural trade between China and ASEAN in 2005 (%)*

Agricultural Products	China's Export to ASEAN	China's Import from ASEAN
Fruits and vegetables	40.9	13.8
Processed food	23.2	4.9
Fish products	13.8	2.8
Grain	7.2	3.7
Livestock	4.2	0.1
Sugar	3.2	0.9
Oilseeds	1.8	0.1
Rubber	1.7	33.1
Vegetable oil	1.5	36.9
Other agricultural products	2.5	3.8

Source: Data are from the United Nations Statistics Division, Commodity Trade Statistics Database, COMTRADE.

fruits and vegetables dominate agricultural exports of ASEAN to China, accounting for 83 per cent of the total. The large bilateral trade in fruits and vegetables implies that at least for those products, the two economies are very complementary; ASEAN can provide tropical fruits such as mangoes and bananas, whereas China can provide temperate fruits such as apples and pears.

Trends in trade patterns parallel the comparative advantages of the two sides. China has comparative advantage in labour-intensive products, whereas ASEAN has comparative advantage in land-intensive products. Although, overall, China has a trade deficit with ASEAN in agricultural products, China has always shown a net trade surplus in labour-intensive agricultural products, which has increased from US$170 million in 2001 to US$630 million in 2005. On the other hand, in terms of land-intensive agricultural products, ASEAN's exports to China have maintained a very high growth rate. For example, China imported US$1.5 billion in land-intensive products from ASEAN in 2001, and US$3.9 billion in 2005. Table 10.2 reveals that agricultural trade between China and ASEAN has grown steadily in the past decade. China's agricultural exports to ASEAN countries have doubled, whereas ASEAN's agricultural exports to China have increased six-fold since 1992. The last column in Table 10.2 also shows that China has become a major importer of agricultural products from ASEAN. China accounted for more than 10 per cent of ASEAN's total agricultural exports in 2005.

Table 10.2 Total and agricultural trade between China and ASEAN (1992–05)

Year	Exports from China to ASEAN (100 million US$)		Exports from ASEAN to China (100 million US$)		Share of Bilateral Agricultural Exports in Total Agricultural Exports (%)	
	Total	Agriculture	Total	Agriculture	China	ASEAN
1992	46.7	10.5	37.9	8.7	9.2	3.3
1993	53.4	11.4	50.7	8.1	9.9	3.1
1994	71.6	15.9	64.6	19.2	11.0	5.9
1995	104.7	16.9	83.1	25.6	11.7	6.7
1996	103.1	14.6	95.5	26.9	10.1	7.2
1997	127.1	15.9	106.7	28.9	10.4	7.4
1998	111.6	17.5	100.9	21.8	12.5	6.1
1999	122.7	13.9	114.2	16.8	10.1	4.8
2000	173.4	15.2	162.1	21.0	9.5	6.1
2001	183.8	13.0	165.8	22.3	8.0	6.7
2002	246.5	18.2	236.4	31.4	9.6	8.1
2003	309.3	23.3	307.0	40.4	10.8	9.1
2004	429.0	21.0	413.5	53.0	9.0	10.2
2005	553.7	24.4	522.3	58.7	8.8	10.2

Source: Data are from the United Nations Statistics Division, Commodity Trade Statistics Database, COMTRADE.

METHODOLOGY AND POLICY SCENARIOS

The analysis undertaken links two general equilibrium models: the Global Trade Analysis Project (GTAP), which evaluates the impact of ACFTA on China's international trade, and the China Agricultural Decision Support System (CHINAGRO), which examines ACFTA's impact on the various regions of China. The national-level economic impact of ACFTA, assessed with the GTAP model, and the simulated price changes of international agricultural products were fed into the multiregional equilibrium model, CHINAGRO, which analysed the impact of ACFTA on China's regional agricultural development. Such forms of model linkage have been used in many studies. For example, Adams et al. (1998) linked GTAP with the Australian ORANI-G applied general equilibrium model. Horridge and Zhai (2006) provided a general description on how to link GTAP with regional models.

GTAP is a well-known multicountry, multisector computable general equilibrium model, and is often used for international trade analysis (Hertel, 1997). The model is based on the assumptions that producers minimize their production costs and consumers maximize their utility under certain constraints. Supply and demand of all commodities clear by adjusting prices in a perfectly competitive market. Representative consumers of each country or region are determined with a non-homothetic constant difference of elasticity (CDE) demand function. On the production side, firms combine intermediate inputs and primary factors (for example, land, labour and capital) to produce commodities with constant-returns-to-scale technology. Intermediate inputs consist of domestic and foreign components, with the foreign component differentiated by region of origin (the Armington assumption). The data used for this study was based on the GTAP Database Version 6. The classifications of regions/countries and commodities are shown in Appendix Tables 10A.1 and 10A.2.

In GTAP, China is only one region, so we selected CHINAGRO to explore the impact of agricultural development in the different regions. CHINAGRO is a 17–commodity, eight-region general equilibrium welfare model,[3] which has been successfully used for policy analysis of China's regional agricultural development (Keyzer and van Veen, 2005; Fisher et al., 2006; Huang et al., 2007). The model consists of six income groups per region, with farm supply represented at the county level. For each county, the model comprizes 28 products and a range of 14 farm types involved in cropping and livestock production. The 28 products encompass most of China's agricultural products, including rice, maize, wheat, sugarcane, oil crops, pork and poultry. The 14 farm types include categories such as irrigated cropping, rain-fed cropping, tree cropping, traditional livestock farms and specialized livestock farms. Consumption is depicted at the regional level separately for urban and rural populations, and domestic trade is interregional (Keyzer and van Veen, 2005).

Because we are interested in assessing the economic impact of ACFTA on China's agricultural development at national and regional level, we developed two scenarios, a baseline scenario and a fully implemented ACFTA scenario. We estimated the impact of ACFTA by comparing the results from the two scenarios in 2010.

Baseline Scenario

The baselines were constructed using a recursive dynamic approach to reflect the changes over time in the endowments of the countries. This procedure has been used in several other studies (for example, Hertel and Martin, 1999; Tongeren and Huang, 2004). The growth in endowments

(GDP, population, skilled and unskilled labour, capital and natural resources) were mainly taken from similar studies (Huang and Yang, 2006; Tongeren and Huang, 2004; Walmsley, Betina and Robert, 2000).

The baseline projection assumes a continuation of existing policies and the effectuation of important policy events related to international trade as they are known to date. The important policy changes are: implementation of the remaining commitments from the GATT Uruguay Round agreements; China's WTO accession commitments between 2001 and 2010; the global phase-out of the Multi-fibre Agreement under the WTO Agreement on Textiles and Clothing (ATC) by January 2005; EU enlargement with Central and Eastern European Countries (CEECs); and the implementation of a free trade area among ASEAN member countries.

ACFTA Scenario

In the scenario of full implementation of ACFTA, we assumed that the tariffs between China and the older ASEAN members will be reduced to zero by 2010 for all commodities except those on the Special Products List, for which we assume that the tariffs will be reduced to 5 per cent. ACFTA permits newer ASEAN members to remove all import tariffs as late as 2015, but they must eliminate the import tariffs on commodities listed in the EHP by 2010. Therefore, in this simulation, we assume newer ASEAN members will not liberalize except for the commodities under the EHP, whereas China will impose no import tariffs on commodities imported from those countries in 2010.

SIMULATION RESULTS

The Macro Effects of ACFTA

The simulation results indicate that ACFTA will improve economic welfare and stimulate economic growth of both China and ASEAN. The older ASEAN countries will be the biggest winners in terms of absolute social economic welfare gains (US$1507 million), followed by China whose welfare will increase by US$517 million. The net welfare increase of newer ASEAN members will be US$117 million. The GDP growth of all participants will benefit from ACFTA.

Compared with the baseline results, GDP growth rates of China, of an older member of ASEAN and of a newer member of ASEAN will increase by 0.2 per cent, 0.6 per cent and 0.5 per cent, respectively (Table 10.3). International trade of all members will also expand. Total exports and

Table 10.3   *General impact of ACFTA on the economies of China and ASEAN by 2010*

	China	Older ASEAN Members	Newer ASEAN Members
Welfare change (EV, million $US)	517	1507	117
GDP change (%)	0.20	0.58	0.46
Export increase (million $US)	7764	3664	128
Import increase (million $US)	9769	5805	268
Price of land (% increase)	0.32	0.68	1.73
Unskilled labour wage (% increase)	0.32	0.94	0.44
Skilled labour wage (% increase)	0.28	0.93	0.42
Price of capital (% increase)	0.42	0.94	0.43

Source: Simulation results.

imports of China will increase by US$7764 million and US$9769 million, respectively, and the exports and imports for all ASEAN countries (older and newer members) will increase by US$3792 million and US$6073 million, respectively.

The returns to primary inputs (that is, land, capital and labour) increase for all participating countries in the ACFTA scenario. As trade liberalization promotes production in all the participating countries, the demand for primary factors increases, leading to increases in primary factor prices. The rent of land increases by 0.32 per cent in China, 0.68 per cent in older ASEAN members, and 1.73 per cent in newer ASEAN members. Wages of all countries grow; however, the wage increase for unskilled labour is marginally higher than for skilled labour in all member countries (Table 10.3).

ACFTA will have significant impacts on China's agricultural trade as well as on the international prices faced by China, and the impacts vary remarkably among commodities. Table 10.4 shows that ACFTA will increase most commodity prices faced by China on the world market, except the prices of sugar and vegetable oil, which will decrease by 0.06 per cent and 0.10 per cent, respectively. China's exports of sugar, tea/horticultural products and fruits and vegetables will expand dramatically in the ACFTA scenario by 76.6 per cent, 11.17 per cent and 8.28 per cent respectively. Imports of vegetable oil, sugar and fruits and vegetables increase by 27.6 per cent, 10.8 per cent and 5.29 per cent (Table 10.4). As we have explained, since the fruits and vegetables produced by ASEAN

Table 10.4   *Impact of ACFTA on world prices and China's agricultural trade in 2010*

Agricultural Products	World Price Increase (%)	Exports		Imports	
		Increase (%)	Value (million $US)	Increase (%)	Value (million $US)
Rice	0.28	2.68	16	2.62	6
Wheat	0.22	7.20	2	0.65	3
Other grains	0.26	0.33	2	0.43	4
Vegetables/fruits	0.33	8.28	135	5.29	89
Oilseeds	0.16	3.18	10	0.28	23
Sugar	−0.06	76.63	16	10.80	43
Cotton	0.13	0.87	1	0.42	11
Vegetable oil	−0.10	3.08	4	27.60	243
Tea/horticulture	1.15	11.17	137	5.40	87
Beef and mutton	0.26	0.10	0	0.71	5
Pork and poultry	0.28	2.65	114	3.63	154
Milk	0.23	0.75	0	1.04	7
Fish	0.09	0.16	1	1.58	2

Source: Simulation results.

and China (especially Northern China) are quite different, one would expect both the exports and imports of these products to increase substantially when the free trade area is fully implemented. China's net exports of tea/horticultural products and fruits and vegetables will increase by US$50 million and US$46 million respectively (Table 10.4), while ACFTA will increase China's net imports of vegetable oil (mostly palm oil) by US$239 million. ACFTA will also increase China's net imports of sugar, pork and poultry.

Impact of ACFTA at the Regional Level, by Agricultural Commodity

It is necessary and very valuable to analyse the impact of ACFTA on China's agricultural development by region because of the vast differences among China's regions. First, there exists large diversity across provinces in cropping patterns. As shown in Appendix Table 10A.3, there are provinces (for example, Heilongjiang, Jilin, Shanxi and Hebei) in which farmers are producing wheat, maize, soybeans and cotton. In contrast, there are provinces such as Shandong, Zhejiang and Guangdong that have relatively large shares of their farming areas in horticultural production. There

Table 10.5   Price effects of ACFTA for different regions of China by 2010 (%)

Regions	Rice	Wheat	Vegetable Oil	Sugar	Fruits	Vegetables	Livestock
North	1.02	0.00	−1.47	−0.74	1.99	2.13	−1.77
Northeast	1.71	0.00	−1.31	−1.15	1.73	1.82	−1.75
East	0.60	0.78	−1.30	−0.37	1.94	2.02	−1.51
Central	0.64	0.75	−1.47	−0.74	1.87	1.96	−1.60
South	−1.49	0.65	−2.08	−3.45	−4.63	2.15	−1.24
Southwest	−0.52	0.71	−1.29	−3.02	−0.28	1.90	−1.36
Tibet	–	0.00	–	–	1.69	1.96	−1.44
Northwest	0.51	0.71	−1.48	−1.12	2.61	2.06	−1.70

Source: Simulation results.

also is great diversity in the production of livestock across provinces, as shown by Appendix Table 10A.4.

Second, even within the same group of agricultural products, the commodities produced across regions can be very different. For example, although they are classified into the same commodity group, the fruits produced in the Southern part of China are mainly tropical varieties (quite similar to the fruits from ASEAN), while the fruits produced in the Central and Northern parts of China are temperate varieties (different from the fruits produced in ASEAN countries). Third, transportation infrastructure and other market developments vary by regions and this can affect price transmission. Last but not least, supply elasticities differ by regions, so that production responds more to price changes in some regions than in others.

Table 10.5 presents the price effects of ACFTA by agricultural products in different regions of China. As a result of ACFTA, the prices of vegetable oils, sugar and livestock products in all regions decrease, but prices increase for the commodities in which China has a comparative advantage, such as vegetables.

For certain group of commodities, ACFTA lowers prices in some regions of and raise them in others. These differences primarily result from differences among the products themselves. Rice and fruits, for example, are similar in Southern China and in ASEAN countries, but the products produced in Northern China are more complementary with those of ASEAN countries. So, after tariff reductions under the ACFTA agreement, more rice and tropical fruits will be imported into Northern China from ASEAN countries, and exports of rice and fruits produced in Northern China to ASEAN will also increase. As a result, farmers in

Table 10.6   *Effects of ACFTA on regional agricultural production in China in 2010 (%)*

Regions	Rice	Wheat	Vegetable Oil	Sugar	Fruit	Vegetables	Livestock
North	0.40	0.00	−0.66	−0.59	0.66	1.13	−0.23
Northeast	0.88	0.16	−0.57	−0.64	0.55	1.02	−0.36
East	0.79	−0.28	−1.03	−1.00	0.66	0.02	−0.34
Central	0.77	−0.41	−1.28	−1.20	0.59	0.13	−0.38
South	−0.20	0.61	−0.13	−1.75	−1.03	1.08	−0.33
Southwest	−0.11	−0.33	−1.06	−1.69	−0.09	0.57	−0.35
Tibet	–	–	−0.39	–	0.60	0.96	0.00
Northwest	0.10	0.06	−0.45	−0.34	0.67	1.09	−0.11
China	0.44	−0.07	−0.82	−1.50	0.27	0.70	−0.31

Source: Simulation results.

Northern China will receive higher prices for their rice and fruits, while those in Southern China will receive lower prices.

Price changes will have an impact on the allocation of factor inputs and hence on the outputs of different commodities in each region. In our simulation, regional changes in outputs are strongly correlated with regional price changes. For example, as prices increase for vegetables in all regions, the output of vegetables in all regions rises. The uneven increases in output (highest in Northern China at 1.13 per cent and lowest in Eastern China at 0.02 per cent) result from the differences in price increases and the different supply elasticities. By contrast, ACFTA will reduce China's production of vegetable oils and sugar by 0.82 per cent and 1.5 per cent, respectively (Table 10.6). As expected, the agreement will reduce production of rice and fruits in Southern and Southwest regions of China, but increase them in other regions. For example, rice production will increase in the Northeast region by 0.88 per cent (Table 10.6).

One exception is wheat production. Although wheat prices in all regions increase in the ACFTA scenario, China's total wheat production decreases by 0.07 per cent (Table 10.6). Wheat production in the Northeast, Northwest and Southern regions is expected to increase, but production in the East, Central and Southwest regions will decline moderately. The differences between the simulated effects on price and production can be explained by fixed factors of production in agriculture, including land and labour constraints. In the East and Central regions, although the wheat price increases in the ACFTA scenario, the price of fruits and vegetables increases more (Table 10.5), implying that the opportunity cost of growing wheat increases more than the increase in wheat price. Because the total available cultivated land and agricultural labour remain fixed, when more resources are moved away from the wheat sector, its production might be expected to decline even if its price increases.

Aggregate Impact of ACFTA on Agriculture at the Regional Level

Table 10.7 shows the impact of ACFTA on each region and the national level of China in total and net agricultural output. At the national level, compared with baseline scenario results, total and net agricultural outputs under ACFTA increase by 0.18 per cent and 0.35 per cent (US$52.9 million and US$79.4 million), respectively. Net output rises by a larger percentage than total output because ACFTA improves production efficiency and profit margins.

At the regional level, South China loses out under ACFTA, with total agricultural output declining by 0.99 per cent, and net agricultural output declining by 1.06 per cent (Table 10.7). This result is consistent with our expectations. As discussed above, primary agricultural products in South China, such as fruits and sugar, will face fierce competition from ASEAN products, and both the prices and outputs of those products will decrease. Although outputs of wheat and vegetables increase in the ACFTA scenario, the shares of those products are very low in South China, so the increases in these products cannot compensate for the decline of the main products in this region.

Table 10.7   Impact of ACFTA on China's national and regional total and net agricultural output in 2010

	Total Agricultural Output		Net Agricultural Output	
	Value (million $US)	Percentage change (%)	Value (million $US)	Percentage change (%)
North	25.4	0.35	32.5	0.68
Northeast	8.9	0.34	15.0	0.87
East	28.8	0.70	31.3	0.92
Central	10.9	0.28	12.5	0.38
South	−47.0	−0.99	−43.1	−1.06
Southwest	18.0	0.37	19.4	0.54
Tibet	−0.6	−0.16	−0.6	−0.18
Northwest	8.6	0.34	12.5	0.67
China	52.9	0.18	79.4	0.35

Source: Simulation results.

Another region that loses in the ACFTA scenario is Tibet, but only to a limited extent. The total and net agricultural outputs of this region decline by 0.16 per cent and 0.18 per cent respectively (Table 10.7). The main negative effect on Tibet comes from the livestock sector, which suffers from an increase in the maize price and a decline in the milk price.

Other regions gain from ACFTA. The East gains the most; net agricultural output increases by 0.92 per cent, followed by the Northeast (0.87 per cent), the North (0.68 per cent), and the Northwest (0.67 per cent). In terms of the value of net agricultural output, North China, the East, the Southwest and the Northeast gain US$32.5 million, US$31.3 million, US$19.4 million and US$15.0 million, respectively (Table 10.7). Gains for the North and East regions mainly come from production increases in fruits and vegetables, while the increase in the rice price and production accounts for most of the net output increase in the East region.

For the Northeast, the production increase of rice and vegetables accounts for 70 per cent of the overall gain, with the rest coming from fruits and wheat. The increase in production and price of fruits, vegetables and wheat contributes to the increase of net agricultural output in the Northwest. The Central and Southwest regions will have only a very moderate gain from the ACFTA.

CONCLUSIONS

The creation of ACFTA will promote agricultural trade between China and ASEAN countries, and will improve the economic welfare and stimulate the economic growth of both China and ASEAN countries. The economic welfare of ASEAN countries is projected to increase by about US$1624 million, and China's economic welfare to increase by about US$517 million.

Trade will increase in all ACFTA countries. China's total exports and imports will increase by US$7764 million and US$9769 million, respectively, and the exports and imports of ASEAN countries will increase by US$3792 million and US$6073 million, respectively. The development of agricultural trade clearly follows the comparative advantage of each side. China's net export of fruits and vegetables will increase by US$46 million. On the import side, China's imports of vegetable oils and sugar will increase by US$239 million and US$75.8 million, respectively. ACFTA will also bring a large increase in China's net imports of pork and poultry.

However, ACFTA has some disadvantages. It reduces trade barriers only between China and ASEAN. It can therefore promote production of some commodities for which neither side has a comparative advantage, and harm some sectors in other countries outside ACFTA. For example, although ASEAN countries do not have a comparative advantage in the production of sugar and livestock products, with the reduction of China's import tariffs, the production of these commodities in ASEAN countries will increase. The countries that have comparative advantage in these commodities, such as Brazil and Australia, will lose part of their international market.

The impact of ACFTA on China's agricultural development differs significantly among its regions. For the production of some commodities, such as sugar, the impact has the same sign for all regions, but the magnitudes differ. For other groups of commodities, such as rice and fruits, impacts are of opposite signs in different regions, largely because the particular products differ between Northern and Southern regions. Generally, products in the South are closer substitutes for ASEAN products than those produced in the North.

From the overall impacts on regional total and net agricultural outputs, South China loses in the ACFTA scenario, with the total value of agricultural output declining by 0.99 per cent, and net value of agricultural output declining by 1.06 per cent. Northern regions of China will gain. The East will see its net value of agricultural output increase by 0.92 per cent, followed by the Northeast (0.87 per cent), the North (0.68 per cent) and the Northwest (0.67 per cent). ACFTA has no significant impact on the total and net value of agricultural output in Tibet, the Southwest and Central China.

Most studies of the impact of multilateral trade agreements, such as the WTO, on different regions of China have found that Southern regions of China will gain significantly from trade liberalization, whereas Northern regions of China will see moderate gains or even losses. However, ACFTA may have the opposite pattern of regional effects in agriculture, which would have important implications for China's regional development policies.

NOTES

1. All trade values in this chapter are in 2000 constant US dollar prices.
2. We use the Standard International Trade Classification (SITC revision 3) to classify agricultural products. Agricultural products in this study include: SITC0 (Food and Live Animals), SITC1 (Beverages and Tobacco), SITC4 (Animals and Vegetable Oils, Fats and Waxes), and some subgroups of SITC2 (Crude Materials, Non-edibles, except Fuels). The agricultural trade data are from the United National Statistics Division, Commodity Trade Statistics Database (COMTRADE). All values of agricultural trade are in 2000 constant US dollar prices.
3. In the CHINAGRO model, China is disaggregated into eight areas, which are the

North (Beijing, Tianjin, Hebei, Henan and Shanxi), the Northeast (Heilongjiang, Jilin and Liaoning), the East (Shanghai, Jiangsu, Zhejiang and Anhui), the Central (Hubei, Hunan and Jiangxi), the South (Guangdong, Guangxi, Fujian and Hainan), the Southwest (Sichuan, Chongqing, Guizhou and Yunnan), Tibet (Qinghai and Xizang) and the Northwest (Xinjiang, Gansu, Inner Mongolia, Shaanxi and Ningxia). China's Hong Kong, Macao and Taiwan are not included in the current database.

REFERENCES

Adams, P., M. Horridge, B. Parmenter and X. Zhang (1998), 'Long Run Effects on China of APEC Trade Liberalization', General Paper No. G-130, Centre of Policy Studies, The Impact Project, Monash University, Melbourne.

Ahearne, A., J. Fernald, P. Loungani and J. Schindler (2006), 'Flying Geese or Sitting Ducks: China's Impact on the Trade Fortunes of Other Asian Economies', Working Paper, Board of Governors of the Federal Reserve System, No. 887.

Chirathivat, S. (2002), 'ASEAN-China Free Trade Area: background, implications, and future development', *Journal of Asia Economics*, **13** (5), 671–86.

Fisher, G., J. Huang, M. Keyzer, H. Qiu, L. Sun and W. van Veen (2006), 'Managing a Successful Transition of China's Agricultural Transition', Summary Report of the Chinagro Project on the Sustainable Adaptation of China's Agriculture to Globalization, International Scientific Cooperation Project ICA4-CT-2001-10085.

Fukase, E. and L. Winters (2003), 'Possible dynamic effects of AFTA for the new member countries', *The World Economy*, **26** (6), 853–71.

Hertel, T. (ed.) (1997), *Global Trade Analysis: Modelling and Applications*, Cambridge, UK: Cambridge University Press.

Hertel, T. and W. Martin (1999), 'Would Developing Countries Gain from Inclusion of Manufactures in the WTO Negotiations?', GTAP Working Paper, Purdue University.

Holst, D. and J. Weiss (2004), 'ASEAN and China: export rivals or partners in regional growth?', *The World Economy*, **27** (8), 1255–74.

Horridge, M. and F. Zhai (2006), 'Shocking A Single-country CGE Model with Export Prices and Quantities from a Global Model', in T. Hertel and L. Winters (eds), *Poverty and the WTO: Impacts of the Doha Development Agenda*, New York: Palgrave-MacMillan, pp. 38–45.

Huang, J. and J. Yang (2006), 'China's rapid economic growth and its implications for agriculture and food security in China and the rest of world', *Management World* (1), 67–76.

Huang, J., H. Qiu, M. Keyzer and E. Meng (2007), 'Potential Impacts of Bioethanol Development in China's Pearl River Basin', Study Report submitted to International Maize and Wheat Improvement Center, Mexico.

Keyzer, M. and W. van Veen (2005), 'Towards a Spatially and Socially Explicit Agricultural Policy Analysis for China', Working Paper No. 5, Centre for World Food Studies, Amsterdam.

Lu, L. (2006), 'The analysis on the similarity of China and ASEAN's agricultural products', *World Agricultural Economy* (in Chinese) (1), 36–40.

Ministry of Agriculture of China (2007), *China Animal Statistical Yearbook 2007*, Beijing: China Agricultural Press.

National Bureau of Statistics of China (NBS) (various issues), *China Statistical Yearbook*, Beijing: China Statistics Press.

Rong, J. and C. Yang (2006), 'Empirical study on competitiveness and complementarity of China and ASEAN's agricultural products', *International Trade Problems* (in Chinese) (8), 45–50.

Tongeren, F. and J. Huang (2004), 'China's Food Economy in the Early 21st Century', Study Report No. 6.04.04, Agricultural Economics Research Institute (LEI), The Hague.

Tongzon, J. (2005), 'ASEAN-China Free Trade Area: a bane or boon for ASEAN countries?', *The World Economy*, **28** (2), 191–210.

United Nations Statistics Division, *Commodity Trade Statistics Database*, COMTRADE. http://unstats.un.org/unsd/comtrade/default.aspx.

Walmsley, T., V. Betina and A. Robert (2000), 'A Base Case Scenario for the Dynamic GTAP Model', Center for Global Trade Analysis, Purdue University, West Lafayette.

Yang, J., H. Zhang and J. Huang (2005), 'The impact of phasing out MFA on China and world economy', *Management World* (3), 64–74.

APPENDIX

Table 10A.1   Regional aggregations

	Description	Original GTAP Version 6 Regional Aggregation
China	Mainland, China	Mainland, China
HK	Hong Kong, China	Hong Kong, China
TW	Taiwan, China	Taiwan, China
JapKor	Japan and South Korea	Japan, South Korea
ASEAN	Older ASEAN members	Indonesia, Malaysia, Philippines, Thailand, Singapore, Vietnam, rest of Southeast Asia
OthAsia	Other Asia	India, Bangladesh, Sri Lanka, rest of East Asia, rest of South Asia
AusNzl	Australia and New Zealand	Australia and New Zealand
NAFTA	North American Free Trade Area	Canada, United States, Mexico
SAM	South and Central America	Central America, Caribbean, Colombia, Peru, Venezuela, rest of Andean Pact, Argentina, Brazil, Chile, Uruguay, rest of South America, rest of the Caribbean
EU-15	European Union	Austria, Belgium, Denmark, Finland, France, Germany, United Kingdom, Greece, Ireland, Italy, Luxembourg, Netherlands, Portugal, Spain, Sweden
CEEC	Central European Associates	Hungary, Poland, Albania, Bulgaria, Croatia, Cyprus, Czech Republic, Malta, Romania, Slovakia, Slovenia, Estonia, rest of Europe
ROW	Rest of world	Switzerland, rest of EFTA, Turkey, rest of Middle East, Morocco, rest of North Africa, Malawi, Mozambique, Tanzania, Zambia, Zimbabwe, other Southern Africa, Uganda, rest of Sub-Saharan Africa, Former Soviet Union, Botswana, rest of SACU, Russia, rest of world

Note: As the GTAP Version 6 Database has no detailed information on Brunei, only the other five members are included as representative of the original ASEAN members.

Table 10A.2   Sector aggregation

	Original GTAP Version 6 Sector Aggregation
Rice	Paddy rice, processed rice
Wheat	Wheat
Coarse grain	Cereals, grains nec
Vegetables and fruits	Vegetables, fruit, nuts
Oilseeds	Oilseeds
Sugar	Sugar cane, sugar beet, sugar
Cotton	Plant-based fibres
Other crops	Crops nec
Vegetable oil	Vegetable oils and fats
Cattle and mutton	Cattle, sheep, goats, horses and their meats
Pork and poultry	Animal products nec, wool, silkworm cocoons, meat products
Milk	Raw milk, dairy products
Fish	Fish
Processed food	Food products nec, beverages & tobacco products
Nature resources	Forestry, coal, oil, gas, minerals nec
Textiles and apparel	Textiles, wearing apparel, leather products
Natural industry	Wood products, paper products & publishing, petroleum, coal products; chemicals, rubber, plastic products; mineral products
Metal and machinery	Ferrous metals; metals nec; metal products; machinery and equipment nec
Transportation	Motor vehicles and parts; transport equipment nec
Electronics	Electronic equipment
Manufactures	Manufactures nec
Services	Electricity, gas manufacture, distribution, water, construction, trade, transport nec, sea transport, air transport, communication, financial services nec, insurance, business services nec, recreation and other, public admin/defence/health/educat, dwellings

Note: nec – not elsewhere classified.

Table 10A.3 Shares of sown area by crops and provinces in China in 2006 (%)

	Rice	Wheat	Corn	Soybean	Tuber	Oilseed	Cotton	Sugar	Vegetable	Orchard	Others	Total
Beijing	0.2	16.7	36.0	3.5	1.1	1.9	0.6	0.0	21.6	18.5	0.0	100
Tianjin	3.2	20.3	27.0	4.2	0.2	0.9	14.8	0.0	22.7	6.8	0.0	100
Hebei	1.0	26.3	28.9	3.3	3.3	5.8	6.8	0.2	12.2	11.9	0.3	100
Shanxi	0.1	20.9	34.8	10.2	9.7	6.4	3.1	0.1	6.9	7.7	0.2	100
Inner Mongolia	1.8	8.0	36.2	21.3	11.7	12.9	0.0	1.0	4.9	1.0	1.2	100
Liaoning	16.6	0.4	50.3	6.9	3.4	4.2	0.0	0.0	9.5	8.3	0.3	100
Jilin	13.8	0.2	58.2	12.3	3.1	6.0	0.0	0.1	4.5	1.3	0.6	100
Heilongjiang	19.4	2.5	24.8	38.7	3.3	4.3	0.0	1.1	3.3	0.4	2.0	100
Shanghai	32.1	9.1	1.1	2.8	0.3	6.9	0.3	0.4	39.5	7.0	0.4	100
Jiangsu	30.5	23.7	5.2	4.6	1.2	11.1	4.8	0.0	15.8	2.6	0.4	100
Zhejiang	35.5	2.4	2.3	7.3	3.8	8.1	0.6	0.5	23.1	10.4	6.0	100
Anhui	24.4	23.8	7.8	11.9	3.8	13.0	4.4	0.1	7.9	1.2	1.7	100
Fujian	30.8	0.2	1.3	3.8	11.0	4.1	0.0	0.5	21.6	18.4	8.3	100
Jiangxi	62.9	0.2	0.3	3.1	2.3	11.4	1.3	0.3	10.8	5.9	1.5	100
Shandong	1.1	30.4	25.0	2.1	2.6	7.9	8.4	0.0	15.8	6.3	0.4	100
Henan	4.3	36.1	18.6	4.2	3.0	11.2	5.8	0.0	12.5	3.0	1.4	100
Hubei	28.6	10.9	6.0	3.8	5.6	18.5	5.5	0.1	13.9	3.9	3.3	100
Hunan	49.5	0.8	3.5	3.6	5.0	12.0	2.2	0.3	13.7	5.9	3.4	100

Table 10A.3 (continued)

	Rice	Wheat	Corn	Soybean	Tuber	Oilseed	Cotton	Sugar	Vegetable	Orchard	Others	Total
Guangdong	37.2	0.1	2.4	1.9	6.9	5.6	0.0	2.9	20.9	17.9	4.2	100
Guangxi	31.0	0.2	7.0	3.6	3.3	4.2	0.0	11.4	15.3	11.8	12.3	100
Hainan	32.5	0.0	1.5	1.1	10.2	4.4	0.0	6.8	19.3	17.3	6.9	100
Chongqing	21.9	7.7	13.3	6.9	22.0	7.6	0.0	0.1	12.3	5.6	2.6	100
Sichuan	21.9	13.4	12.6	5.0	14.6	11.3	0.3	0.3	12.4	5.0	3.3	100
Guizhou	15.9	9.0	16.4	7.2	18.7	12.5	0.0	0.4	11.0	2.6	6.1	100
Yunnan	17.0	8.4	19.2	7.6	11.8	3.7	0.0	4.7	8.5	3.9	15.3	100
Tibet	1.0	41.9	3.4	8.1	0.6	24.4	0.0	0.0	19.2	1.2	0.1	100
Shaanxi	3.0	24.8	23.1	7.9	6.8	5.5	1.7	0.0	7.4	17.7	2.0	100
Gansu	0.2	29.1	14.4	6.6	16.6	9.5	2.2	0.1	9.3	10.9	0.9	100
Qinghai	0.0	23.6	0.2	11.0	19.2	38.2	0.0	0.0	6.6	1.0	0.1	100
Ningxia	8.8	24.6	18.8	5.9	20.2	8.9	0.0	0.0	6.6	6.0	0.1	100
Xinjiang	1.7	19.4	13.9	2.6	0.6	4.0	33.8	2.5	5.0	13.4	3.1	100

Source: National Bureau of Statistics of China (various issues), *China Statistical Yearbook*, Beijing: China Statistics Press.

Table 10A.4   Shares of animal production by provinces in China in 2006 (%)

	Pork	Beef	Mutton	Poultry	Eggs	Milk	Fish
Beijing	0.6	0.5	0.6	2.1	0.5	1.9	0.1
Tianjin	0.7	0.8	0.6	0.9	0.8	2.1	0.7
Hebei	6.8	12.0	7.5	6.8	15.8	12.6	2.1
Shanxi	1.0	1.0	1.6	0.3	1.8	2.5	0.1
Inner Mongolia	1.8	5.1	17.2	1.9	1.7	26.6	0.2
Liaoning	3.8	5.9	1.6	7.1	8.1	2.9	8.4
Jilin	2.2	7.1	0.9	6.5	3.4	1.1	0.2
Heilongjiang	2.0	4.3	2.5	2.1	3.7	14.1	0.9
Shanghai	0.3	0.0	0.1	0.4	0.2	0.7	0.7
Jiangsu	4.2	0.7	3.8	7.3	6.3	1.8	7.7
Zhejiang	2.5	0.2	0.8	2.1	1.4	0.8	9.2
Anhui	4.4	4.6	3.7	5.4	4.2	0.4	3.5
Fujian	2.6	0.4	0.5	1.7	1.5	0.5	11.4
Jiangxi	3.6	1.4	0.4	3.3	1.5	0.4	3.4
Shandong	7.3	10.8	7.8	16.5	14.6	7.2	14.2
Henan	9.0	14.6	10.9	5.9	13.6	4.7	1.2
Hubei	4.9	2.1	1.4	3.4	4.2	0.4	6.3
Hunan	8.7	2.5	2.8	4.4	3.2	0.2	3.5
Guangdong	5.0	1.0	0.2	8.1	1.2	0.4	13.8
Guangxi	3.8	2.5	0.9	2.1	0.6	0.2	5.6
Hainan	0.8	0.4	0.3	1.1	0.1	0.0	3.2
Chongqing	2.7	0.8	0.9	1.5	1.3	0.3	0.4
Sichuan	10.4	3.9	4.5	4.8	5.8	1.9	2.1
Guizhou	2.7	1.8	1.3	0.8	0.4	0.1	0.2
Yunnan	5.0	3.2	2.4	1.4	0.7	1.2	0.6
Tibet	0.0	1.8	1.7	0.0	0.0	0.8	0.0
Shaanxi	1.3	1.7	2.2	0.7	1.7	4.8	0.2
Gansu	1.0	1.9	3.1	0.3	0.5	1.1	0.0
Qinghai	0.2	1.0	2.0	0.0	0.0	0.8	0.0
Ningxia	0.2	0.8	1.5	0.2	0.2	2.0	0.1
Xinjiang	0.6	5.1	14.3	1.0	0.9	5.7	0.2
Total	100	100	100	100	100	100	100

Sources: National Bureau of Statistics of China (NBS) (various issues), *China Statistical Yearbook*, Beijing: China Statistics Press and Ministry of Agriculture of China (2007), *China Animal Statistical Yearbook 2007*, Beijing: China Agricultural Press.

11. Linking economic development with demand for energy: a discontinuous estimation of energy demand elasticity

Ligang Song and Yu Sheng

INTRODUCTION

It is generally accepted that there is a strong causal relationship between national income and energy demand, with the price of energy products playing an important role in affecting the relationship, as shown in many studies examining the relationship between economic growth and energy consumption (Taylor, 1975; Bohi and Zimmerman, 1984; Dahl and Sterner, 1991; Brenton, 1997; Ferguson, Wilkinson and Hill 2000). Despite the existence of significant income and price elasticities found in these studies, there appears to be a lack of general agreement on represent-ative values for the income and price elasticities of energy products, and in particular on why the magnitude of these elasticities may differ across countries with disparate incomes or over time for the same country. In a comprehensive survey of quantitative studies on country-specific energy consumption, Dahl (1992) showed that the demand for energy was price inelastic and slightly income elastic at the aggregate level but there was no clear-cut evidence that the developing world's energy demand is less price elastic or more income elastic than for the industrial world. Brenton (1997) and Ferguson et al. (2000) used some cross-country energy consumption data to estimate different energy demand equations respectively, and found that the own-price elasticity for energy is higher in the poor than in the rich countries, and income elasticity for energy declines with the rising of income.

To explain the above phenomenon, some recent studies, including Maddala et al. (1997), Garcia-Cerrutti (2000), Lowe (2003), Bernstein and Griffin (2005) and Yoo (2006), attempted to incorporate some region-specific characteristics, such as different consumption preferences and different energy-usage techniques in production across countries, into the estimation of the cross-country energy consumption function. Those studies provided some interesting results with respect to the relationship between economic growth and energy consumption through improving the accuracy of estimating the income and price elasticities of energy products. However, they could not explain two important phenomena (Bernstein and Griffin, 2005): (1) the estimated energy consumptions in cross-country studies generally lack price elasticity, which is significantly different from those in country-specific studies; (2) the estimated energy consumptions in country-specific studies usually show different trends over different time periods, which is probably due to the differences in country-specific characteristics. The above two phenomena raise an interesting question as to whether there is a common feature that can be identified linking economic growth with energy consumption of different countries at different phases of development and income levels.

This chapter intends to use the structural economic development theory from Chenery, Robinson and Syrquin (1986) to examine how significant changes in national income level of a country may affect its energy consumption behaviour over time. We argue that since different economic development stages are characterized with different industrial structures, the energy demand in different stages of economic development may demonstrate different and specific income and price elasticities even after controlling the energy consumption preference and the energy-usage technology. Moreover, when structural economic development takes place in different countries sequentially, the aggregate energy consumption may show some regular changing trends, which could not be captured by country-specific characteristics (usually constant over time). This, differing from the previous studies, provides some explanations on how the wave-by-wave economic development across countries may lead to cyclical fluctuations of global energy demand during the past four decades. This approach can be used to predict the changing trade pattern of energy products in the world markets.

The second section summarizes classical economic growth theory from the perspective of development economics and links it to the structural change in energy demand in some major countries. As the experience of development shows, there are often significant structural changes in energy demand when a country moves from the lower economic growth stage to the higher one. This provides us with a theoretical basis for using the development economic theory as an explanation for the changing trend of energy demand. The third section develops an error correction model, which incorporates the impact of different economic growth stages into the estimation of energy demand function through using a series of dummy variables and interaction terms, and specifies the 65-country and

40-year data for the panel data regression. The fourth section presents the estimated results, which show that countries at different economic growth stages may be characterized by different elasticities of energy consumption. Generally speaking, economic growth tends to increase the income (expenditure) elasticity of energy and decrease the price elasticity of energy in a country that undergoes the process of industrialization. This trend tends to generate an increase in the overall demand for energy, thereby posing a shock to the world energy market (if this country's demand share in the world market is sufficiently large). This provides some sound explanation on the cyclical price and demand fluctuations in energy that are observed with the waves of economic growth in East Asia during the past four decades. The fifth section applies the empirical results for analysing the case of China and India. Some implications are drawn on the impact of these two countries' booming economies on the future demand and international trade in the world energy market. The final section concludes the chapter.

CHANGING WORLD ENERGY DEMAND AND ITS DETERMINANTS

The world primary energy demand has experienced rapid growth over the past four decades, despite a slight drop due to the supply shock in the late 1970s. Up to 2005, the total world primary energy demand reached 10.54 billion tonnes of oil equivalent, which is 2.5 times that (3.86 billion tonnes of oil equivalent) in 1965. Behind the steady increasing trend of world primary energy demand, countries with different levels of development have demonstrated different energy demand patterns. Three characteristics of cross-country primary energy consumption trends in the world can be summarized as follows (International Energy Agency [IEA], 2006). First, the primary energy demand in developed countries is still dominant in the total world primary energy consumption, though it increased slowly. Second, the primary energy demand in developing countries, in particular the newly industrializing economies (NIEs) in East Asia, increased rapidly and was becoming a new engine of the total world energy consumption growth. Third, the newly increased part of the world primary energy demand came in a wave-by-wave pattern and has been dominated by different countries with different stages of development over time.

Based on the data from Statistical Review of World Energy (British Petroleum [BP], 2006), from 1965 to 2005, the annual growth rate of primary energy demand from the United States, the European Union,

Japan and Russia is on average 1.5 per cent, which is far lower than that from developing countries in East Asia, such as South Korea, Taiwan, ASEAN, China and India, which is around 5.8 per cent on average. As a consequence, the share of the primary energy demand from the United States, the EU, Japan and Russia over the total demand of the world, declined from 79.3 per cent to 53.1 per cent (but still dominant in world primary energy consumption) while that from South Korea, Taiwan, ASEAN, China and India increased from 6.9 per cent to 24.7 per cent over this period. This implies that developing countries are increasingly becoming a major driving force of the primary energy demand in the world. Moreover, the driving force for the primary energy demand seemed to come from different countries over different time periods. The newly increased primary energy demand mainly came from the EU and Japan during the period 1965–70, the major driving force for the primary energy demand came from the newly industrializing economies, such as South Korea, Taiwan and ASEAN, during the period 1980–90, and the major driving force for the primary energy demand came from China, followed by India, during the period 1990–2005. This implies that the newly increased world primary energy demands have been waved up and increased as more and more countries have entered the process of industrialization.

The above phenomena raised a number of questions: why could East Asia, rather than any other part of the world, have become the new engine of world primary energy demand? What are the underlying factors that can be used to explain the changing trend in world primary energy demand? Is there any common feature associated with those factors across countries? How can changing world income and energy price affect world energy consumption? To answer those questions, a number of previous studies, such as Karki, Mann and Salehfar (2005), IEA (2006) and Yoo (2006) argued that the rapid increase in world income and the vibrating oil price in the international market changed the demand pattern of world energy consumption. Figure 11.1 shows changes of GDP per capita across different countries during the period 1965–2005. The major structural changes in primary energy consumption in different countries tended to agglomerate in two specific ranges of GDP per capita levels, US$5000–10 000 and US$20 000–30 000. This suggests that it was GDP per capita range rather than GDP per capita level that seemed to play a more important role in affecting the primary energy demand both across different countries and over different periods of time. This observation provided us with a perspective for carrying out our empirical work.

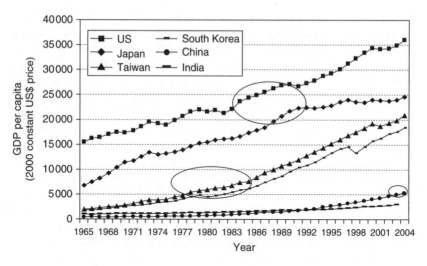

Source: Authors' calculation from the Penn World Table 6.2 (CIC, 2008).

Figure 11.1   GDP per capita across countries: 1965–2005

STRUCTURAL ECONOMIC DEVELOPMENT AND ENERGY DEMAND: THEORY, METHODOLOGY AND DATA

It is commonly accepted in development economics that the economic growth in a country is usually driven by two main forces: one is the growth of population, capital accumulation and technological progress; and the other is the wave-by-wave economic structural changes moving an economy from primary stage to a more advanced stage of development. The former force is continuous and can generate the long-term and steady development while the latter force resulting from the working of the first force plus the implementation of appropriate policies and institutions can generate the short-term catch-up development. The combination or inter-action of the two forces tends to form the spirally increasing economic growth path and splits the economic growth into different stages with some associated specific features (Lewis, 1965; Chenery et al., 1986).

Following the classical development theory (that is, Chenery et al., 1986), the economic development of a country usually consists of four stages: agricultural economic stage, industrialization economic stage, commercialization economic stage and advanced economic stage. Each stage of economic development has its own significant features. More specifically, the agricultural economic stage is the initial development stage of an economy, which is characterized by the relatively large proportion of agricultural population and the relatively low level of industrialization. In this stage, the core of the economic development is to overcome the 'dual economy'. When economic growth moves on and the national income increases to some extent, the economy may enter into the second and the third development stages sequentially – that is, the industrialization and the commercialization economic stages. At these stages of development, the core of economic development is industrialization and urbanization and as a consequence, the economy will experience dramatic changes in industrial structure. Finally, after both secondary and tertiary industries are mature and primary industry declines below 10 per cent of total output, the economy can achieve the integration and step into the advanced economic stage. From then on, the economic growth will be mainly driven by technological progress and population growth.

Combining the structural economic development theory with the changing pattern of energy consumption associated with economic development, one can easily find that: since different economic development stages are corresponding to different industrial structures (which in turn may generate different patterns of energy consumption), the relationship between economic growth of a country and its primary energy demand would vary along the economic development path. Thus, it is necessary to incorporate the economic development stages into the estimation of energy consumption function so that the impact of economic structural change on the fall and rise of energy consumption along the economic growth path can be examined.

Based on the standard consumption function with utility maximizing theory, we assume that the demand for energy products is determined not only by changes in income and price but also varies with different economic development stages with which a particular country is associated. Thus, the demand function for energy products in double-log form for panel data regression can be written as:

$$\ln ED_{it} = \beta_0 + \beta_1 \ln P_t + \beta_2 \ln Y_{it} + \gamma S_{it} + u_i + \varepsilon_{it} \qquad (11.1)$$

where ED_{it} is the aggregate demand for all energy products in country i at time t, which is measured with tonnes of oil equivalent and Y_{it} is the national income of country i at time t, which is measured with US dollars with constant price (which is calculated by using the current price adjusted by purchasing power parity across countries and over time). Both of those variables are measured on a per capita basis so as to control for any variation in population growth. Data for the price variable P_t is the real price of crude oil in the world market, which is calculated using the spot price in the international market adjusted by the consumer price index in each country.[1] In addition, u_i is defined as the country-specific effect that does not change over time and ε_{it} is defined as the random effect. A key assumption of equation (11.1) is that the income and price elasticities of each country for energy products are independent of their development stages or stable over time.

The appropriate measure of the different economic development stages of a country has been a controversial topic in the literature on economic development. Many authors prefer to use some trend proxies, such as the industrialization rate (or the share of secondary and tertiary industrial output over total GDP), the urbanization rate (the share of the number of urban population over that of the total) and the industrial structural index of workforce, for this variable. Although those proxies reflect some characteristics of different stages of economic development, they may be generally biased when being incorporated into the estimation of energy consumption function since energy consumption is usually related to changes of the whole economy. For this reason, we use different ranges of GDP per capita (measured with 1984 constant price and adjusted with the purchasing power parity across countries) to generate six dummy variables designed to capture the characteristics associated with different stages of industrialization, commercialization and an advanced level of economic development. Such design is consistent with Chenery et al. (1986).

$$\gamma S_{it} = \gamma_i \sum_{i=1}^{6} IND_{it} \tag{11.2}$$

Estimation of our general model would seem to be quite simple using the standard ordinary least squares (OLS) method. However, it would be misleading with respect to its estimation due to the fact that most economic variables are non-stationary and this high auto-correlation may generate inconsistent estimators and inaccurate hypothesis tests (Granger and Newbold, 1974). To deal with this econometric problem, we use the dynamic panel data (DPD) regression technique developed by Arellano and Bond (1991), Arellano and Bover (1995) and Blundell and Bond (1998) in this study. The advantage of the method is that it can make full use of the combinations of different variables to eliminate the endogeneity between independent variables and the residuals (or the cointegration of the non-stationary series) and as a result, both the long-term and short-term elasticities of energy consumption can be specified.

For a group of non-stationary series, equation (11.1) can be rearranged in a structural form to detail the long-run and short-run dynamics of a group of integrated variables:

$$\Delta Z_{it} = \eta + \sum_{j=1}^{n} \Gamma_j \Delta Z_{jt-ji} + \pi Z_{it-1} + \gamma S_{it} + u_i + \varepsilon_{it} \qquad (11.3)$$

where Z_{it} is a vector of $I(d)$ variables, ε_{it} is a vector of white noise residuals and η is a constant vector (representing the time trend). The adjustments to disequilibrium are captured over n lagged periods in the coefficient matrix Γ_j.

Following Roodman (2006), we can specify suitable instrumental variables from the lagged or differentiated dependent and independent variables and use the difference and system GMM (generalized method of moment) methods to investigate the relationship between integrated series with dynamic panel data.[2] Obviously, for a long-run relationship to exist, at least the first column must contain non-zero elements. Thus, this cointegrating relationship specified in equation (11.3) represents the foundation of a complete dynamic panel model and the regression, which allows us to compare the immediate and overall average elasticities of energy demand across countries.

Finally, the data used in the above regression covered 65 countries for the period 1965–2005. The data for energy consumption in each country and that for the real price of crude oil come from BP 'Statistical Review of World Energy' (2006). The data for population and GDP (calculated with the constant price and adjusted for purchasing power parity) come from the Penn Word Table 6.2 (CIC, 2008).

EMPIRICAL RESULTS

Before estimating any relationship between energy consumption and its explanatory variables, we need some identification strategy either from economic or statistical perspectives. Specifically, we assume that all lagged independent variables on the right-hand side of equation (11.3) are exogenous so that their further lagged or differentiated items can be used as the instrument variables for GMM estimation.[3] Based on Roodman (2006), we first differentiate the regression function (say, equation (11.3)) to remove u_i and thereafter produce an equation that is estimable by instrumental variable method and use a generalized method of moments estimator for coefficients with the instruments as lagged levels of the dependent variable and the predetermined variables and differences of the strictly exogenous variables. The results from both a difference GMM and a system GMM estimation are shown in Table 11.1.

To choose between the difference and system GMM method, we first use an AR(1) model with the control of different time dummies for each period from 1965–2005 to examine the autocorrelation of the logged energy consumption (with equation (11.4)).

Table 11.1 The difference in GMM and the system GMM estimations

	Difference GMM	System GMM
Dependent variable is $\ln(C_t)$		
Constant	–	–19.642***
	–	(0.596)
T	0.036***	0.005***
	(0.002)	(0.000)
$\ln(C_{t-1})$	–0.868***	–0.315***
	(0.064)	(0.035)
$\ln(C_{t-2})$	–0.832***	0.237***
	(0.054)	(0.022)
$\ln(P_t)$	–0.004	–0.013***
	(0.006)	(0.003)
$\ln(P_{t-2})$	–0.014**	0.006*
	(0.006)	(0.003)
$\ln(Y_t)$	0.525	0.631***
	(0.038)	(0.020)
$\ln(Y_{t-2})$	0.617	0.403***
	(0.047)	(0.022)
S_1	0.037	0.257***
	(0.032)	(0.008)
S_2	0.093**	0.534***
	(0.042)	(0.014)
S_3	0.113**	0.459***
	(0.050)	(0.013)
S_4	0.144***	0.716***
	(0.052)	(0.019)
S_5	0.146***	0.704***
	(0.053)	(0.019)
S_6	0.093*	0.809***
	(0.051)	(0.021)
Number of observations	2045	2110
Number of countries	65	65
m_1	0.000	0.000
m_2	0.000	0.735
Sargan–Hansen test	0.000	0.503

Note: The numbers in brackets are the standard errors. *, ** and *** = coefficients are significant at 10 per cent, 5 per cent and 1 per cent level respectively. m_1 and m_2 are Arellano–Bond tests for AR(1) and AR(2) in first differences.

Source: Authors' own estimations.

$$\ln C_{it} = \theta \ln C_{it-1} + \sum_{t=1}^{T} D_{it} + u_i + \varepsilon_{it} \qquad (11.4)$$

The results show that the coefficient of $\ln(C_{t-1})$ is 0.95 and the significance level is ($Z = 58.45$) close to 1 per cent ($m_1 = 0.002$, $m_2 = 0.026$, Sargan–Hansen test =1). Due to Blundell and Bond (1998), this suggests that a system GMM estimate will be more suitable than the difference GMM estimation, which can be supported by the comparison between the difference and system GMM estimates as reported in Table 11.1. Furthermore, we use the Arellano–Bond test for AR(1) and AR(2) in first differences to choose the suitable lagged periods for dependent and independent variables and the Sargan–Hansen test to specify the combination of instrumental variables for the system GMM estimation. Finally, we eliminate the insignificant independent variables from the regressions and the results are shown in column (2) of Table 11.1. There are two interesting findings.

First, there exist some significant income and price elasticities for energy demand with the cross-country data over time and in particular there are significant time structures for these income and price elasticities for energy demand, which is different from the results obtained from the previous studies on cross-country studies (Dahl, 1992). From Table 11.1, we have the estimated energy demand function as below:

$$\Delta \ln C_{i,t} = -19.64 + 0.005t - 0.237\Delta \ln C_{i,t-1} - 0.013\Delta \ln P_{i,t}$$

$$- 0.006\Delta \ln P_{i,t-1} + 0.631\Delta \ln Y_{i,t} - 0.403\Delta \ln Y_{i,t-1}$$

$$- 1.078(\ln C_{i,t-1} + 0.006\ln P_{i,t-1} - 0.959\Delta \ln Y_{i,t-1}) \qquad (11.5)$$

From equation (11.5), both the short-run and long-run income and price elasticities can be calculated. The short-run and the long-run price elasticities are –0.015 and –0.006 respectively. That is, the absolute value of the short-run price elasticity is higher than the long-run one. A feasible explanation is that energy products have lack of substitutes in production and consumption and thus the short-run price shock can only reduce the temporary energy demand. Equation (11.5) also shows that the short-run and the long-run income elasticities are 0.184 and 0.959 respectively. That is, the absolute value of the short-run price elasticity is lower than the long-run one. A possible explanation is that as income is permanently increased, more and more energy products would be consumed through more channels and thus demand for energy products will be increased in the long run. Meanwhile, the above finding also helps to explain the inconsistency between the cross-country and country-specific estimates on energy demand (the former shows no significant price elasticity, which is inconsistent with the impact of international oil price on demand; see *World Energy Outlook 2006* (IEA, 2006), since the analytical approach adopted only allows them to show the long-run effects.

Second, the different stages of economic development play an important role in affecting the energy demand in addition to the income and price effects. To illustrate this point, we make use of the coefficients of GDP and its lags to estimate the income elasticity of energy consumption for different stages of a country's development. Figure 11.2(a) shows how energy demand will evolve over time when a country is going through different stages of economic development based on the estimates obtained using the dynamic panel regression. As it is shown, as GDP per capita increased from US$5 000 to US$10 000 (at 2000 constant US dollar prices) (or at the industrialization stage), there will be a significant increase in energy demand in addition to the income effects. An explanation for this phenomenon is that: when the economy is being transformed from an agricultural society to an industrialized society the more capital- and energy-intensive sectors will substitute the labour-intensive sectors in dominating the production (Humphrey and Stanislaw, 1979). Figure 11.2(b) provides the decomposition of energy consumption between changes in income and stages of economic development, which shows that the contribution of industrialization towards percentage changes in energy consumption would not reach the peak until the per capita income level reaches US$10 000. These findings can be used to explain the pattern of wave-by-wave increases in energy demand from East Asia following the development process of different countries in this region during the past four decades. This also helps us to identify the future trend of changing world energy demand as countries such as China and India move along the path characterized with the 'continuous change and breaking points'.

ECONOMIC DEVELOPMENT AND ENERGY DEMAND: THE CASE OF CHINA

China, as one of the largest developing countries in the world, has achieved high economic growth by expanding its GDP by more than 10 times during the past four decades up to 2006. In particular, after its accession to the WTO in 2001, the annual economic growth rate has reached 10.7 per cent and its total GDP reached US$2.7 trillion in 2006. The rapid economic growth in China is accompanied with industrial structure transformation and the rapid pace of urbanization. According to *China Statistical Yearbook 2007* (NBS, 2007), the urbanization rate and the

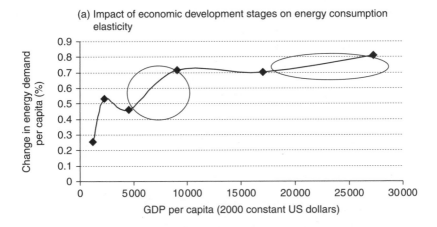

(a) Impact of economic development stages on energy consumption elasticity

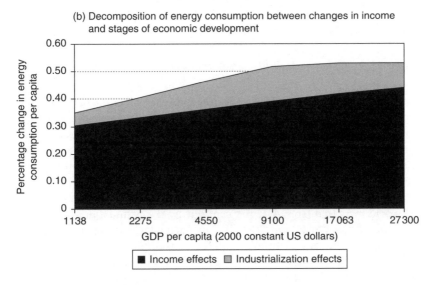

(b) Decomposition of energy consumption between changes in income and stages of economic development

Source: Authors' own calculation.

Figure 11.2   Impact of economic development stages on energy demand

industrialization rate (the share of secondary industry over total GDP) in 2006 reached 43.9 per cent and 48.9 per cent respectively.

Rapid economic growth and development structural changes generate a strong demand for energy products in China as predicted by the theory. The total primary energy consumption increased by 36.3 per cent during

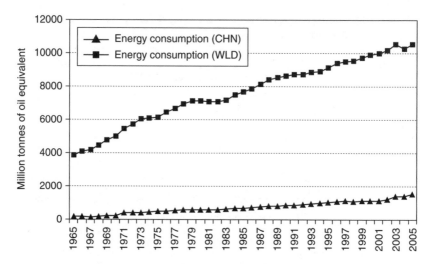

Source: World Bank, World Development Indicators Online Database.

Figure 11.3   China and world energy consumption: 1965–2005

the past decade and reached 1.55 billion tonnes of oil equivalent in 2005.
Figure 11.3 shows the total consumption of primary energy products in
China as compared with that of the world since 1965. As it is shown, there
is rapid growth in China's total primary energy consumption. The share
of total primary energy consumption of China over that of the world
increased from 4.72 per cent in 1965 to 14.7 per cent in 2005. The share
of newly increased primary energy consumption of China over that of
the world increased from 4.42 per cent during the period 1965–70 to 12.6
per cent during the period 2000–05. In particular, during the past five
years, the growth rate of primary energy consumption of China is much
higher than that of the world of 6.1 per cent. As a consequence, China is
becoming one of the largest consumers for energy consumption.

Similar to the experiences of other economies such as South Korea,
Taiwan and ASEAN in East Asia, rapid economic growth plus structural
changes is a major driving force behind China's ever-increasing energy
demand. Figure 11.4 shows the relationship between energy consumption
per capita and GDP per capita in China for the last four decades (1965–
2006). As it is shown, a rapid increase in the energy consumption intensity in China started to take place after China's GDP per capita reached
around US$1100, driving China's energy consumption per capita over 1
tonne. From the past experience of South Korea, Taiwan and ASEAN,
this implies that the structural change will lead to a rapid increase in

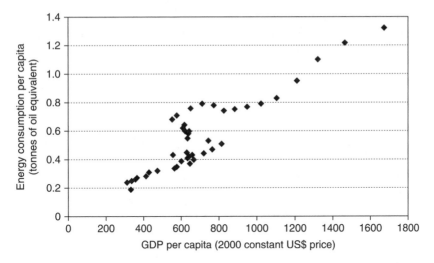

Source: BP (2006), 'Statistical Review of World Energy 2006'.

Figure 11.4 The relationship between energy consumption per capita and GDP per capita in China

energy demand in China from now on. Given the estimate of the IEA on Chinese annual economic growth rate as 6.4 per cent over the next 20 years, the real GDP per capita of China may rise from US$1445 (in 2000 constant US dollar prices) in 2005 to US$2687 in 2015, and further to US$4996 in 2025. This suggests that the world will witness China's level of energy consumption per capita doubled or even tripled in the next 10 to 20 years.

CONCLUSION

This study uses a dynamic panel regression technique to estimate a cross-country demand equation for energy products with 65-country and 40-year panel data and examines the cross-country income and price elasticities of energy consumption during the period 1965–2005. We found that a country in different stages of economic development would demonstrate different levels of demand for energy consumption. This, combined with the relatively stable energy supply, can be used to explain why and how the wave-by-wave pattern of economic development across countries may lead to a cyclical fluctuation of energy prices and the changing trade pattern of energy products in the world market. This finding can also be used to shed light on explaining the recent boom in China's and India's ever-increasing demand for energy products, which foreshadows a prolonged cycle of high demand for world energy.

NOTES

1. Based on the BP 'Statistical Review of World Energy' (2006), the spot price of crude oil before 1984 is set as the price of Arabian Light posted at Ras Tanura and that after 1984 is set as Brent dated price.
2. The Johansen (1991) test orders linear combinations of the different variables using eigenvalues, and then sequentially tests whether the columns of the α matrix are jointly zeros.
3. This assumption is only made for simplicity, and the results from the endogenous independent variables are shown in Appendix Table 11A.1.

REFERENCES

Arellano, M. and S. Bond (1991), 'Some tests of specification for panel data: Monte Carlo evidence and an application to employment equations', *The Review of Economic Studies*, **58** (2), 277–97.
Arellano, M. and O. Bover (1995), 'Another look at the instrumental variable estimation of error-components models', *Journal of Econometrics*, **68** (1), 29–51.
Bernstein, M. and J. Griffin (2005), 'Regional Differences in the Price-elasticity of Demand for Energy', Research Report No. TR-2920NREL, Rand Corporation, https://www.rand.org/publications/electronic/enviro.html, accessed 14 April 2008.
Blundell, R. and S. Bond (1998), 'GMM Estimation with Persistent Panel Data: An Application to Production Functions', IFS Working Paper No. W99/4, http://www.nuffield.ox.ac.uk/users/bond/wp9904.pdf, accessed 14 April 2008.
Bohi, D. and M. Zimmerman (1984), 'An update on econometric studies of energy demand behavior', *Annual Review of Energy*, **9** (1), 105–54.
Brenton, P. (1997), 'Estimates of the demand for energy using: cross-country consumption data', *Applied Economics*, **29** (7), 851–9.
British Petroleum Global Ltd (BP) (2006), 'Statistical Review of World Energy', http://www.bp.com, accessed 14 April 2008.
Center for International Comparison (CIC) (2008), Penn World Table 6.2, University of Pennsylvania, http://pwt.econ.upenn.edu/, accessed 14 April 2008.
Chenery H., S. Robinson and M. Syrquin (1986), *Industrialization and Growth: A Comparative Study*, Oxford: Oxford University Press.
Dahl, C. (1992), 'A survey of energy demand elasticities for the developing world', *Journal of Energy and Development*, **18** (1), 1–47.
Dahl, C. and T. Sterner (1991), 'Analyzing gasoline demand elasticities: a survey', *Energy Economics*, **13** (3), 203–10.
Ferguson, R., W. Wilkinson and R. Hill (2000), 'Electricity use and economic development', *Energy Policy*, **28** (13), 923–34.

Garcia-Cerrutti, P. (2000), 'Estimating elasticities of residential energy demand from panel county data using dynamic random variables models with heteroskedastic and correlated error terms', *Resource and Energy Economics*, **22** (4), 355–66.

Granger, C. and P. Newbold (1974), 'Spurious regressions in econometrics', *Journal of Econometrics*, **2** (2), 111–20.

Humphrey, W. and J. Stanislaw (1979), 'Economic growth and energy consumption in the UK: 1700–1975', *Energy Policy*, **7** (1), 29–43.

International Energy Agency (IEA) (2006), *World Energy Outlook*, International Energy Agency, London.

Johansen, S. (1991), 'Estimation and hypothesis testing of cointegration vectors in Gaussian vector autoregressive models', *Econometrica*, **59** (6), 1551–80.

Karki, S., M. Mann and H. Salehfar (2005), 'Energy and environment in the ASEAN: challenges and opportunities', *Energy Policy*, **33** (4), 499–509.

Lewis, W. (1965), 'A review of economic development', *American Economic Review*, **55** (2), 1–16.

Lowe, R. (2003), 'A theoretical analysis of price elasticity of energy demand in multi-stage energy-conversion systems', *Energy Policy*, **31** (5),1699–704.

Maddala, G., R. Trost, H. Li and F. Joutz (1997), 'Estimation of short-run and long-run elasticity of energy demand from panel data using shrinkage estimation', *Journal of Business & Economic Statistics*, **15** (1), 90–101.

National Bureau of Statistics China (NBS) (2007), *China Statistical Yearbook 2007*, Beijing: China Statistics Press.

Roodman, D. (2006), 'Aid Project Proliferation and Absorptive Capacity', Working Paper No. 75, Center for Global Development, http://ideas.repec.org/n/nep-dev/2006-07-21.html, accessed 14 April 2008.

Taylor, L. (1975), 'The demand for electricity: a survey', *Bell Journal of Economics*, **6** (1), 74–110.

World Bank, World Development Indicators Online Database, http://publications.worldbank.org/WDI, accessed 14 April 2008.

Yoo, S. (2006), 'The causal relationship between electricity consumption and economic growth in the ASEAN countries', *Energy Policy*, **34** (18), 3573–82.

APPENDIX

Table 11A.1 *Dynamic panel estimation on energy consumption with endogenous independent variables*

	Difference GMM Endogenous	System GMM
Dependent variable is $\ln(C_t)$		
$\ln(C_{t-1})$	0.914***	0.979***
	(0.017)	(0.002)
$\ln(P_t)$	−0.008	−0.008
	0.009	0.009
$\ln(P_{t-1})$	0.019*	0.019*
	(0.011)	(0.011)
$\ln(P_{t-2})$	−0.010	−0.006
	0.007	0.008
$\ln(Y_t)$	0.261***	0.304***
	(0.088)	(0.027)
$\ln(Y_{t-1})$	−0.218**	−0.291***
	(0.088)	(0.026)
S_1	0.047**	0.012**
	(0.022)	(0.006)
S_2	0.073***	0.019***
	(0.025)	(0.007)
S_3	0.101***	0.017**
	(0.028)	0.008
S_4	0.126***	0.025**
	(0.029)	(0.010)
S_5	0.110***	0.021*
	(0.030)	(0.011)
S_6	0.090***	0.029***
	(0.029)	(0.010)
Num. of observations	2045	2110
Num. of countries	65	65
m_1	0.06	0.00
m_2	0.20	0.00
Sargan–Hansen test	1.00	0.04

Note: The numbers in brackets are the standard errors. *, ** and *** = coefficients significant at 10 per cent, 5 per cent and 1 per cent level respectively. m_1 and m_2 are Arellano–Bond tests for AR(1) and AR(2) in first differences.

Source: Authors' own calculation.

Index